The Poor Relation:

Irish Foreign Policy and the Third World

The Poor Relation:

Irish Foreign Policy and the Third World

Michael Holmes, Nicholas Rees, Bernadette Whelan

 TRÓCAIRE
and
GILL and MACMILLAN

Published in Ireland by

TRÓCAIRE

Catholic Agency for World Development
169 Booterstown Ave.,
Blackrock, Co. Dublin
and
Gill and Macmillan Ltd,
Goldenbridge, Inchicore, Dublin 8
with associated companies in
Auckland, Budapest, Gaborone, Harare, Hong Kong,
Kampala, Kuala Lumpur, Lagos, London, Madras, Manzini,
Melbourne, Mexico City, Nairobi, New York, Singapore,
Sydney, Tokyo, Windhoek

© Trócaire 1993
ISBN 0 7171 1970 X

Index: Fergus Mulligan
Design: The Graphiconies
Print origination by Typeform Ltd
Printed in Ireland by Genprint Ltd

*The illustration on the front cover is Iveagh House, headquarters of
the Department of Foreign Affairs, Dublin.*

Contents

List of Tables

List of Figures

Acknowledgments

This book was written with the help of a number of individuals and the cooperation of governmental and non-governmental agencies, without whom this project would not have been possible. First and foremost, we would like to thank Trócaire for inviting us to undertake this study. We have found it a most interesting and stimulating subject, and we hope that our interest has been adequately conveyed in the book.

The project was commissioned by the Research Advisory Group of Trócaire. We received many helpful comments and criticisms from the members of the Group, Frank Barry, Packie Commins, Tony Fahey, Connell Fanning, Mary Jennings, Alan Matthews and Eoin O'Malley, and also from Sally O'Neill, Trócaire's Deputy Director. Particular thanks are due to Andy Storey, Trócaire's Research Adviser, who supervised the project from beginning to end with skill and wit. We also received invaluable assistance from Trócaire's librarian, Anne Kinsella, whose kind assistance went well beyond the call of duty.

The Department of Foreign Affairs gave invaluable help and support for the study. Members of the Department gave freely of their time and their knowledge in responding to interviews and questionnaires, providing material which was immensely valuable to our research. They also took the time and the care to provide a valuable set of comments on parts of our earlier drafts, which again proved a great asset to the study.

A number of other government departments, political parties and non-governmental agencies also provided us with interviews and other material that was invaluable: the Departments of Finance, of Industry and Commerce, of Defence and of the Taoiseach; Fianna Fáil, Fine Gael, the Labour Party, Democratic Left and the Progressive Democrats; Congood, Oxfam Ireland, Concern, Action from Ireland, the Irish Missionary Union, the Association of Missionary Societies, Christian Aid, Comhlámh, the Methodist World Development and Relief Committee and the Irish Congress of Trade Unions.

We would also like to acknowledge the support provided by our institutions, University College, Dublin and the University of Limerick. In particular, we would like to thank a number of colleagues who provided important insights into aspects of Irish foreign policy and contributed their ideas and comments on the work: Anna Murphy in UCD, and Jim Deegan, Emir Kader, John Logan and Eddie Moxon-Browne in UL. The staff of the

Development Studies libraries in UCD and Mary Immaculate College in Limerick and the Official Publications desk in the UCD library were also very helpful throughout the work. Alan Byrne provided great help in augmenting our minimal computer skills and in designing the figures and diagrams. Research assistance was undertaken at an early stage by Edel Clancy and Dolores Aherne and later by Peter Holmes and Kathy Kennedy, and great assistance and advice came from Denis Holmes. All errors, of fact or judgement, are of course the responsibility of the authors.

Michael Holmes, Nicholas Rees, Bernadette Whelan
January 1993

Chapter 1

The Irish Foreign Policy Environment

Good intentions are no guarantee of good behaviour, so that although Ireland has always expressed its desire for good relations with the other countries of the world, that sentiment has not always been matched by deeds as well as might be hoped. This is especially true for the countries of the Third World. Ireland has consistently voiced support and sympathy for the interests of those countries, but it has rarely paid them the level of attention that it has given to others, such as Britain, the other countries of Europe and the United States. In the overall framework of Ireland's international relations, the Third World has been left as something of a poor relation by comparison. Ireland's geographical and historical experience of being "an island behind an island" has allowed the development of a perception of Ireland as a remote and isolated country. However, the oceans and seas which separate Ireland can also be seen as channels for contact and communication with all corners of the world. Ireland's relations with the wider world have developed from these two conflicting conceptions, on the one hand emphasising the isolation and peripherality of the country, on the other its extensive international links and relations.

This is of direct relevance in Ireland's dealings with the countries of Africa, Asia and Central and South America which constitute the Third World. Despite Ireland's physical distance from them, considerable links have evolved. Relations have been established with states as diverse as Argentina, Zaire, and the Philippines, either on a direct country-to-country level or through international organisations such as the European Community (EC) or the United Nations (UN). Furthermore, the relations between Ireland and the Third World are set to develop and expand considerably because the physical distance is being rendered increasingly inconsequential by technological advances. Events in Africa, Asia and Latin America are increasingly having direct consequences in Ireland, and Ireland's own actions and activities are directly relevant for those countries in turn. However, although the physical distances involved are no longer significant, there remains the problem of overcoming a perceptual distance which has tended in the past to consign the Third World to a low status in Ireland's priorities.

This book sets out to analyse Ireland's links with the countries of Africa, Asia and Latin America and to assess the nature of Irish foreign policy towards the Third World. The focus of the study is on both the formulation and conduct of this aspect of Irish foreign policy. The formulation of Irish foreign policy is taken to refer to the process by which foreign policy is made. We will examine the actors involved, how they identify foreign policy goals, issues and problems, how they arrive at decisions and how they seek to implement policy. The process is, of course, not always as rational as this might suggest. In many instances Irish foreign policy is formulated in reaction to world events and particular problems the state faces rather than in a planned manner, and the policy decided on in theory is not necessarily the one that emerges in practice. The conduct of Irish foreign policy refers to the actions taken in pursuit of foreign policy in practice. We will examine the actual implementation of Irish foreign policy towards the Third World, how it can be assessed and how it feeds back into the overall Irish foreign policy environment.

Organisation of the study

In the rest of Chapter 1, we begin by defining the key terms used in the book and then concentrate on clarifying the Irish foreign policy environment, which forms the background for dealings with the Third World. Relations with the Third World do not exist in isolation, but in conjunction with relations with the rest of the world. Part of this study is aimed at assessing the relative importance accorded to each strand of Irish foreign policy. We will look first at the levels at which foreign policy is carried out. Traditionally, the main level of activity was the bilateral one of direct country-to-country contacts. However, in recent years multilateral contacts through international organisations have become increasingly important, both at a regional level (particularly EC) and at a global level. At all three levels, we shall examine the general structure of Irish relations, and then place relations with Third World countries specifically within that general context. Second, we will look at the values and goals that are apparent in the foreign policy environment, and once more we shall do so in a general context and then with particular reference to the way in which such values and goals impinge upon relations with the Third World.

In Chapter 2, we move from looking at the general environment of Irish foreign policy to a detailed analysis of the processes by which policy towards the Third World is formed. We examine the different actors involved in the process and attempt to assess the roles and the influence each has in that process. While the Department of Foreign Affairs is identified as the key actor involved, other actors cannot be ignored. We shall look at the input of other government actors, including state-sponsored agencies, at the involvement of non-governmental organisations (NGOs), particularly missionary, aid and solidarity groups, and at non-organised sources of influence on foreign policy, particularly the media and public opinion. From this, we develop a picture of the institutional processes involved in foreign policy, not just within Ireland but also at the regional and the global levels.

Having established the overall background to formulation and the conduct of Irish foreign policy towards the Third World, we proceed to analyse it in greater detail in the central three chapters of the book. Chapter 3 looks at the bilateral relations between Ireland and the Third World. We examine the historical development of these relations and focus in particular on the development of formal, official foreign policy links. As well as doing this in a broad fashion for the overall relationship between Ireland and the countries of the Third World, we shall focus on three case studies. India shares with Ireland the cultural and historical circumstances of British colonisation and was the site of Ireland's first Embassy in Asia. The Philippines share a Catholic heritage and identity with Ireland, although formal diplomatic relations remain at a non-resident, consular level. Egypt is one of Ireland's two resident embassies in Africa and has also been a major trading partner in recent years.

In Chapter 4, the focus shifts to the regional level of foreign policy. This does not simply deal with the regional organisations of which Ireland is a member, but also encompasses Ireland's relations with the Third World's own regional organisations. However, the conceptual distinction between these two forms of involvement is blurred in reality, because Ireland's relations with regional organisations in the Third World have largely emerged through Ireland's own regional affiliations. Ireland's involvement in regional organisations is very heavily concentrated on the EC, so the Community dominates the discussion in Chapter 4. We will examine the ways in which the Community impinges on foreign policy actions and on more general relations with the Third World, before detailing the degree of Ireland's involvement in such areas. Two case studies will be used to give more detailed illumination. The first looks at Ireland's involvement in the Lomé Conventions, which are agreements regulating trade and aid relations between the EC and a number of Third World countries. The second looks at the Community's relations with regional groupings in Central and South America, again examining Ireland's contribution.

Chapter 5 concentrates on the global level of relations. Such relations are concentrated around one organisation, the UN, which in turn encompasses a number of affiliated agencies and organisations. We shall examine how the UN impinges on foreign policy and Third World relations, and at the way in which Ireland's relationship with the UN, and through it with Third World states, has developed. We shall concentrate on three case studies to give a more thorough picture. First, Ireland's involvement in UN peacekeeping operations will be examined, and in particular the Irish contribution to the Congo operation of 1960-64. Second, Ireland's voting record in the UN General Assembly will be assessed to demonstrate a more purely foreign policy oriented activity. Finally, we shall examine Ireland's actions through another global organisation, the General Agreement on Tariffs and Trade (GATT), in particular the most recent round of GATT negotiations begun in Uruguay.

Finally, in Chapter 6 we draw together our conclusions about the way in which Irish foreign policy towards the Third World has evolved. The objective throughout the study is to explain the background factors, to identify how and why Irish people have come into contact with the countries of the Third World. From that, a detailed analysis of the way in which official foreign policy has evolved is given. We shall look at which countries Ireland's formal relations are concentrated on, which issues and goals are pursued, and the channels and fora through which this takes place. Finally, we shall assess the conduct of Irish foreign policy: its success in achieving its goals, its impact and the validity of the goals and values being pursued, and the possible means of improvement of Ireland's foreign policy towards the Third World. In general, our analysis will argue that although foreign policy is consistently sympathetic and supportive of Third World concerns, this rarely translates into effective action in support of those concerns.

To examine a topic as broad-ranging as Ireland's relations with the Third World has meant drawing on a very wide range of primary and secondary sources. The research for this study has also made particular use of a set of interviews and a questionnaire. Sixteen interviews were carried out, with officials from the Department of Foreign Affairs, with representatives of a number of NGOs and with representatives from the political parties. They were conducted in the period October 1991 to June 1992. A questionnaire was sent to twelve Irish Embassies, Consulates and Development Cooperation Offices in Third World countries in December 1991, with replies being received from eight of them between December 1991 and March 1992.

Defining the study: foreign policy

Before proceeding with the study, it is necessary to devote a little time to clarifying the two key phrases in the title: foreign policy and Third World. In both instances, there is no agreed definition available for use, and the approaches adopted here are intended more as useful working definitions than exhaustive and precise meanings. In considering foreign policy, it is useful to distinguish two elements. First, this study does not consider all forms of contact between Ireland and other countries as foreign policy. The presence of an Irish person in another country does not in itself constitute foreign policy, so that economic and trading links, tourist traffic and missionary activities are seen as distinct from the process. That should not be taken to imply that they have no bearing on foreign policy. For example, economic ties can lead to trade agreements, tourism can cause consular problems and missionaries can – and have – been expelled, leading to diplomatic confrontations. But while these sorts of non-governmental ties can and do form an important consideration behind foreign policy, they remain as informal and essentially unofficial contacts and are more accurately considered as part of the broader category of international relations. The second element is formal governmental contacts between countries, and it is these official ties which are taken here to constitute foreign policy.

Nevertheless, it is important to respect the fact that both elements need to be considered when assessing Irish foreign policy towards the Third World. The various ways in which Irish people have come into contact with what we now term Third World countries form a backdrop for official ties. Historically, much early contact came about through colonial structures. Irish men served in the British colonial system, both as administrators and as soldiers. The framework of the British empire also provided scope for Irish traders to extend contacts around the world, though economic ties with the Third World were slight and remain so. A more significant contact came through the large number of Irish missionaries who worked in Third World areas, starting in the 1840s with missions to China and India. In more recent times Irish citizens have worked in the Third World as aid volunteers. Thus, there is a historical background and context of relations with the Third World which needs to be taken into account. Such unofficial, informal links have created an Irish presence in the Third World, which has in turn stimulated more formal diplomatic contacts.

Clearly, an identifiably Irish stance (at the level of official contacts) could only emerge with independence, but since 1922 the Irish state has gradually built up a range of formal relations and policies towards the rest of the world. These did not emerge entirely haphazardly. They were structured to some extent by the historical factors mentioned above, but also by the requirements of the foreign policy process. While the traditional agenda of the foreign policy establishment has been concentrated on Europe and North America, and the Third World has always been something of a poor relation, formal relations with the Third World have expanded in recent years. The range of issues that Ireland has presented and has had to react to have included many connected with the Third World. The actions employed by Ireland have increasingly impinged on these countries. And the various kinds of foreign policy fora Ireland has joined have again opened the country to contact with the countries of the Third World and have given Ireland the opportunity of developing policies towards them.

One final point should be made in considering a definition of foreign policy for this study. The issue of aid and questions of development cooperation policy occupy a special position with regard to relations with Third World countries. Clearly, aid constitutes one strand within what we have called international relations. Volunteer workers are an informal, non-governmental contact between Ireland and the Third World, but contribute to the background factors affecting foreign policy. Equally, aid policy can also fall within the ambit of formal governmental policy, and is organised and implemented by the Department of Foreign Affairs in Ireland. However, aid and development cooperation is also slightly distinct from foreign policy. Many of the questions relating to aid policy are technical ones concerning the efficacy of aid, and these will not be considered as central to this study. They have been dealt with in some detail elsewhere.[1] However, some questions of aid policy do coincide with foreign policy, and these will be addressed in this book. Questions such as the decision to approve aid to a particular country or the political role played by Irish Development Cooperation Offices will be considered in full. It should however be borne in mind that aid is only one among a number of issues that can be found within Third World foreign policy, and will not be accorded any undue priority.

Defining the study: the Third World

The second key term that needs to be given at least a working definition before the study proceeds is the Third World. The phrase is one that can be readily understood in some contexts, but that defies accurate definition. Certainly, it conjures up immediate connotations of certain countries wracked by poverty and hunger in Africa, Asia and Latin America. However, beyond what might be termed these "core" countries, the phrase has been applied with an increasing lack of precision to virtually all the countries of those three continents and of the Pacific region. Any attempt to define a term which has thus been applied to well over a hundred states in all areas of the globe is therefore fraught with difficulty. Nevertheless, it is also an important task, particularly from an Irish point of view. One Irish official recalls an informal conversation with a Spanish representative in the UN in the 1960s, where the Spaniard pointed out that both his own country and Ireland faced the same quandary: should they identify themselves as part of the Third World, and be the richest of the poor, or should they identify instead with the First World, and be the poorest of the rich?

There can be little doubt that the official Irish response has been to associate with the First World, and that provides a useful channel to build a definition for the purposes of this book.[2] It is easier to begin by identifying those countries that the book is not primarily concerned with. First, the group of high-income industrialised countries that Ireland belongs to is excluded. This group covers North America, Western Europe, Japan, Australia and New Zealand. Second, industrialised countries of the one-time communist bloc are also excluded. This covers the countries of Eastern Europe and the republics of the former Soviet Union, as foreign policy dealings with these states until now have been quite distinct from dealings with Third World countries. What remains is still a vast and disparate collection of states, but one which we shall treat for the purposes of this book as the Third World.

The Third World is thus taken to cover all the countries of Africa, Asia (except Japan and the Soviet Asian republics), Central and South America and the Pacific region. There are a number of reasons for adopting such an approach. First, in the absence of an agreed and precise definition of the Third World, we prefer to be as inclusive as possible. Second, a narrow approach concentrating on the poorest countries would greatly restrict the number of cases available for study, because such countries have relatively limited diplomatic dealings and capacities. Third, a concentration on the poorest countries would also limit the study to a far narrower range of policy issues, whereas the broader approach adopted gives much more scope for comparisons and contrasts between different parts of the world.

However, we do recognise that an approach which lumps together Venezuela and Vanuatu, South Korea and El Salvador, Bahrain and Burundi, ignores the reality of massive differences within the category. In order to accommodate these differences, we will distinguish (where appropriate) between the countries of the Third World on the same basis used by the Development Assistance Committee (DAC) of the Organisation for Economic Cooperation and Development (OECD), that of average income levels. The basic distinction employed is that of low-income, middle-income and high-income countries (LICs, MICs and HICs), with a further distinction in the low-income bracket of least-developed countries (LLDCs) and a further sub-division of the middle-income bracket into lower and upper bands (LMICs and UMICs).[3]

Appendix 1 gives a list of the countries that fall within our overall definition of Third World, classified by continent and by income bracket. It also presents a slightly more detailed discussion of the various different approaches to defining the Third World. It should be recognised that some countries included under our rubric of Third World might regard this as something of a slight on their status. Certainly, in some quarters the term Third World does carry pejorative connotations. But in this work we do not intend to imply any criticism or condescension in the use of the phrase. A value statement regarding our attitudes towards the Third World, however defined, is appropriate here. Although we will approach our analysis of foreign policy towards the Third World in a neutral and unbiased fashion, we will base some of our conclusions on the premise that this policy ought to attempt to be progressive, in the sense of being in some way supportive of the interests of the Third World. Foreign policy relations with the Third World should at some level be consistent with a goal of alleviating the problems that exist overall in North-South relations.

Levels: bilateral, regional and international

Ireland's foreign relations can be seen as being conducted at three levels: bilateral, regional and global or international. These three levels are of course not mutually exclusive categories and the links between and within them are important to understanding the way in which Ireland formulates and conducts its foreign policy.

(a) The bilateral level

Ireland's bilateral links both generally, and specifically with the Third World, have developed in an ad hoc and sporadic manner over the years, often reflecting occasional interests and chance meetings rather than any fundamentally rational plan. Indeed, at the founding of the state, some argued that there was no need for Ireland to have a Department of Foreign Affairs at all, branding such notions as "ridiculous theatricals".[4] A Department was established nonetheless, and the earliest diplomatic relations were with the UK and the US, established in 1923 and 1924 respectively, followed by the Holy See, France and Germany in 1929. As Table 1.1 shows, bilateral diplomatic contact remains heavily concentrated on European and North American states (see also Appendix 2).

Anglo-Irish and US-Irish relationships have dominated Ireland's foreign policy agenda since the formation of the state. Relations with Britain are significant for a panoply of reasons, reflecting Britain's position as Ireland's nearest neighbour, its role as colonising power, and as a global power in its own right. Extensive economic, social, cultural and political links have constantly placed the Anglo-Irish relationship high on Ireland's agenda,[5] even before the issue of partition is taken into

Table 1.1: Ireland's bilateral diplomatic links, by region, 1992

	resident embs	non-res. embs	H.C. only	DCOs	total	%[a]
W Europe	15	5	1	0	21	87.50
N America	2	0	0	0	2	66.66
Asia	7	17	1	0	25	62.50
E Europe	2	8	0	0	10	58.82[b]
Africa	2	7	6	3	17[c]	32.08
C/L Am.	1	3	3	0	7	15.22
Oceania	1	1	0	0	2	11.76
Sub-total	30	41	11	3	84	54.90
Internat. Orgs.	2	3	na	na	5	na
Total	32	44	11	3	89	

Notes:

(a) This column gives a percentage figure for the number of countries with which there are diplomatic ties as a proportion of the total number of countries in the region.

(b) The number of countries deemed to be in Eastern Europe is 17, based on ten former Soviet republics which lie to the west of the Urals (Russia, Lithuania, Latvia, Estonia, Byelorussia, Ukraine, Moldavia, Armenia, Azerbaijan and Georgia) and seven other states (Poland, Czechoslovakia, Hungary, Bulgaria, Romania, Albania and Yugoslavia).

(c) Tanzania is covered both by a Development Cooperation Office and by non-resident accreditation, and has been included in both these columns.

H.C. Honorary Consulate

DCO Development Cooperation Office

na not applicable to international organisations

Source: Information supplied by Department of Foreign Affairs (1992)

consideration. Ireland has also enjoyed a long and predominantly good relationship with the US, based largely on a significant Irish immigrant population there and also on a common language. The relationship was strengthened in the post-war period by economic support under the Marshall Plan, US investment in the Irish economy and the development of such projects as the transatlantic airport at Shannon.[6] Ireland's bilateral links elsewhere have been very limited, extending predominantly to Europe. The views of the Vatican seem at one stage to have been of particular import to the Department of External Affairs,[7] but the key embassies now are in Paris and Bonn.

Relations with Third World states have never been a priority. Although another early contributor to the Dáil suggested that Ireland should try "to get a slice of Africa" to start a colony,[8] the Department declined to follow this up, so that unlike most of its

European counterparts Ireland had no overseas colonies.[9] Formal diplomatic links were few and slow to develop. The first Dáil (1919), which attempted to initiate relations with other countries prior to Irish independence, established unofficial missions in a number of countries, including Argentina and Chile,[10] but those two South American outposts were not succeeded by formal missions once independence was achieved. The first Irish Embassy in the Third World was opened in Argentina in 1947, to be followed by Nigeria in 1960 and India in 1964. These three embassies appear to have been seen as listening-posts for most of their respective continents, fulfilling little more than token representation.

Membership of the EC acted as a catalyst for the expansion of the Irish foreign service, not just in Europe but in the Third World as well. This was perhaps most noticeable in the case of Africa. The Lagos embassy was joined by Egypt in 1974 and Kenya in 1979. At the same time, the Fine Gael-Labour coalition government of 1973-77 introduced Ireland's first Bilateral Aid Programme, again partly as a reaction to Community membership, and four of the five countries initially targeted for assistance were in Africa. A Development Cooperation Office was established in each of those four (Lesotho, Sudan, Tanzania and Zambia). Finally, during the 1970s and 1980s, non-resident diplomatic relations were set up with Morocco, Algeria, Tunisia and Libya in North Africa and with Zimbabwe. Relations with Africa are thus concentrated on English-speaking countries and on North African Arab states.

The same pattern of expansion following EC membership is evident in Asia and the Middle East, where attention fell overwhelmingly on the newly-industrialising countries (NICs) and oil-exporting countries. Full Embassies were established in China, South Korea, Japan, Saudi Arabia, Lebanon, Iran and Iraq; non-resident relations were established with Malaysia, Singapore, Thailand, the Philippines, Indonesia, Kuwait, Bahrain, the UAE and Brunei. Although India was originally identified as a recipient of Irish bilateral aid, this relationship did not develop. The Indian Embassy has been the base for non-resident accreditation in South East Asia rather than more immediate neighbours such as Bangladesh and Sri Lanka. Relations with Asia remain focussed on the wealthier states.

Despite the fact that the Embassy in Buenos Aires is Ireland's longest-established mission to a Third World country, relations with Central and Latin America have developed to a far lesser extent than with Africa and Asia. No further embassies have been set up, and the only non-resident missions are in Mexico, Brazil and Venezuela. In 1981 the then Foreign Minister, Brian Lenihan, envisaged further expansion: "We are contemplating doing something on these lines in so far as Venezuela is concerned. That is a very obvious area. It is a democratic government".[11] But by the late 1980s the situation had retrenched, with Lenihan noting that "the present constraints on public expenditure make the establishment of formal relations with other states in Latin America unlikely for the time being ... there are contacts in the UN General Assembly in New York and elsewhere".[12] Even that level of contact surpasses the extent of relations with the states of the Pacific. Although the island of New Ireland forms part of Papua New Guinea, there is no Irish diplomatic presence in the region beyond Australia and New Zealand.

(b) The regional level

Ireland's bilateral relations have, then, been quite limited and predominantly with Europe and the United States. This pattern is reinforced through membership of regional organisations, the most important of which in recent years has been the EC. Ireland has, nevertheless, also participated in and been a member of a number of other regional organisations. Some of these have no significant relations with the Third World or any foreign policy element, such as the Council of Europe and the Conference on Security and Co-operation in Europe (CSCE). Of more relevance is the OECD, which Ireland joined in 1948 when the body was known as the OEEC (Organisation for European Economic Co-operation). As the name suggests, the OECD is concerned largely with economic matters, and it has concentrated on encouraging market orientated economic growth. It has an active Development Assistance Committee (DAC), which Ireland joined in 1985. The DAC acts as something of a "conscience of the rich nations"[13] by being a forum for monitoring development cooperation. It works as a "consultative process for accumulating and exchanging experience, harmonizing aid policies and programmes, and critically reviewing and evaluating assistance efforts"[14], and is thus limited to aid issues rather than broader foreign policy matters.

The regional organisation that has changed Ireland's external relations most significantly is the EC. Of course, the impact of membership was felt not just in the sphere of foreign policy, but throughout political and economic life in Ireland.[15] The

Community, by its nature, is itself far more than simply an organisation for cooperation between member states, and has pretensions to being a supranational agency controlling many policy areas. If this were to come about, it would have far-reaching implications for the foreign policies of member states, but even in its present guise the EC has increasingly been impacting on the foreign policy domains of the member states. While the EC lacks a fully fledged foreign policy, it does act in international affairs on behalf of its members in a number of fora.

There are two distinct channels through which this occurs. First, the Community acts for its members regarding trade relations with non-EC states under the terms of the Common Commercial Policy (Article 113), and plays a significant role in overseas development assistance to the Third World.[16] Second, the member states seek to coordinate their foreign policies and actions in international relations through European Political Cooperation (EPC), although this is a distinct decision-making process that operates on the basis of intergovernmental cooperation rather than on the basis of majority voting. Decisions taken under EPC are therefore not binding, and states may choose distinctly different paths in foreign policy, though there is clear and growing pressure to act together. Community concertation of foreign policy has affected Ireland particularly in terms of the contact the country has had with the Third World. Both in terms of quality and quantity, such dealings have mushroomed since EC accession. The expansion of diplomatic ties and the development of an aid programme demonstrate the impact that EC membership has had at a bilateral level. EC membership has not only affected Ireland's bilateral relationships but has required Ireland to adopt active stances on issues it would previously have devoted little time to in the past, such as the Middle East.

(c) The international level

The other international forum in which Ireland has been an active participant has been the UN and its specialised agencies. The UN is relevant to a consideration of Third World issues and problems in a number of ways. First, a number of its affiliated agencies are involved solely with development issues (United Nations Development Programme, International Finance Corporation) or with particular regions of the Third World (Economic Commission for Latin America, United Nations Fund for Namibia). Second, a number of UN bodies have taken on Third World issues as a dominant part of their work, again with a distinction between those concerned with purely development issues (United Nations Children's Fund, Food and Agriculture Organisation) and more general ones (United Nations High Commissioner for Refugees and the General Assembly). The form that such UN involvement takes varies as much as does the range of UN bodies. At one level, exemplified by the UN General Assembly, activity is little more than debate and discussion of issues, whereas agencies such as the UNDP, the FAO, and the World Health Organisation (WHO) are involved in practical implementation of more concrete programmes of action. This more active intervention by UN agencies is strongest in cases where the UN has become directly involved in conflicts through observation and peacekeeping forces.

Ireland sought membership of the UN immediately after World War Two, but was baulked by the USSR until 1955. Once admitted, Ireland began to develop the UN as a major forum for its foreign policy concerns. At that time, in the late 1950s and early 1960s, the nature of the UN was undergoing a considerable transformation. The UN General Assembly was becoming increasingly concerned with the issues of decolonisation as the major colonial empires disintegrated, so of necessity Ireland was cast into a theatre where not only was decolonisation itself a major part of the script, but also whose cast was changing rapidly. Indeed, there was a noticeable shift in the priorities of the UN agenda away from the interests of the two Cold War blocs towards the concerns of the Third World states.[17] Irish membership of the UN meant of necessity a much greater degree of exposure to the countries and interests of the Third World.

Of course, the UN also influences Irish foreign policy on more than simply Third World issues. It has been an important focus for Irish foreign policy on a number of other issues, most notably disarmament and human rights questions. For a brief period in the late 1950s, Ireland devoted much time and effort to pursuing an active and independent policy at the UN, and it remains an important forum for Irish policy. Only Anglo-Irish relations and, more latterly, relations with the EC have regularly received more attention. The UN has also offered significant opportunities for Irish involvement in wider issues of international relations, in particular on the economic front, where a number of agencies founded under UN auspices are involved such as the World Bank and International Monetary Fund (IMF). It is also worth noting the role of the General Agreement on Tariffs and Trade (GATT), which is a major influence on global economic relations, although it is outside any UN competences.[18]

Goals and issues

States can be assumed to pursue sets of foreign policy goals in the international arena. All states have in mind objectives they wish to achieve. Some states, such as the USA and the former Soviet Union, have or had truly global goals that were associated with strong views about the way the world should be, and were based on ideological considerations. The Irish state's goals are much more modest at whatever level they are articulated. As an Irish official observed: "we don't have goals in the sense of great global strategies".[19] Irish foreign policy goals are seldom distinguishable from immediate issues with which the state is dealing.

The issues on the foreign policy agenda of any state fall into two very broad categories: those issues the state itself wishes to raise or to pursue, and those which have been placed on the agenda by other states or forces. Within the first category, there are certain features which appear regularly. The basic distinguishing feature of an independent state is its borders, and in situations where there is any debate or dispute over borders, a political assertion of sovereignty is usually a strong feature of foreign policy. A second feature is the pursuit of economic interests internationally. Another common theme is that of security. No state relies purely or even largely on military policy to ensure defence, so there is always a foreign policy element attached. The second category, which might be termed the international milieu faced by a state, again throws up certain common themes. Most states pursue some sort of international order, certain rules of the international relations/foreign policy game which attempt to control relations between states. Most states also have some conception of international justice, some plan for how relations between states should be.

(a) Sovereignty

For Ireland, the political assertion of sovereignty has been of particular importance throughout the life of the state. The independence achieved in 1922 was highly ill-defined, as the country was granted the rather ambiguous status of being a Free State within the British Commonwealth. The legal competences of this status were not established, and much of the early foreign policy of the Irish Free State was bound up in carving out as much sovereignty and autonomy from Britain as possible. Even in later years, when Ireland's status as a fully independent, sovereign state was no longer contested, the issue of partition and the continued separate existence of Northern Ireland kept issues of sovereignty high on the Irish foreign policy agenda. Until Irish assertiveness on this issue began to wane in the 1970s, partition was raised by Irish delegates at every available forum and at every available opportunity. This approach was condemned by some, who felt that "our parliamentary delegates to the Council of Europe seemed to devote their time to making speeches about partition: speeches which were designed to be read at home, but unfortunately had to be listened to abroad",[20] and certainly seem to have baffled and bored the country's partners.[21] However, it also served to keep an awareness of the injustices of imperialism and colonialism alive and fresh in Irish minds, which, as we shall see, has informed Irish policy towards the Third World quite extensively.

(b) Economic

Traditionally, Irish economic interests were closely aligned with those of Britain, Ireland's major trading partner. More broadly, Ireland is a part of the Western economic camp and the countries of the OECD. As a member of the EC Ireland enjoys a privileged trading relationship with its European partners. Beyond the EC Ireland's external trade is largely governed by the rules and regulations laid down by the European Community under the Common Commercial Policy.

Ireland's economic ties with the Third World range from quite significant links in cases such as Parc Hospital Services in Iraq, the beef trade with a number of Middle Eastern countries, and the investments of the Smurfit Group in Latin America,[22] to some unusual individual links, such as the Wicklow game warden employed on a Tanzanian conservation programme for elephants and rhinoceroses[23] and the employment of one-time Irish soccer international Joe Kinnear as manager of the Nepalese team for the qualifying matches for the 1990 World Cup.[24] Guinness has breweries in Malaysia, Nigeria (where one of the strongest Guinness stouts is brewed), Ghana and the Cameroons, and has licensing deals with a number of other Third World states. However, this might more accurately be seen as a cultural link, since Guinness is owned and operated from the UK, despite its very strong Irish connotations. But in general Irish trading links with the Third World have never been particularly strong. As Table 1.2 shows, the Third World accounts for only a small proportion of Irish imports and exports, amounting to some 6 per cent in 1988.

However, Ireland does have a voice in international economic

Table 1.2: Geographical structure of Irish trade,
1970, 1980 and 1988

Area	Exports			Imports		
	1970 %	1980 %	1988 %	1970 %	1980 %	1988 %
EC	75	68	74	69	71	66
Extra-EC industrial	20	15	23	21	20	28
Extra-EC developing	5	9	7	10	9	6
of which						
OPEC	1	4	3	4	5	0
other LDC	3	5	4	5	4	6
Unclassified	–	1	1	–	1	1
Total	100	100	100	100	100	100
Memo item: value, IR£m	456	4,083	12,301	677	5,421	10,213

Source: Matthews (1991: 30)

fora which contribute significantly to the economic circumstances facing Third World states. In such fora as GATT and the OECD Ireland has adopted a relatively conservative posture in respect of the international trading system. For example, in the most recent round of GATT negotiations the Irish Government has had a very clear interest in defending the maintenance of subsidies for certain agricultural products and textiles, even though these are detrimental to the interests of some developing countries. These issues pose an apparent dilemma to the Irish Government, since while on the one hand in its relations with the Third World it seeks to promote economic growth and prosperity, on the other hand it must attempt to ensure its own economic prosperity. These two goals are not always mutually reinforcing, and indeed are often in conflict with one another.[25]

(c) Security

In respect of security, Ireland has traditionally adopted a neutral stance in international affairs. Ireland's neutrality, which has been a central tenet of Irish foreign policy, is both more ambiguous and less definitive in comparison to its European counterparts such as Sweden, Switzerland, Finland and Austria.[26] It is, nevertheless, significant in terms of what Irish foreign policy-makers do and do not do in international affairs, and in terms of its public popularity. Ireland is not a member of any military alliance, such as the North Atlantic Treaty Organisation (NATO) or the Western European Union (WEU), and therefore does not contribute military forces to any military pacts. Furthermore, Ireland's neutrality and its support for international justice and humanitarian measures in the UN have made it a frequent participant in UN peacekeeping forces. Such activities date from Ireland's initial participation in the Middle East in 1958. Neutrality has served to give Ireland a more distinctive international posture, and has contributed to a general feeling that Irish foreign policy is and should be altruistic and peaceful.

Fundamental questions are now being raised about Irish neutrality, especially in the light of ratification of the Maastricht Treaty and any possible future EC intergovernmental conferences, such as that planned for 1996.[27] It is proposed that a degree of security cooperation be accepted by the EC, though the EC is likely to be enlarged before any significant development on security cooperation occurs. Since the next rounds of enlargement seem sure to see the accession of a number of neutral states, such as Austria, Sweden and Finland, this would greatly enhance Ireland's ability to maintain its neutrality should it so desire. How this would affect Ireland's relations with the Third World is not yet clear, if indeed it would do so at all. Neutrality can be seen as a bridge to the Non-Aligned Movement, which encompasses most Third World states, but neither Ireland nor the other European neutrals have maintained particularly close relations with the Movement in the past,[28] and the collapse of the Cold War is far more of a challenge to non-aligned status than it is to neutrality.

(d) International order

Issues presented by the overall international milieu may, as we have stated before, be divided into issues of international order and international justice. All states have an interest in seeing a relatively well-ordered international environment around them, but conceptions of how that order is to be achieved vary considerably. More powerful states can seek to impose their own preferred order on others, either globally or regionally. Ireland, in common with most smaller states, adopts a very different stance. Two consequences follow from Ireland's relatively small and powerless circumstances. Policy has generally been to pursue peaceful, negotiated solutions to problems, on the profoundly reasonable grounds that any other path could be disastrous for Ireland. Policy has also been to encourage the growth and use of international organisations as the best fora for any such negotiations. Bodies such as the UN or the EC give Ireland a greater opportunity for influence with global and regional powers than would an entirely anarchic international environment.

Of course, this presents certain dilemmas for Ireland. As a strong supporter of the UN, it has to face the fact that this body is viewed less favourably by some of the country's traditional partners, particularly the US and the UK. Furthermore, there is a developing paradox arising from Ireland's relationship with the EC. Ireland cannot be seen purely as a small state in world affairs, because it is also part of a powerful bloc, whose collective views on how best to achieve world order might differ from what Ireland has espoused so far. Ireland, of course, is not the only small state in the EC, nor even the only one which is generally supportive of the UN, but it is certainly a problem that the Community's smaller states need to consider.

(e) International justice

Finally, the international environment also poses questions of international justice. For a variety of reasons, largely stemming from the country's historical experiences, Ireland has generally adopted what might be termed a progressive stance on such issues. Ireland's own colonial experience is still remembered; the situation in Northern Ireland keeps conflict to the forefront in Ireland; and the country's peripheral location creates problems of economic performance. All these factors contribute to the ways in which Irish people interpret events elsewhere. In particular, the colonial past has given the country considerable sympathy for decolonisation struggles elsewhere and has contributed to a lingering suspicion concerning the activities and motivations of more powerful states. The Northern Irish situation creates a particular awareness and appreciation of the complexities involved in any conflict or border dispute. And the country's own economic problems encourage a degree of understanding on issues such as demands for a New International Economic Order, although they may at the same time lessen the desire to act on these demands.

It should of course be pointed out that these various types of issues are by no means intrinsically complementary. Indeed, contradictions can and do emerge both within and between these issue headings. For example, Ireland's experience as a colony leads it to support liberation movements elsewhere, but that is constrained by the current circumstances in Northern Ireland, as Irish Governments have been anxious to avoid being seen to support any liberation groups advocating violence. Contradictions also emerge between the kinds of issues. Security interests can clash with economic objectives, for example when the US sought to prevent its European allies from trading technology to the USSR for a gas pipeline in the 1980s. Ireland's support for decolonisation movements is not always compatible with the aim of encouraging a degree of world order, since such groups represent a challenge to the existing order. The interplay of these issues is an important element in Irish foreign policy.

Conclusion

The analysis of the goals and the levels of Irish foreign policy that has been presented so far already suggests three features of that foreign policy. First, the formal foreign policy sphere has been gradually expanding since the foundation of the state. Bilateral diplomatic relations have spread to many countries, and Ireland's involvement in international organisations at both the regional and the global level has also grown. At the same time, a wider range of goals of foreign policy is being taken on now. From a concentration on the issues of independence and sovereignty to begin with, Irish concerns have been expanded to include many more issues. The pursuit of sovereignty has declined in importance as Ireland has become more assured of its place among the nations of the world, and instead attention has turned to what roles the country can play. Economic goals are perhaps slightly more important, especially since joining the UN.

The second feature is that the balance between the different levels of policy has changed. Understandably, given the dearth of opportunities for involvement in international organisations at the time, the bilateral level dominated Irish foreign policy until the post-war era. However, developments since then have not simply added new dimensions to Irish foreign policy but have changed their relationships as well. The UN became a particularly important focus for Irish foreign policy after accession in 1955. But since joining the EC in 1973, the UN has in turn become a less central level of foreign policy. The EC is now the more important focus, ahead of both the bilateral and the global levels, though all three are significant components of Irish foreign policy activity.

The third feature is that although the boundaries of foreign policy have been expanding, the development of relations with the Third World has tended to lag behind other developments. The importance of the EC and the UN in Irish foreign policy has benefitted relations with the Third World. Both organisations have exposed Ireland to a far greater extent of involvement with the concerns and interests of the Third World. But despite the increased opportunity for involvement through the regional and global foreign policy levels, bilateral links remain weak. Ireland has fewer embassies in the Third World than elsewhere, and the foreign policy goals which might most readily be associated with the Third World – those of international justice and international order – are more recent additions to Ireland's foreign policy interests. This suggests that relations with the Third World do not rank quite as significantly as relations with other parts of the globe, emphasising that the Third World is something of a poor relation in Irish foreign policy.

This will be examined in more detail later on. For the moment, it is necessary to clarify further the frameworks that Irish foreign policy finds itself in. The levels and the goals represent in a way the "how and why" of putting policy across. However, it is also important to assess the process by which that policy emerges in the first place, to look at the "how and why" of formulation rather than implementation. The following chapter therefore examines in a general manner the Irish foreign policy-making process and the actors who participate in the different decision-making structures. In particular, we consider the place of Third World issues in this process and the weight accorded to such concerns relative to Ireland's other foreign policy interests.

Footnotes

1   O'Neill 1982; Trócaire 1985; O'Neill 1991.
2   Alternative responses have been suggested, as for instance in Caherty et. al. (1992), which argues *inter alia* that the conditions for some communities in Ireland (for instance, women, Travellers, the unemployed, Northern nationalists) are directly analogous with conditions in the Third World. There is certainly a case for arguing that Third World conditions are to be found in parts of New York, London and Dublin, and that First World lifestyles are equally to be found for example in Nairobi or New Delhi. However, such cross-state conceptions are not appropriate to a book dealing first and foremost with a form of inter-state behaviour such as foreign policy.

3 The 1990 DAC Report, using data for 1988, defines LICs as countries with a GNP per capita of $545 or less, MICs as countries with a GNP per capita between $545 and $6,000, and HICs as ones with a GNP per capita of over $6,000. The LLDCs are a group of countries deemed to have particularly severe problems of development, with general characteristics of having a low per capita income, a low adult literacy rate and low contribution of manufacturing to GDP, with other less quantifiable elements taken into consideration also. The cut-off point between LMICs and UMICs is $2,200. A full list of countries in each group and sub-group is provided in Appendix 1.

4 *Dáil debates*, 16 November 1923, 5: 940.

5 Keatinge 1982: 308-319.

6 Whelan 1992.

7 Keogh 1989: passim.

8 *Dáil debates*, 13 May 1925, 11: 1448-1449.

9 Indeed, Ireland's own experience of colonisation and liberation make it more sympathetic to liberation movements elsewhere. The country has been a willing supporter of UN resolutions for causes such as the anti-apartheid movement and Palestinian liberation.

10 Keatinge 1973: 108.

11 *Dáil debates*, 1 April 1981, 1: 729.

12 Kirby 1992: 119-20.

13 Rubin 1966.

14 Thorp 1985: 45.

15 Coombes 1983; Keatinge 1991a.

16 Matthews 1991.

17 Lindemann 1982: 111.

18 GATT emerged from the UN-planned International Trade Organisation which was never instituted.

19 Interview, Department of Foreign Affairs official, October 1991.

20 O'Brien 1962: 14.

21 Hederman 1983: 35-36.

22 Kirby 1992: 129.

23 *The Irish Times*, 15 January 1992.

24 *Sunday Tribune*, 22 March 1992.

25 Matthews (1991) argues that maintaining protectionist barriers is not in Ireland's own long-term interests either.

26 Salmon 1990.

27 Connolly 1992.

28 Keatinge 1984a: 52.

Chapter 2

Foreign Policy-Making in Ireland

The purpose of this chapter is to set out the factors which influence the formulation of foreign policy in Ireland. We begin by providing a brief explanation of the foreign policy process, not just in Ireland but also in terms of more broadly applicable explanations of how and why countries make their foreign policy. The chapter then moves on to a detailed breakdown of the influence that a number of important actors have on foreign policy in Ireland. These actors include not only governmental ones such as the Minister for Foreign Affairs and the Department of Foreign Affairs, but also non-governmental actors ranging from pressure groups to political parties and non-organised influences such as public opinion and the media. The role and influence of each actor will be assessed. Finally, the chapter presents summaries of how Irish foreign policy is formed at each of the three levels: the domestic level, dealing with bilateral affairs, the regional level of the EC and the global level of the UN.

The foreign policy process

The making and conduct of foreign policy is predominantly the preserve of the government, and within the government the executive branch. As Michael D. Higgins has observed, "Irish foreign policy is a pragmatic amalgam of positions on issues of the day decided by the executive arm of diplomacy rather than a representative assembly. Almost unique in its lack of a Foreign Policy Committee, the Irish Oireachtas is viewed with suspicion by the permanent mandarins in the executive".[1] Irish foreign policy, however, is not entirely an ad hoc and piecemeal process. Irish Governments have pursued a range of different and sometimes conflicting goals in the international arena. In many respects these goals relate for historic, economic and political reasons to the First World rather than the Third World. Ireland is only in the process of coming to terms with and constructing a relationship with the countries of the Third World.

The Irish case in many ways fits into the traditional West European model of foreign policy-making, since the foreign policy process is dominated, as mentioned above, by a small professional civil service concentrated within the Department of Foreign Affairs, and presided over at the political level by the Minister for Foreign Affairs and a junior minister. While other departments, such as Finance, Justice, Agriculture and Industry and Commerce, are involved, they do not exercise the authority over foreign policy that the Department of Foreign Affairs displays. There is also little legislative oversight of this process, with a weak parliamentary tradition of accountability and scrutiny, alongside a poorly developed parliamentary committee system.

We can, however, attempt to describe this foreign policy-making process, relating the various actors to the process of decision-making in the different fora in which Ireland participates. The types of actors involved in the policy-making process range from the governmental (the executive and legislative, the Department of Foreign Affairs), to the non-governmental organised (political parties, interest groups) and the non-governmental, non-organised interests (public opinion). But this only tells us part of the story, and it is necessary to consider particular examples to illustrate how this policy process functions, which we do in the next three chapters. For example, in some instances Irish missionaries and other NGOs have played an important part in the foreign policy-making process. In many ways, the influence of such NGOs is subtle and therefore difficult to assess, but nevertheless they constitute an important part of the policy-making process, and one worth noting and examining.

It is also possible to assume that policy-making, whilst it may differ by area and issue, does engender some broad similarities across issues and time. First, in the governmental context foreign policy comprises the actors who make the foreign policy, the organisational-bureaucratic setting in which it is made, and the broader political environment which sanctions such actions. It is the relationship between these forces that largely determines foreign policy, and which provides the back-drop within which the foreign policy-makers go about their daily business. In comparison with many other West European states this involves relatively few actors and is marked by a simple organisational structure. Within Foreign Affairs a small professional staff work together under quite difficult conditions to make and carry out policy. They are generally under-resourced and therefore overstretched, but nevertheless they sit at the apex of the foreign policy-making process mediating demands from other governmental and non-governmental actors. Second, foreign policy is influenced both directly and indirectly by a range of other non-governmental actors. The impact of the non-governmental actors on the policy process is difficult to measure, especially in what we assume to be an executive-dominated foreign policy process, but nevertheless they do have a role to play in the formulation of policy. The Irish Government acknowledged this, in part, through the establishment of the Advisory Council on Development Cooperation (ACDC), an agency which was created to advise the Irish Government on aid policy, but which was abolished in 1991 (see pages 46 and 48).

It is, then, possible to distinguish between the different sources of foreign policy at two broad levels: the governmental and the societal. What is more difficult to assess is the relationship between the two levels, and the impact of societal forces on the governmental setting. In many respects it differs in relation to the situation and the issue under discussion. For example, in Ireland the GATT talks and the EC's proposals for the reform of agriculture have been highly visible, and have led to considerable opposition from the Irish Farmers' Association (IFA). By contrast, other topics, such as the Lomé Convention, have attracted little attention, and therefore have been predominantly discussed behind closed doors with little public debate.

On a day-to-day basis the Department of Foreign Affairs has been principally responsible for the formulation and practice of foreign policy. Most foreign policy issues are dealt with by the Department of Foreign Affairs on a routine basis. The Department serves and represents the Minister at meetings with other departments. In most instances, matters are dealt with at an official level by civil servants who formulate policy for ministerial approval, usually within the framework of the Cabinet. They collect information, undertake analysis and coordinate with other departments in the formulation of policy and in reacting to daily international events. Finally, they have to implement the policy, ensuring that the desired objectives are achieved. The foreign policy-making process is nevertheless never quite so clear-cut. In practice, as Wallace notes, "the process of policy-making is less one of a series of discrete and identifiable decisions than of a continuous flow of policy".[2] "Governments are rarely unified, objectives rarely entirely clear; information is seldom adequate, and the consequences of a particular line of action are never certain".[3]

Governmental actors

We have already distinguished three broadly different categories of actors. The first of these are governmental actors, and in this category we will make a further distinction between three types. First, there are the political actors of government, in other words the executive and the parliament. The second type of governmental actor is the Department of Foreign Affairs itself. The third is made up of the other government departments and also the various semi-state agencies attached to them and to Foreign Affairs.

(a) Executive and parliament

In foreign policy matters, the authority of the executive is virtually unquestioned. As Keatinge has commented,[4] "the role of the cabinet and especially of its leader and Foreign Minister is paramount". Interestingly, both of those actors have tended to downplay Third World issues. This is evident from an analysis of the official visits overseas by Irish Presidents, Taoisaigh and Foreign Ministers (Table 2.1).[5] In the period 1986-90, only 21 out of 72 such visits were to Third World countries, most of them to countries with which Ireland has reasonably significant trade relations.

There is considerable scope for Foreign Ministers and Taoisaigh to influence the direction and the concerns of foreign policy according to personal preferences. The roles played by individual politicians have been quite significant in the development of policy. This was first evident under de Valera, who combined the jobs of Taoiseach and Foreign Minister. He placed a very clear personal stamp on the direction and style of foreign policy, by emphasising independence and sovereignty at all opportunities, by endorsing an active role for Ireland in the League of Nations and by deciding on a policy of neutrality during the Second World War. De Valera was also strongly given to an intensely personalised decision-making style which minimised the influence played by others in foreign policy matters.[6]

This personal input into foreign policy has continued. Seán MacBride, Foreign Minister of the Coalition Government of

Table 2.1: Official visits to and from Ireland, 1986-90[a]

	Visits to Ireland		Visits from Ireland	
	total	Third World	total	Third World
1986	6	2	6	2
1987	5	0	4	0
1988	4	2	7	1
1989	7	1	13[b]	2
1990[c]	13	1	42	16
Total	35	6[d]	72	21[e]

Notes:

(a) visits by President, Taoiseach or Foreign Minister, and their equivalents for other countries, including President of European Commission.

(b) including visit by Minister for Foreign Affairs to Paris for Euro-Arab Dialogue talks, not included as Third World.

(c) For the first half of 1990, Ireland held the Presidency of the EC, which accounts for most of the increased activity.

(d) official visits to Ireland from Third World countries: China (2), India, Nicaragua, Saudi Arabia, Turkey.

(e) official visits from Ireland to Third World countries: Bahrain, Brunei, China, Egypt (3), Iran, Jordan, Kuwait, Morocco, Namibia, Saudi Arabia (3), South Africa (2), Singapore, South Korea, Tunisia (2), Zambia.

Sources: Keatinge (1987, 1988, 1989, 1990, 1991) Annual review – Ireland's foreign relations *Irish studies in international affairs* 2 (3, 4), 3 (1, 2, 3): appendix c.

1948-51, pursued rather contradictory aims of a more European policy but also one that continued to emphasise partition. When Ireland joined the UN, Frank Aiken, Fianna Fáil Foreign Minister from 1957 to 1969, fully supported the extension of foreign policy and particularly emphasised the issue of disarmament. In the late 1950s and the early 1960s, the Taoiseach, Seán Lemass, oversaw a shift towards Europe, and in this period the economic aspect of foreign policy goals began to come more into play. In more recent years, Garret FitzGerald was very strongly associated with a commitment to developing an aid programme and improving links with the Third World, both as Foreign Minister in 1973-77 and as Taoiseach in the early 1980s, and David Andrews, who became Minister for Foreign Affairs in 1992, has long been associated with a concern for development issues.

However, although personal commitments to the Third World

on the part of leading politicians have played some role, in general there is little political capital to be made from such concerns. Not all Taosaigh or Foreign Ministers have the same level of commitment or interest in foreign affairs, and certainly not all of them would place the Third World high among their foreign policy concerns. In 1972, the Foreign Minister, Patrick Hillery, attempted to rank foreign policy priorities in terms of "concentric circles". He placed Anglo-Irish relations innermost, then relations with the EC, in third place bilateral relations with other developed countries, fourth involvement with other international organisations, particularly the UN, and finally relations with Third World states.[7] This order is still applicable, although the EC has probably closed the gap with Anglo-Irish relations to a considerable degree at this stage.

Foreign policy matters have generally been accorded a very low priority in Irish political life. At the ballot box, few votes are decided on foreign policy issues. The experience of Labour Party TD Michael D. Higgins is informative in this respect. Higgins is widely known for his extensive involvement in foreign policy issues, particularly Third World matters, leading to jibes that he was more a member of the Dáil for Managua than for Galway West. Higgins has stated, however, that his international commitments have told against him on only one occasion. He noted a clear decline in support due to his strong opposition to the visit to Ireland by US President Reagan, even though that was paradoxically the most broadly supported of his many stances.[8] How typical this case might be is open to debate, but there are only a handful of TDs and Senators who are regularly active on foreign policy issues, although that handful make a very considerable contribution to the issues. As one commentator has put it, "special knowledge of foreign affairs is not a qualification that recommends itself to Irish electors"[9], unless it can be applied to the benefit of one's local constituency. When Gerard Collins was made Foreign Minister, he is reputed to have stated that "development aid begins in Limerick West"[10], his own Dáil constituency.

This is reflective of the overall relationship between the political executive and the parliament when it comes to foreign policy. The Dáil has proved very ineffective in maintaining supervision over foreign policy. Very few Oireachtas members contribute to foreign policy debates, and when they do few show any real understanding of the issues: "The contribution of the majority of TDs is minimal and nebulous".[11] This can be interpreted as a self-perpetuating situation: because the Dáil pays little attention to foreign policy issues, governments accord it little respect when it does attempt to act, reinforcing a tendency towards elitism and isolation in Irish foreign policy decision-making. At times, the procedure seems to have been that when the Dáil wants information to say that it is a matter for the government and the people, but when public opinion demands information, to say it is a matter for government and Oireachtas.[12]

The experiences of Oireachtas committees on foreign policy issues underline the problems faced. The Joint Committee on Cooperation with Developing Countries, established in 1982, regularly attempted to expand its influence on aid issues, but was baulked in that aim when it was not reinstated in 1985. Attempts to establish a more comprehensive Joint Committee on Foreign Policy were similarly delayed.[13] The formation of such a committee has been debated on and off since 1924, and although the government eventually consented to establish one in 1991, it has not yet come into existence. This has left only one Oireachtas committee with any degree of responsibility for foreign policy matters, the Joint Committee on Secondary Legislation of the European Community. However, it has no authority over EPC matters, and Third World trade or aid questions form only a small proportion of the EC legislation that the committee oversees. In general, as O'Leary has observed, "the Irish Parliament has not had a tradition of parliamentary committees" which may in part account for the continuing problems in establishing a foreign policy committee.[14]

(b) The Department of Foreign Affairs

The principal foreign policy actor has undoubtedly been the Department of Foreign Affairs (or the Department of External Affairs, as it was known until 1971). Its role is relatively simple: "the primary function of the Department of Foreign Affairs is to advise the government on Ireland's external relations and to act as the channel of official communication with foreign governments and international organisations".[15] This entails the following:

(a) collecting information on all political, economic and other developments abroad that are of interest to Ireland;

(b) presentation and explanation of Irish Government policy to foreign governments and organisations;

(c) representing Ireland at the UN and at international conferences;

(d) negotiating and ratifying international treaties;
(e) encouraging the development of trade;
(f) disseminating information on Ireland;
(g) looking after consular issues, including responsibility for passports and visas;
(h) dealing with questions of international law.[16]

The same source also makes special mention of three further competences of the Department. It makes particular reference to the work of the Department with the Permanent Representation to the EC and it notes that it is responsible for monitoring and coordinating relations with Northern Ireland and for administering the development cooperation programme.[17]

However, as Table 2.2 indicates, the Department is noticeably weaker in terms of overseas representation than its counterparts in many European countries. On a number of measures, such as personnel and missions, the Irish foreign ministry is clearly under-resourced in contrast to comparable countries. These figures do not cover an even worse situation prior to a marked improvement that took place following accession to the EC. Membership led to an increase in personnel in the Department and an expansion in the number of diplomatic missions – twelve resident embassies have been established since 1973, 36 non-resident links and four Development Cooperation Offices. Of course, bearing in mind what has already been said about the geographical spread of Irish embassies (Table 1.1 above), it requires little imagination to realise that the comparative dearth of Irish embassies weighs most heavily on the Third World – under a third are in the Third World, compared to over a half in the other countries examined.

The Department is divided into seven divisions (see Figure 2.1), three of which have a direct role with Third World affairs. The Development Cooperation Division is responsible for co-ordinating Ireland's development assistance programmes, both bilaterally and multilaterally; the Political Division contains sections dealing with Latin America, Africa and Asia; the European Communities Division includes sections dealing with the Third World through the EC. In terms of staff numbers, the Department is quite small. This can be seen to be both an advantage and a hindrance. The small size allows for very easy liaison between desks, so that the person in charge of EC-Latin American relations can keep in close contact with the person in charge of Ireland's bilateral links with Latin America. But it also

Table 2.2: Resident embassies of selected European countries[a]

	Europe	other DAC	Africa	C/S Am.	Asia/Oc.	total	% Third World[b]
Netherlands	24	5	22	16	21	88	67.0
Sweden	27	5	20	12	24	88	63.6
Denmark	29	4	17	6	19	75	56.0
Switzerland	24	5	16	10	17	72	59.7
Austria	24	4	13	8	19	68	58.8
Finland	24	4	11	9	15	63	55.6
Norway	22	4	7	6	15	54	51.9
Ireland	17	4	2	1	6	30	30.0

Notes:

(a) Because the material is drawn from different years, the lists are not directly comparable, as the older sources would for example still include the GDR among their embassies, while newer sources would include new embassies in the Baltic states. However, the general picture holds true.

(b) Percent of embassies in Africa, Central and South America and Asia/Oceania out of total embassies.

Sources:

Royal Swedish Ministry for Foreign Affairs, 1991
Royal Dutch Ministry for Foreign Affairs, n.d.
Royal Danish Ministry for Foreign Affairs, n.d.
Swiss Federal Department of Foreign Affairs, May 1990
Austrian Federal Ministry of Foreign Affairs, n.d.
Finnish Ministry for Foreign Affairs, April 1991
Royal Norwegian Ministry for Foreign Affairs, 1991
State Directory, Republic of Ireland, 1991

Figure 2.1: Structure of Department of Foreign Affairs, Dublin, 1991

Minister/private secretary	
Minister of state/private secretary	
Secretary/private secretary	

ANGLO-IRISH INFORMATION & CULTURAL DIVISION Asst. Sec.	CULTURAL & INFORMATION SECTION 1 Councillor (Clr.), 3 1st Sec, 1 3rd Sec. PRESS SECTION 1 Clr., 1 1st Sec, 1 3rd Sec. ANGLO-IRISH SECTION 4 Clr., 7 1st Sec, 6 3rd Sec., 2 HEO
ADMINISTRATION DIVISION Asst. Sec.	PERSONNEL SECTION & FINANCE UNIT 1 Clr., 3 1st Sec., 1 HEO ORGANISATION AND MANAGEMENT SERVICES 1 Clr., 8 staff CONSULAR SECTION including PASSPORT OFFICE (2 officers) 1 Clr., 2 1st Sec., 1 3rd Sec., 2 HEO PROTOCOL SECTION 1 Clr., 2 1st Sec., 1 3rd Sec., 2 HEO
EUROPEAN COMMUNITIES DIVISION Asst. Sec.	3 Clr., 6 1st Sec., 7 3rd Sec.
FOREIGN EARNINGS DIVISION Asst. Sec	2 Clr., 3 1st Sec., 2 3rd Sec.
LEGAL DIVISION Asst. Sec.	4 Legal Adviser, 1 HEO
POLITICAL DIVISION Asst. Sec.	4 Clr., 10 1st Sec., 7 3rd Sec.
DEVELOPMENT COOPERATION DIVISION Asst. Sec.	2 Clr., 6 1st Sec., 3 3rd Sec., 2 HEO

means that civil servants are being asked to be experts on a huge range of countries and political problems at any one time, imposing perhaps an unnecessarily heavy demand.

(c) Other government departments and agencies

Other government departments have played lesser roles in the making of foreign policy, but have nonetheless been important in certain issue areas. The Department of the Taoiseach has emerged as an important contributor, particularly on Northern Ireland and EC issues, but has tended to concentrate on what are deemed important issues. In that light, it is interesting to note that the Department has played little role on Third World issues. A number of other departments have also had inputs, mostly associated with their own particular concerns. For example, the Department of Industry and Commerce has been the major contributor for Ireland in GATT negotiations; the Department of Defence has had a particular involvement through peacekeeping activities and the Department of Agriculture has participated regularly in fora such as the Food and Agriculture Organisation (FAO).

The Department of Justice is responsible for the conduct of an increasingly sensitive aspect of Irish relations with the Third World – the attitude towards, and treatment of, Third World refugees and migrants. Ireland has certainly assisted refugees through contributions to the UN. In 1974, for example, the UN asked Ireland to take a number of Chilean refugees after the coup. The Government agreed to do so; however, most of these had returned to Chile by the mid-1980s.[18] In 1979, Ireland was asked by the UN to take 2,000 Vietnamese "boat people", but the Government agreed to accept just 200. The Government subsequently indicated that "it had not decided on any precise figure for the total number of refugees to be accepted here",[19] but has generally followed a very restrictive line.

The Irish Government has not incorporated the UN Convention on Refugees Status into domestic law, and a study conducted by the Irish Refugee Council indicates that of 212 applications for political asylum to the Department of Justice from 1986 to 1990, only 23 were granted.[20] Ireland's doors are not open to refugees or immigrants, and in particular those from the Third World. This is similar to the approach pursued by the Department of Justice towards Jewish emigrants fleeing Germany at the time of the Second World War who sought asylum here in Ireland. Though the numbers were minuscule compared to requests to Britain and the US, the Department of Justice did not encourage Jewish immigration.[21] Many were allowed to stay only after personal requests were made to Eamon de Valera on their behalf by prominent individuals and organisations. Comparisons can be made between these attitudes and those pertaining towards Third World nations now.

The role of the Department of Finance is also worthy of attention. Although it does not have a direct role in the making of foreign policy, it holds the purse strings for Foreign Affairs because of its role in scrutinising and assessing the financial activities of all departments. The Department's rubrics for decisions are general ones that would apply to all departments, basically that expenditures be justified and kept to a minimum. Finance would be involved in questions such as the opening of an embassy or the negotiation of an international treaty which required financial commitments. Beyond that, Finance is prepared to be swayed and has no particular preference among Ireland's foreign policy goals.

In times of financial stringency it is difficult to maintain the Department of Foreign Affairs, much less to try any expansion. Finance does not seem to insist on any particular kind of cutback, for example closure of specific embassies or programmes, but by limiting the total budget available to Foreign Affairs it forces those decisions onto that Department. In 1987, at a time of general cutbacks in public finances, Foreign Affairs was forced to close the Embassy in Kenya and the Development Cooperation Office in Sudan and to cut back drastically on expenditure on development assistance. Official Development Assistance was cut from 0.25 per cent of GNP in 1986 to 0.18 per cent in 1991,[22] and most of that reduction has affected the Bilateral Aid Programme rather than multilateral aid commitments, which are less easy to renege upon.

In view of these cutbacks, it is interesting to note that the cost of maintaining embassies in the Third World is considerably lower than elsewhere, as can be seen in Table 2.3. The first two sections of the Table give figures for the estimated total cost per embassy and per diplomat in different regions, with cost in North American and European missions emerging clearly higher than in Africa and South America. The figures in the third section of the Table give a comparison between the expenditures on salaries, wages and allowances for all embassies, DCOs and permanent representations in 1991. This expenditure accounted for roughly 62 per cent of the Department of Foreign Affairs spending in that year (excluding development assistance), although it usually accounts for closer to 70 per cent of expenditure. The figures

Table 2.3: Costs of maintaining embassies (IR£)

Average cost of placing an Irish diplomat overseas in: (1980)	Ambassador	Counsellor	First Sec.	Third Sec.
A North American capital	105,000	33,300	28,000	19,750
A West European capital	88,500	36,700	30,300	22,250
An East European capital	81,000	–	27,600	22,000
An African capital	72,500	37,700	–	–
A South American capital	57,500	–	–	17,000

Total average annual cost of an embassy overseas (1980)

North America	317,000
Western Europe	280,000
Eastern Europe	230,000
Africa	145,000
South America	120,000

Average cost of embassy salaries, wages and allowances (1991)

Western Europe	529,600
North America	479,700
Other OECD	381,000
Eastern Europe	237,000
Asia (excl. Japan)	206,700
South America	152,200

Source: *Dáil debates*, 18 June 1980, 322: 971-974; Revised Estimate for Public Expenditure 1992

suggest a similar pattern, with costs in North American and West European missions in particular outstripping those of other missions. By way of reference, the estimated annual cost of maintaining non-resident relations with countries was IR£5,000 which applied in most cases where such accreditation is established by Ireland.[23]

In addition to governmental departments, there are also a number of semi-state agencies involved in the foreign policy domain. Some of these include Third World or development issues as part of a wider vista of work, for instance the Irish Trade Board (An Bord Tráchtála).[24] The lack of importance of Third World markets is evident from the spread of the office network of the Trade Board (Table 2.4). The Board has 22 offices outside Ireland with none in Africa or Latin America. In Asia, there are offices in Japan, Singapore, Hong Kong and China. The trade consultant network consists of 35 contacts, including four in Africa, one in Latin America and seven in Asia.

The Trade Board is ready to provide "market information, advisory services and field assistance" to exporters to Africa, South and East Asia.[25] But the Board's plans for 1991 were to continue support for existing links: electronics and services suppliers to Asian markets and sales opportunities in African markets "will be pursued on a tactical basis".[26] This can be contrasted with the response of the Trade Board to the opening up of Central and Eastern Europe. New pilot offices were rapidly established in Warsaw, Prague and Budapest. But developing markets in less-developed countries is not a priority with the Board. This creates difficulties for Irish exporters wishing to start commercial activities in Third World countries who do not have existing contacts there.

Other semi-state agencies involved in the foreign policy process, such as the Agency for Personal Service Overseas (APSO), the Advisory Council on Development Cooperation (ACDC), Higher Education for Development Cooperation (HEDCO) and the State Agencies Development Cooperation Organisation (DEVCO), are concerned more exclusively with development issues. The objective of these agencies is to better coordinate Ireland's official and voluntary activities overseas. For example, APSO's objective is to supervise the recruitment and improve the training of Irish personnel working on Third World activities. The Government refused to adopt a recommendation made by the Irish Commission for Justice and Peace, DEVCO and APSO for the creation of a single state-sponsored agency to implement Ireland's development assistance policy, and indeed in 1991 the

Table 2.4: Irish Trade Board international network, 1991

	(a) Offices	(b) Consultants
W. Europe:	London Manchester Glasgow Brussels Amsterdam Copenhagen Dusseldorf Paris Milan Madrid Stockholm	Athens Helsinki Lisbon Marseille Oslo Nicosia Rome Reykjavik Zurich
E. Europe:	Moscow Budapest Prague Warsaw	
N. America:	New York Toronto	Atlanta Boston Chicago San Francisco
Oceania:		Sydney Auckland
Asia:	Riyadh Tokyo Beijing Hong Kong Singapore	Amman Bangkok Istanbul Jakarta Karachi Kuala Lumpur Kuwait Manila Seoul Shanghai Taipei Tel Aviv
Africa:		Kampala Lagos Lusaka Nairobi
South America:		Quito

Source: CTT (1991)
Note: The Irish Livestock and Meat Board (Córas Beostoic agus Feola) also has an overseas office network, but it is confined to five offices in Western Europe: London, Paris, Dusseldorf, Milan and Madrid.

ACDC, which was trying to develop such a role, was disbanded. The agency described this move as "consistent with what must be regarded as a downgrading of the role to be played by Ireland, as one of the world's richest countries, in assisting the Third World".[27]

Non-governmental organisations

In Ireland a multiplicity of non-governmental organisations (NGOs) have played an increasingly important part in the conduct of Irish foreign policy towards the Third World. Some of these organisations are broad-based ones which cover the Third World as one among many topics. The political parties may be considered here. They constitute organisations which express foreign policy stances and opinions and, obviously enough, seek to express their views when in government. The major political parties in Ireland have all shared a common attitude towards the Third World: when out of power all express sympathy with their problems; all have pursued generally similar lines on key political issues such as South Africa and Central America; all have made statements committing themselves to increase ODA targets. However, performance when in government is different: both "the National Coalition and Fianna Fáil administrations have reneged on their policy commitments",[28] and the UN targets were effectively postponed entirely throughout the late 1980s.

The Labour Party has perhaps a slightly more developed international network, having an international secretary and having been involved in the Socialist International since 1968. However, all the main parties are affiliated at the very least to an EC party grouping, if not a global grouping. Apart from once again demonstrating the Europeanisation of Irish politics, this indicates the possibilities the parties have for access to information and ideas about other countries, including those of the Third World. For example, in 1982 the European People's Party, of which Fine Gael is a member, held a study meeting in Limerick on the environment and on Euro-African relations.[29] It is interesting to examine the subject matter of foreign policy questions put by the political parties in the Dáil. Table 2.5 demonstrates that those relating to Third World political issues account for almost a quarter of all questions in the period from 1980 to 1985. South Africa is the subject of 48 of those 217 questions, El Salvador of 35, Nicaragua and other Central American countries of a further 23 questions, and the Philippines,

Table 2.5: Dáil questions to Minister and Minister of State for Foreign Affairs, by subject, 1980-85

	1980	1981	1982	1983	1984	1985	Total	%
Third World politics	51	42	21	32	33	38	217	22.7
Development and aid	32	15	8	4	8	6	73	7.7
International organisations[a]	23	8	7	4	8	17	67	7.0
Neutrality and disarmament	13	1	5	19	4	9	51	5.3
European Community	19	11	8	8	14	14	74	7.8
W Europe (incl. UK)	13	1	8	14	10	14	60	6.3
E Europe (incl. USSR)	25	1	13	5	4	2	50	5.2
North America (incl. US)	1	0	0	2	9	6	18	1.9
Territorial rights[b]	4	2	22	9	6	9	52	5.5
Northern Ireland	29	10	10	27	36	24	136	14.3
Department issues[c]	24	12	20	16	24	21	117	12.3
General foreign policy[d]	2	4	9	7	8	9	39	4.1
Total	236	107	131	147	164	169	954	100

Notes:
(a) including UN and CSCE
(b) mostly questions concerning status of Rockall, extent of territorial waters, territorial violations and visits to Ireland by foreign military ships and aircraft
(c) including questions about ministerial expenses and staff employment conditions
(d) including questions relating to the whole Irish diplomatic network

Source: Part 2, *Index to Dáil Debates*, 1980-85, 318-62

Chile, Israel and Iran have all featured regularly. In total, thirty-six Third World countries or regions have been brought up in Dáil questions in those six years, ranging from Afghanistan, Cambodia and Grenada to Sierra Leone, Angola and Sri Lanka. In addition, a further 7.7 per cent of questions relate specifically to aid matters and a significant proportion of categories such as international organisations (which includes questions dealing with the UNIFIL force in the Lebanon, for instance) and general questions (which includes a number of questions on the extent of Ireland's diplomatic network) have a Third World element.

It is worth adding that of the questions that can be categorised as relating primarily to Third World countries, either on political or aid matters, the Labour Party has been the most frequent contributor (see Table 2.6). It should also be borne in mind that the Labour Party and the Workers Party had fewer members than Fianna Fáil and Fine Gael, and would seem therefore to have devoted proportionately more of their available time to Third World matters. However, political parties face certain problems in raising Third World issues domestically. First, as mentioned previously, foreign affairs issues sway very few votes in Ireland, and this applies all the more strongly to Third World issues. Second, the parties face very limited participation structures for debating foreign policy matters. Parliamentary questions provide

Table 2.6: Dáil questions on foreign policy, by party, 1980-85

	FF	FG	LP	WP	Other[a]	Total
Total foreign policy questions	290	284	190	100	90	954
%	30.4	29.8	19.9	10.5	9.4	100.0
Third World politics	45	47	63	44	18	217
%	20.7	21.7	29.0	20.3	8.3	100.0
Development & aid	17	17	33	0	6	73
%	23.3	23.3	45.2	0.0	8.2	100.0

Notes:
(a) Socialist Labour Party (31 total, 11 on Third World, two on aid), Democratic Socialist Party (three total, all on aid), independents (John O'Connell: six total, three on Third World, Tony Gregory: 31 total, four on Third World, Neil Blaney: 19 total, one on aid)

Source: Part 2, *Index to Dáil debates*, 1980-1985, 318-362

one channel, but very few of the questions tabled are answered – approximately ten per cent in 1990-91.[30] Thus, in the absence of a committee on foreign affairs and European affairs, parties have had to depend on activities such as lobbying ministers and attending political briefings provided by the Department of Foreign Affairs. In this respect, their activities are little different from those of pressure groups.

Other multiple-issue groups include the trade union movement. The Irish Congress of Trade Unions (ICTU) has a specific Third World Committee with representatives of 22 unions. Its principal task is "to encourage contact with and support for trade unions in the developing countries of the Third World and to support the free exercise of trade union rights in these countries".[31] In Ireland it works both to disseminate information on Third World issues through the union movement and to lobby on related issues. No similar institutional expression of interest in the Third World is evident in the Federation of Irish Employers (FIE) nor in the Irish Farmers Association, which are regarded as particularly important pressure groups in the Irish political system.

Another agency which addresses Third World issues as part of a wider-ranging agenda is the Irish Missionary Union. The 1990 Irish Missionary Union Survey revealed that missionaries were

Table 2.7: Irish missionaries in the Third World and the First World

	1975	1981
Africa	3,715	3,585
Asia	1,342	1,084
Oceania	102	98
Central/South America	573	657
Third World sub-total	5,732	5,424
Japan	94	93
Canada	191	198
Australia	559	688
New Zealand	136	226
United States	1,406	2,860
United Kingdom	2,896	3,179
Rest of Europe	432	208
First World sub-total	5,714	7,452

Source: Irish Missionary Union (1976, 1982)

Table 2.8: Irish missionaries in the Third World, top twenty countries, 1990

South Africa	786	Pakistan	99
Nigeria	480	Tanzania	94
Kenya	461	Sierra Leone	88
Zambia	329	Hong Kong	88
Philippines	245	Uganda	82
Brazil	198	Ghana	73
India	184	Malawi	68
Zimbabwe	141	Trinidad & Tobago	62
Peru	117	Chile	61
South Korea	116	Argentina	54

Source: Irish Missionary Union (1990)

active in 85 Third World countries, which provides an interesting comparison with the Irish diplomatic network. Missionaries have constituted one of the strongest links with the Third World in the past, and the links have continued, for the most part concentrated in English-speaking countries. But the missionary presence is by no means confined to the Third World alone. As Table 2.7 shows, there are far more Irish missionaries in the developed world, once again concentrated heavily in the English-speaking world. Nevertheless, the missionary factor is important in the development of Irish foreign policy towards the Third World (see Table 2.8). For long the missionary movement was the only Irish presence and contributed to the formation of domestic viewpoints and policy on the Third World. A recent study of the Irish missionary movement suggests two forms of activity. First, Irish missionaries have travelled to Irish emigrant centres, keeping the Irish diaspora in the developed world Christian. Second, missionaries left to convert non-Christian peoples, predominantly in the Third World. Both Catholic and Protestant Churches have been to the fore in this latter activity with the Protestant Churches starting even earlier than the Catholic church.[32] Much of the work conducted by Irish missionaries in developing countries was in the development field.[33]

Historically, there has been discussion regarding the motives of the European Churches in missionary work but, regardless of this, the network created by Irish missionaries represents a chain of continuous Irish ties with the Third World. The Irish missionary movement constituted an informal Irish presence, particularly before the expansion of official diplomatic contacts in the 1970s. Furthermore, since the Second Vatican Council, the missionary Churches have taken on board a "commitment to authentic human development and liberation" along with evangelisation.[34] Implementing the former has become particularly prominent in the missionary church in Asia, South and Central America and parts of Africa where "exploitation, poverty and oppression were endemic".[35] Though this trend has caused divisions within the Roman Catholic Church, as it has meant an increased involvement for clergy in state politics, it has also meant that there is a greater concern among some sections of the Church with the political and economic situations facing the missionaries. Thus, the pursuit of justice and freedom has become an important principle to be highlighted with policy-makers and the public.

This has fed back into Irish society through the Catholic Church's education system, its publications and its overall status in Irish society. The Church's role in educating the public, stimulating an awareness of the Third World, is crucial and even more so when the issue is not a foreign policy priority. From the publication of its first missionary magazine in Ireland in 1914, the Catholic Church has been engaged in stimulating public interest so that the missionary "movement would be adequately funded and staffed".[36] In recent years major religious-based Third World agencies such as Christian Aid and Trócaire have devoted resources to education of the Irish public and increasing general awareness. The value of missionary experiences and ties is self-evident. In an MRBI survey, 38 per cent of the public indicated that the Church was a major source of "influence and information" about Third World aid.[37] This confirms the importance of the Church and its missionary activities in attitude forming.

In terms of influencing foreign policy, missionaries have probably had greater impact than many non-governmental groups. A number of examples can be given. Perhaps the most significant instance occurred during the Biafran War in Nigeria in 1967. A number of Irish missionaries there supported the break-away Ibo tribe, leading to strained relations between Ireland and Nigeria for a time. The Irish Ambassador remained in Lagos, while the second official in the Embassy travelled to the Biafran side to assist Irish citizens there – most of them missionaries. More recently, the imprisonment of an Irish priest, Fr Niall O'Brien, in the Philippines led to pressure on the Irish Government to intervene on his behalf (see Chapter 3). Again, in 1992 the decision by the Malawian government to expel an Irish bishop, Monsignor John Roche, led to pressure on the Government to respond, and "a Department of Foreign Affairs spokesman in Dublin said it would be guided by the Kiltegan Missionary Society [the bishop's order]".[38] The Government raised the issue with its EC partners and representations were made by the Community to have the Malawian decision reversed. The issue was also raised by an Irish MEP in the European Parliament, and by the Irish Ambassador in London in a meeting with his Malawian counterpart there.[39] The increasing concern of the hierarchy about the Third World could also be credited with contributing to a public environment which encouraged the state to accept the UN target for aid and to establish the bilateral aid programme in the early 1970s.

Other NGOs are more purely concerned with Third World issues, and again provide a major source of Irish contact with that part of the world. At the forefront of these would be the various aid agencies. These have emerged relatively recently, with the majority of agencies in Ireland having been set up since 1970,

Table 2.9: Membership of Congood,[a] 1992

	established
Action from Ireland (AFrI)	1975
Association of Missionary Societies	1973[b]
Christian Aid	1976[c]
Church of Ireland Bishops' Appeal	1969
Comhlámh	1976
Concern	1968
Gorta	1965
Irish Commission for Justice and Peace (ICJP)	1970
Irish Council for Overseas Students (ICOS)	1970
Irish Foundation for Co-operative Development	1978
Irish Missionary Union	1970
Methodist World Development and Relief Committee	1971
Self-Help Development	1985
Trócaire	1973
Voluntary Service International (VSI)	1965

Source: Congood (1991)

Notes:
(a) Congood itself was established in 1979. Its membership does not include all aid agencies operating in Ireland, including some significant ones such as Oxfam Ireland, Goal, UNICEF Ireland and Action Aid.
(b) The decision to establish the Association was taken in 1972; the first meeting took place in the following year.
(c) Date of establishment of Dublin office.

though most Irish agencies were developed from religious organisations which were already active in the Third World (see Table 2.9). A number of non-Irish agencies have also been attracted to the country. There are at present up to 50 development-related NGOs operating in Ireland reflecting the widespread level of interest and concern. This extensive involvement by NGOs meant that "total expenditure by the voluntary agencies in 1990 is estimated at 25 million pounds – roughly twice that of the bilateral [official] programme".[40]

The multiplicity of agencies indicates that varying methods and attitudes prevail on the issue of development and the NGOs identify separate and differing roles for themselves. A certain amount of rivalry between agencies is evident, a competitiveness over resources and a conflict over the best means of development: "each has its own constituency at home to a certain extent, but there is increased competition for funds, media access and political influence".[41] The significance of these groups, whether secular or religious-based, Irish or part of a wider organisation, goes beyond their aid activities. They are involved in political lobbying on aid and general Third World issues in Ireland and at the European level. There is a clear distinction in Ireland between organisations which see political lobbying and campaigning as being part and parcel of their work, and those which regard such campaigns as unnecessary. In the former group are agencies such as Trócaire and Oxfam, where the political aspect of aid and development is given a high priority. In the latter category would be Concern, which lobbies purely on questions of aid, not foreign policy.

The different approaches of NGOs reflect two features. First, the size of a group is important. A small agency, with limited staff and resources, would normally find it difficult to involve itself in any kind of effective lobbying campaign – although a proviso should be attached in situations where the groups do not have a significant funding role, which can free resources for campaigning. Second, among the larger agencies there are those that send large numbers of workers abroad or employ workers in Third World countries, and those whose aid work is carried out mostly through partner organisations in the relevant country. Within both groupings some NGOs have higher profiles than others, and to protect their workers and contacts are often slow to openly criticise a regime. The need to maintain official approval to operate aid schemes – necessary for visas, work and travel permits – militates strongly against being outspoken on political issues. Where the organisation's presence is not so obvious it is easier to make political commentary. These two stances might be complementary but it is frequently difficult to achieve a balance.

Many development commentators differ on the exact nature of the NGOs' lobbying role. For example, according to a Sudanese consultant on the Irish BAP, the role of the NGO should include not sacrificing "the welfare of the poor for the mere sake of appeasing atrocious governments. Their role here is to expose these governments and mobilise other organisations for a positive change in these societies".[42] Though there has not been a similar study conducted in Ireland on the political orientation and approaches of the NGOs to development, in the British context the agencies have been categorised along a spectrum stretching from a conservative apolitical stance to accepting a political view of development. Consequently, this latter stance involves agencies accepting that, along with providing aid, NGOs must seek to change existing power structures through obtaining support within their own political structures, and also that education of the public and politicians alike must involve not just highlighting poverty but the causes of poverty. According to Heatley, both Oxfam and Christian Aid, which have Irish branches, are close to this line of thinking and aware of the political implications of their activities.[43]

In the Irish case lobbying has traditionally been an accepted part of the political system. Trócaire has recognised the necessity and value of lobbying: "It is particularly at the political level, national and international, that crucial decisions are made and we must have a presence and an influence in this area".[44] The needs of Third World communities involve not just aid but also in some cases making political statements and taking a side. One example, is that Trócaire in the 1980s, unlike Oxfam in the 1970s,[45] favoured maintaining a presence in countries where socialist revolution had taken place. Oxfam did not aid liberation movements nor involve itself in countries like "Angola, Guinea-Bissau, Mozambique and Vietnam where socialist revolution had taken place"[46] whereas Trócaire became involved in Laos and Kampuchea, believing that irrespective of human rights problems "it is essential to help people in need in whatever way we can".[47] (In fact, Oxfam changed its policy and became involved in, for example, Kampuchea in the 1980s.) Thus, Trócaire will "sacrifice some of the norms and procedures which we demand in all other countries" in order to "rebuild confidence, help them to avoid isolation, make ourselves acceptable, have an influence, and [be] able to promote the values we stand for." And where justice is sought Trócaire will also plead "their case in all arenas where we have influence".[48]

NGO aid agencies are also involved in development education activities in Ireland designed to generate increased awareness of such issues among the population in general. Finally, aid agencies do not exist in isolation of each other. There is an umbrella body, the Confederation of Non-Governmental Organisations for Overseas Development (CONGOOD), which draws together aid and missionary organisations; there is also an organisation for returned volunteers, Comhlámh, which extends to solidarity group members too.

Another set of organisations which has contributed to Ireland's contacts with the Third World are the various solidarity and friendship groups. These groups grew out of an increased awareness of the Third World in the 1970s, around the same time as similar groups were emerging throughout Europe. Their style is often different from that of the development agencies, they are often able to react quickly to events and may appear to adopt far more emotional positions. Also such groups may not have strong organisational bases and their activity often seems spasmodic, and is thus difficult to catalogue with any degree of reliability. Nevertheless, some solidarity groups have been reasonably successful at catching a corner of the public eye and gaining some kind of audience. Perhaps the best known solidarity group in Ireland has been the Irish Anti-Apartheid Movement (IAAM), which established strong links with the political elite in Ireland from its establishment in 1964.[49] However, it is more an exception than the rule of how solidarity groups can influence affairs.

The more usual pattern would seem to be that solidarity groups gain more attention when there is a simultaneous general groundswell of public interest and sympathy in an issue. It is difficult to judge whether such interest has emerged as a consequence of solidarity group activity, but it should be pointed out that there is a sufficient number of such groups active in Ireland who have not achieved particular success or influence to suggest that it is indeed the case that a successful solidarity group is a consequence rather than a cause of public interest. This puts into perspective the comments made by two Irish diplomats in recent years which were very critical of the influence not just of solidarity groups but of what might be termed the "Third World lobby" in Ireland. In 1989, the Irish Ambassador to the US attacked this lobby, describing them as "small interest groups" trying to dominate the foreign policy debate and "to set an agenda for the conduct of the Irish-American relationship which is essentially dominated by a spirit of anti-Americanism".[50]

In a second incident in 1992, the Irish Ambassador to Russia, Patrick McCabe, gave a radio interview in Moscow in which he said that the Catholic Church influenced Irish opinions to the extent that anti-abortion agitators were often "the same people whom you would find outside the embassy of the USA protesting against US policy in Nicaragua and El Salvador".[51] This raised a number of interesting responses. The official Department of Foreign Affairs response was to emphasise that "the Ambassador clearly did not intend to imply any criticism of any grouping in Ireland".[52] A Fianna Fáil politician, Vincent Brady, seems to have regarded the comments as a slur on anti-abortionists,[53] while many involved in the protests were equally appalled to be associated with the anti-abortion movement. The organisers of the US Embassy picket made the far more significant point that it was disturbing that a Foreign Affairs official should regard a peaceful lobby as "agitation", and that he should be so out of touch with affairs back in Ireland as to make such an inaccurate assertion.[54] The incident suggests that Foreign Affairs has something still to learn about such lobby groups.

Non-governmental, non-organised

The above highlights the importance of public opinion in Irish foreign policy. Irish attitudes towards the Third World are, however, curiously contradictory. Successive surveys carried out by the ACDC show a very high rate of altruistic personal support and commitment to Third World aid in Ireland. However, that is qualified by two further features. First, the support remains personal – it does not extend to support for government actions. Second, the surveys also indicate a low rate of awareness of Third World issues and problems in Ireland. The 1990 report notes that "people have been, and continue to be, highly supportive of Third World aid, yet any questions addressing knowledge of Third World problems, and consequent solutions, continue to produce relatively uninformed answers".[55]

This is not simply a question of attitudes to aid, because there is evidence to suggest that Irish people's images of the Third World are not limited to those of aid and development problems. One unpublished report notes that while Irish people tend to have a predominant image of the Third World in developmental terms, this changed in certain contexts where problems of underdevelopment were seen to have a clearly political basis.[56] These contexts were ones where countries were identified as being in the Third World in foreign policy terms rather than aid terms: "In relation to particular areas of the Third World, such as Central America or South Africa, the issues are clearly perceived as political and justice issues, rather than lack of resources".[57]

This of course leads on to the question of how public opinions are formed. Virtually all of the NGOs mentioned above run development education programmes designed to raise awareness of Third World issues in Ireland. But the most significant channel for influencing and informing the Irish public is the media. As Horgan, Owens and Sutton[58] have noted, with respect to aid questions alone, "the media are, along with the churches, a principal and in some cases dominant source of influence on Irish people", a feature borne out by a 1983 opinion survey (Table 2.10). This applies beyond aid issues as well, particularly when the issues are the more dramatic, newsworthy aspects of foreign events such as coups, wars and elections rather than the more mundane aspects such as trade agreements and diplomatic consultations. The media is an important purveyor of inform- ation about the politics of the Third World.

That raises the issue of how well the media in Ireland does that job. One important feature is the activity of foreign organisations and agencies, usually British ones, in the Irish markets, which has both positive and negative consequences. The availabilty of British media creates more choice and allows for wider coverage, and furthermore a number of British newspapers have now established separate Irish editions. However, the availability of British papers and television throughout Ireland means that many people receive news which has been compiled with a different audience in mind. Even when considering the indigenous print and electronic media, a similar problem exists.

Table 2.10: Sources of influence on thinking on aid, 1983

	%
Media	43
The Church	38
Politicians	7
The Home	5

Source: Horgan, Owens, Sutton (1987)

No Irish media organisation has the resources to maintain a comprehensive international network of correspondents, which again makes them dependent on agency reports or on pooling agreements with British papers. This problem reflects the general position of the Third World in Irish priorities. At this stage, most of the Irish papers and television and radio companies have permanent correspondents in England and on the European mainland, some have representatives as far afield as Washington and Moscow, but none has a permanent correspondent anywhere in the Third World. A survey of articles in the Irish press relating to the Third World shows that most come from foreign agency reports, some from freelance Irish reporters, and some from permanent staff sent out to cover specific issues or problems.[59] Again, this indicates the subsidiary position that the Third World occupies in Irish priorities. Irish people have shown great concern for the Third World, but more out of enthusiasm than understanding.

Decision-making structures

The above gives an idea of the role and the influence of the actors involved in the foreign policy process in Ireland. However, treating each in isolation does not adequately portray the dynamism inherent in any policy-making process. It is necessary to go further to look at how the various actors work together in the overall formulation of foreign policy. Again, there is a risk of giving a picture of formulation that is too rigid or simplified. The precise coalitions of actors involved in foreign policy issues varies virtually from case to case. However, it is possible to present a summary framework of foreign policy formulation at the domestic level, in the European Community and through the UN.

First, we shall examine briefly the general pattern of decision-making in Ireland. Cabinet ministers have a virtual monopoly of policy initiation in the Oireachtas, but "in carrying out their initiation and critical decision-making functions, ministers are powerfully aided by a small number of senior public servants".[60] Although the final power of decision lies with the minister, his or her civil servants play an important role in channelling information and suggestions. Beyond the government and the public service, two important groups of actors can be identified. First, there are a range of influences on policy-making, ranging from the media and public opinion to political parties and

Figure 2.2: Decision-making structure of the Irish Government

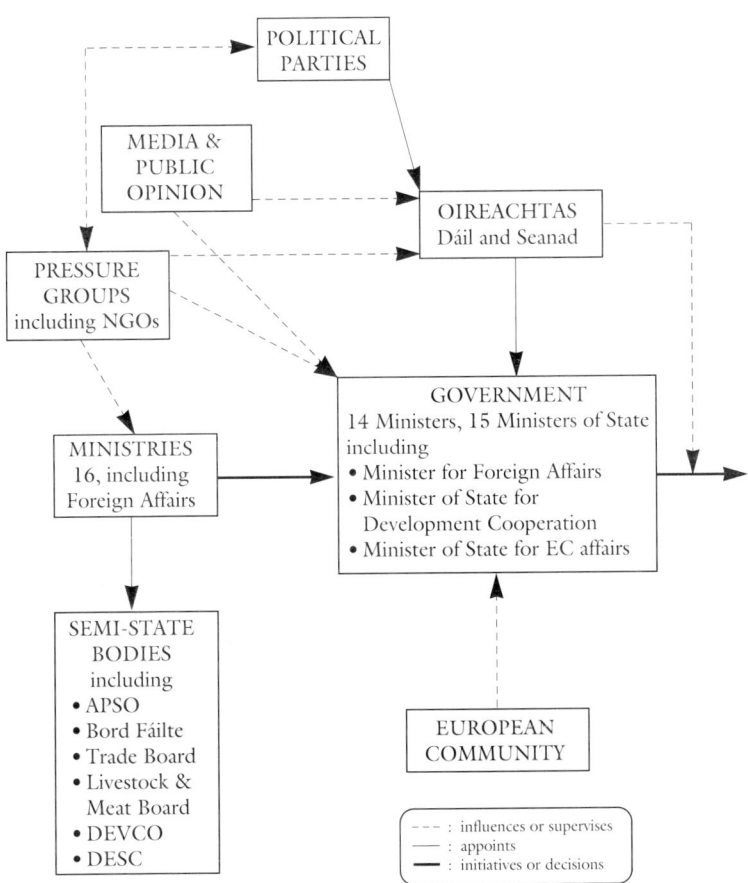

pressure groups, and also including the European Community. Second, actors such as the Oireachtas and the Courts are involved in scrutinising the decisions of government (see Figure 2.2). But Chubb has noted that although there is a far greater degree of consultation with pressure groups in Ireland than previously, "some of those who come into contact with civil servants get the impression that not all of them want genuine consultation, let alone negotiation. They think that some civil servants tend to regard those contacts as a way of getting information and compliance or as a public relations device and do not see policy making as a genuinely cooperative activity".[61]

This point becomes more relevant when the sources of information of the Department of Foreign Affairs in particular are considered. Such sources vary, but a pattern is evident. When the Department does not have a great deal of experience about a particular country or problem, it is more prepared to accept information gratefully from any source. Later on, as the Department develops its expertise, it relies much more heavily on its own sources. Where Irish embassies are available, their own contacts and information are primary, but all embassies also rely to a considerable extent on exchanges of information with the embassies of other European Community countries.[62] Other sources might be availed of occasionally, but not on any systematic basis. These would include local and international press sources, Irish missionaries, business people and aid workers and the information that can be gathered through involvement in committees of the UN, the Lomé Convention and so on.[63] There is however a feeling among some of the latter sources that their experience of Third World countries is not made sufficient use of, that there is a considerable body of expertise that is under-utilised.[64] This does not mean that such groups should be given priority by the Department, rather that some form of regular contact and exchange of information would be mutually beneficial.

Thus, at the domestic level of foreign policy-making there is a limited degree of consultation by the minister and the department, which is perhaps comparable to most other Irish Government departments. However, the element of scrutiny is considerably weaker than for other areas. Very few aspects of foreign policy are amenable to judicial supervision. The 1986 Supreme Court decision that the Single European Act was unconstitutional which forced the Government to hold a referendum on the Act was an exception rather than the rule. And as we have already seen, parliamentary control and scrutiny of foreign policy in Ireland is quite weak.

Second, it is necessary to distinguish between two policy-making structures when the EC is being examined, because EPC is quite distinct from other Community structures. The standard policy-making framework of the EC, which would apply for issues such as the Common Commercial Policy and aid and trade negotiations, is represented in Figure 2.3. The key actors are the Commission and the Council of Ministers. The Commission is in some ways analogous to a civil service for the Community. It is made up of seventeen Commissioners appointed by the member states' governments, and a permanent staff of around 11,000, divided between 23 Directorates-General (DGs), which are comparable to ministries. DG VIII is responsible for development cooperation activities, and Third World matters also fall within the scope of DG I, which is more broadly concerned with external relations. Other DGs would have more occasional contact with Third World matters. The Commission is supposed to represent a European view, and not to hold any national bias or favouritism, and certainly officials in the Department of Foreign Affairs note that although Irish officials in the Commission are quite helpful in clarifying technical matters, they do not lean to the Irish side on substantive questions.[65] The Council of Ministers consists of representatives of the national governments, who operate at a number of different levels. The basic level is that of the working group, consisting of civil servants from each member state. Some working groups are established on a semi-permanent basis, such as that responsible for matters connected with the Lomé Conventions. Others are established on an ad hoc, temporary basis. Above them is Coreper, the Committee of Permanent Representatives, made up of each country's ambassador to the EC. At a higher level still are the full ministerial meetings of the Council, with different ministers attending depending on the subject in question. Finally, there are summit meetings of the heads of government of each member state, known as European Councils.

The Commission is responsible for proposing and drafting all policy, but the Council of Ministers is the body which decides on policy. Around that basic axis, a number of other actors become involved. The Commission does not draw up its proposals in isolation, it consults with other groups in order to try to assemble a proposal which has a realistic chance of approval by the Council. The consultations would normally include the national governments of member states, the European Parliament and interested pressure groups. Pressure groups can thus attempt to exercise an influence, and indeed it is noteworthy that there are now some 600 umbrella bodies for pressure groups based in Brussels. All the major Irish aid NGOs are attached to European umbrella groups,[66] as are business, trade union, consumer and agricultural interests. Of course, the lobbying network is not restricted to seeking consultations with the Commission, and can attempt to influence at all levels, through national governments, through the Commission and through the Council. The European Parliament is also a major target for pressure. Once decisions emerge from the Council, they are implemented either by the Commission or by national administrations. The decisions are also open to scrutiny through the European Court of Justice,

Figure 2.3: Decision-making structure of the EC

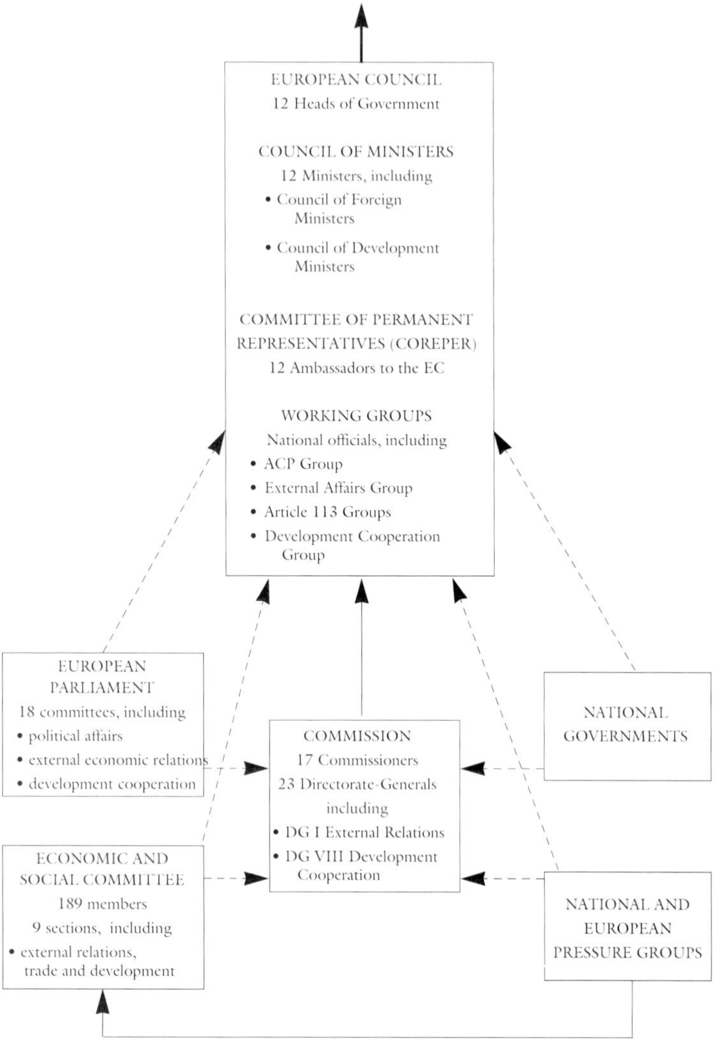

EUROPEAN COUNCIL
12 Heads of Government

COUNCIL OF MINISTERS
12 Ministers, including
• Council of Foreign
  Ministers
• Council of Development
  Ministers

COMMITTEE OF PERMANENT
REPRESENTATIVES (COREPER)
12 Ambassadors to the EC

WORKING GROUPS
National officials, including
• ACP Group
• External Affairs Group
• Article 113 Groups
• Development Cooperation
  Group

EUROPEAN
PARLIAMENT
18 committees, including
• political affairs
• external economic relations
• development cooperation

COMMISSION
17 Commissioners
23 Directorate-Generals
including
• DG I External Relations
• DG VIII Development
  Cooperation

NATIONAL
GOVERNMENTS

ECONOMIC AND
SOCIAL COMMITTEE
189 members
9 sections, including
• external relations,
  trade and development

NATIONAL AND
EUROPEAN
PRESSURE GROUPS

the European Parliament and through the national parliaments of the member states.

However, a different structure applies for the European Political Cooperation procedure (EPC). EPC is formally distinct from Community structures, and is an inter-governmental framework (see Figure 2.4). EPC is based on encouraging co-ordination of the foreign policies of member states, and its day-to-day work consists of exchanges of information between each foreign ministry, co-ordination of policy in fora such as the UN and regular contacts among member state embassies in third countries. On occasion, there are meetings of the foreign ministers of the member states, held both on a regular basis and as emergency responses to foreign policy crises. Responsibility for running the EPC process is rotated between the foreign ministries every six months. The country holding the Presidency of the Community acts as foreign policy spokesperson for all the members and is in charge of the administration of EPC. It is assisted in the latter task by two procedures: the "troika" mechanism, whereby the country holding the Presidency co-ordinates closely with the previous and the incoming Presidency countries; and the EPC Secretariat, which is a small technical support body set up in 1986.[67] The Secretariat, which comprises five civil servants, is organised on geographical and functional lines with each individual responsible for a particular area of the world and a number of functional issue areas.[68]

The Commission has observer status at the meetings of the foreign ministers and is supposed generally to be kept informed of EPC deliberations and developments. Furthermore, there is a degree of overlap between Community and EPC competences which gives the Commission a greater role at times. The European Parliament has power to question the foreign ministers about EPC matters, and the Parliament's Political Affairs Committee maintains a degree of supervision. But essentially, EPC is a process run by the foreign ministries with little other involvement or interference. It is they who decide which foreign

Figure 2.4: Structure of European Political Cooperation

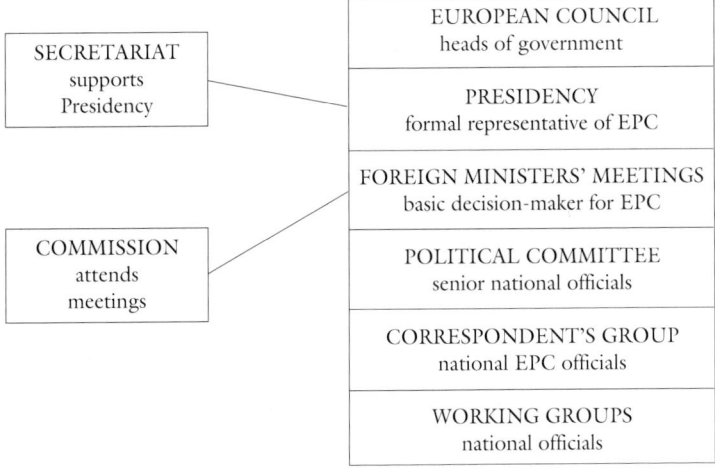

policy issues are dealt with in EPC: for instance Third World issues appear frequently on the agenda (see Table 4.3), whereas relations between the EC states and the US have remained primarily a series of bilateral matters. This is particularly true in the domestic political settings. National parliaments have always been kept at a remove from foreign affairs, and this situation has been exacerbated by EPC. As Hill notes, "there is relatively little scope for accountability in the process",[69] and indeed EPC can often be used as a screen to protect a country from criticism. The Department of Foreign Affairs will very rarely state what the Irish position on a particular issue is, even though one must be presumed to exist. Instead, they wait until a consensus has been agreed and then come out with the EPC policy.

The third structure that needs to be examined is that of the United Nations, though this is a much more simple framework to describe. The central body is the UN General Assembly, which meets both in full plenary sessions and in specialised committees. There are seven main committees of the General Assembly (see Figure 2.5), and agenda items due to be considered by the plenary sessions are normally discussed first at the committee stage. Indeed, "most matters receive their most thorough airing and consideration at this stage, since the press of time permits the Assembly in plenary session to explore extensively only the most politically explosive issues".[70]

Nearly all UN members have permanent missions stationed in New York. These perform "the traditional diplomatic functions of representation, negotiation, information gathering, and reporting. But at the UN this is done multilaterally with more than 160 states", which means that "the UN diplomat deals constantly with many national viewpoints and policies and often operates through procedures more congenial to national parliaments than to chanceries and foreign offices".[71] One particularly important feature of the way in which delegations work is the close cooperation and coordination of positions that is attempted by the EC members through EPC. Furthermore, the diplomatic dealings at the UN are not confined to items on the UN agenda. The UN is a convenient setting for a general exchange of views and opinions, which is particularly helpful for smaller nations which do not have the resources to maintain large diplomatic networks of their own.

However, the decisions of the General Assembly, the resolutions that are voted on in plenary sessions, have no legislative force to support them, and there is a noticeable gap between the power to decide and the ability to implement.[72] This

Figure 2.5: Structure of United Nations

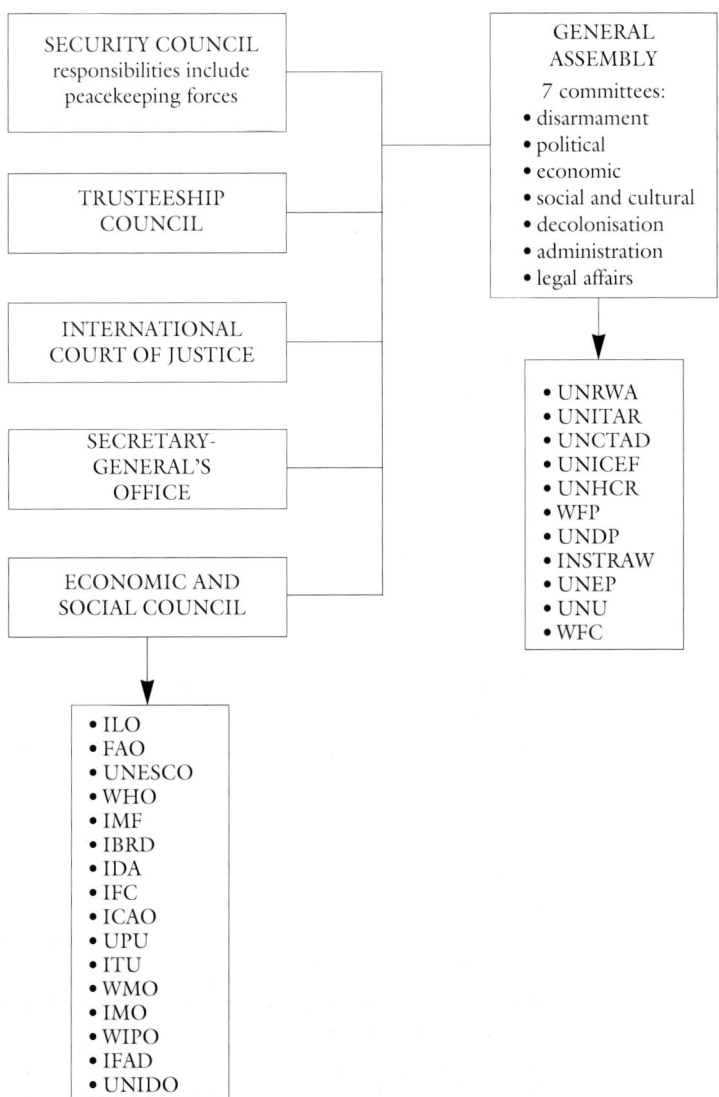

means that the UN Security Council is responsible for the more significant decisions of the UN, as the Security Council does have the authority to try to enforce compliance. The third principal organ of the UN is the Secretariat, which is responsible for trying to steer the work of the UN through the General Assembly, the Security Council and the other UN agencies.

The UN system is relatively open to activity by interest and pressure groups, particularly through monitoring and reporting activities.[73] However, the expense and distance involved mean that such lobbying work is normally the preserve of large international NGOs: Irish groups are very rarely involved directly themselves. For the most part, Ireland's involvement with the UN is carried out through the Permanent Missions in New York and Geneva. The missions have a certain degree of discretion, but all decisions with a political impact would be referred to Dublin for decision by the minister and senior Department officials.[74]

Conclusion

Irish foreign policy is made in an assortment of ways, depending on the forum or the case involved. The precise alignment of actors and influences varies quite considerably. However, certain general features have emerged from the above examination of foreign policy-making at the domestic, the European and the UN levels.

First, the Department of Foreign Affairs is clearly the primary actor in the process, and governmental expertise in dealing with international affairs has become concentrated in that Department. However, other government departments have a significant role when their own particular concerns are at stake, particularly in the European Community and in some of the subsidiary organisations of the UN. In such areas, the Department of Foreign Affairs has more of a coordinating than a leadership role. Second, at the political level the Minister for Foreign Affairs plays an important part in providing policy direction, again particularly through the EC Council of Ministers and EPC Foreign Ministers' meetings. The ministers attached to other departments probably have less influence on foreign affairs than do their departmental officials, but the political leadership role of the Taoiseach should be emphasised. The Taoiseach can readily encourage and pursue particular foreign policy initiatives. Third, the influence of the European Community throughout the different processes is striking, as it is a significant factor at the domestic and the UN levels. Few decisions are taken without consideration of the Community dimension. Fourth, non-governmental actors are afforded only a secondary role throughout the processes and parliamentary supervision of foreign policy is also relatively weak. The Irish foreign policy-making process at all stages operates within a very exclusive framework which is dominated by a relatively small group of people.

Each of these foreign policy-making features has in turn a specific relevance for relations with the Third World. The primacy of the Department of Foreign Affairs is even more in evidence, with administrative expertise in this field being concentrated there, particularly in the Development Cooperation Division, which has been described as "a creative and informed section dealing imaginatively, within Government budget restraints, with development aid to Third World countries."[75] Other government departments have even fewer direct dealings with the Third World than they do with other countries. The overall political direction is weaker. The Minister for Foreign Affairs devotes a greater amount of political attention and time to other issues, particularly EC matters and Anglo-Irish relations, and this lack of primacy given to Third World affairs is further apparent from the foreign policy initiatives of successive Taosaigh, who have also concentrated on these same areas. The EC has reversed this imbalance to a degree, by encouraging far greater contact between Ireland and the Third World, but in general the exclusive framework of foreign affairs, allied to the lack of political attention received by Third World issues, has inhibited the development of relations. The elitism is particularly evident with regard to the involvement of non-governmental actors. The accumulated expertise of aid agencies, missionaries, certain politicians and journalists could be a valuable addition to information sources on Third World issues, but no regular channel exists for accommodating their knowledge.

In relation to these features the attention that Third World issues receive in foreign policy-making is restricted. The Third World is accorded a low political priority within the policy-making process. At the administrative level, within the Department of Foreign Affairs, Third World issues lose out to those issue areas which receive political backing. This is particularly apparent within the Development Cooperation Division. To some extent this division is seen as a career backwater unless the official has a particular commitment to Third World affairs. Ireland has foreign policy goals which might be better advanced by improved relations with the Third World, but the priorities of the foreign policy process have stymied this. This uneven and somewhat incomplete process is further demonstrated in the following chapters which focus on the conduct of foreign policy at three levels.

Footnotes

1 Higgins 1988: 74.

2 Wallace 1975: 5.

3 *Ibid.:* 5-6.

4 Keatinge 1973: 9-10.

5 Since official visits by the President must be sanctioned by the Government, these may also be taken as indicative of the Government's foreign policy interests. However, in the period in question, only nine of the total seventy-two visits from Ireland were by the President, one of which was to a Third World country (China).

6 Whelan 1984: 34.

7 *Dáil debates*, 18 April 1972, 260: 390-403.

8 Interview, March 1992. The suggestion is that most foreign policy issues, though supported by only a small minority, were considered unimportant by the majority, whereas his stance on President Reagan's visit, though more widely supported, also aroused more opposition among the majority.

9 Keatinge 1973: 215.

10 Collins is widely reported to have made this comment which John Bowman raised during an RTE "Questions and Answers" programme in 1992.

11 Keatinge 1973: 217.

12 *Ibid.:* 46.

13 Higgins 1988: 63.

14 1985: 143.

15 Ireland 1991: 70.

16 *Ibid.*

17 *Ibid.*

18 *Dáil debates*, 20 February 1974, 270: 1140.

19 *Dáil debates*, 23 October 1979, 316: 1874.

20 The breakdown of these figures in terms of nationalities is not available; however, those seeking refugee status through the Council in 1992 were from Somalia, Liberia, Ghana, Sri Lanka, China, Russia, Libya and Iraq.

21 Whelan 1985.

22 ACDC 1991: 86.

23 *Dáil debates*, 2 May 1985, 318:448.

24 This was previously known as Córas Tráchtála Teoranta (CTT): references will be made to CTT for documents published under the old name. CTT merged with the Irish Goods Council in 1991 to form the Irish Trade Board.

25 CTT 1990: 13.

26 *Ibid.*

27 *The Irish Times*, 8 November 1991.

28 Higgins 1985: 48.

29 *European Digest 1982.*

30 Interview, party official, March 1992.

31 ICTU (not dated)

32 Hogan 1990: 7.

33 Quinn 1980: 31.

34 Hogan 1990: 187.

35 *Ibid.:* 186.

36 *Ibid.:* 145.

37 Horgan, Owens, Sutton 1987, Part 1: 9.

38 *The Irish Times*, 20 April 1992.
39 See press reports, 20-23 April 1992.
40 ACDC 1991: 111.
41 *Ibid.*
42 *Ibid.*: 135.
43 Heatley 1979: 39.
44 Trócaire 1985: 129
45 Oxfam is, in general, quite politically active, and its Irish branch has, for example, worked with Trócaire on a number of projects and campaigns.
46 Heatley 1979: 41.
47 Trócaire 1985: 128.
48 *Ibid.*: 127-8.
49 Laffan 1988: 26.
50 Quoted in Kirby 1992: 177.
51 *The Irish Times*, 20 March 1992.
52 Letter to *The Irish Times*, 21 March 1992.
53 *The Irish Times*, 21 March 1992.
54 Letter to *The Irish Times*, 26 March 1992.
55 ACDC 1990: 9.
56 Trócaire 1985: 5.
57 Horgan, Owens and Sutton 1987, part 3: 4
58 *Ibid.* part 1: 9
59 Horgan 1987: 20-21
60 Chubb 1982: 172
61 *Ibid.*: 137.
62 Questionnaire, 1991.
63 Interview, October 1991.
64 Interview, December 1991.
65 Interview, March 1992.
66 There are a number of umbrella groupings for aid agencies at a European level which have to some extent overlapping memberships. Three of the more important agencies are CIDSE (which comprises predominantly Catholic agencies), EUROSTEP (most other agencies), and EURODAD (which coordinates agency programmes on debt and development), all of which are based in Brussels. It is also worth mentioning the role played by two further organisations, which provide additional support and information facilities for aid agencies. These are the EC's NGO Liaison Committee, located in Brussels, and the UN NGO Liaison Service, based in Geneva.
67 The Secretariat was established by the Single European Act, which also incorporated EPC for the first time into a Treaty framework. Prior to then, EPC was nominally a completely separate activity which just happened to involve the same states as were in the Community.
68 The Secretariat is divided along the following lines with one official responsible for each group of tasks: (a) General affairs, CSCE, Eastern Europe, disarmament and questions of security, cooperation among the twelve in delegations to member states; (b) Africa, planning, communications; (c) Liaison with Presidency and European Parliament, Middle East; (d) Latin America and the nuclear non-proliferation protocol; and (e) Asia, United Nations and legal cooperation.
69 Hill 1983: 188.
70 Riggs and Plano 1988: 29.

71 *Ibid.:* 67
72 *Ibid.:* 75
73 Willets 1988: 30
74 Interview, Department of Foreign Affairs, November 1991.
75 McSweeney 1988: 202

Chapter 3

Ireland, Diplomacy and the Third World

The foreign policy of a state begins with the establishment of a functioning self-government in the state concerned. Consequently, in Ireland's case it did not have a foreign policy prior to 1922 let alone formal relations with the Third World. Earlier declarations on external relations by nationalist groups, though influential and useful, cannot be considered as foreign policy. Accordingly, Irish foreign policy had in essence to be created in 1922 and is still evolving. In this chapter, we begin by examining that evolution and argue that the development of Ireland's bilateral diplomatic relations with the developing world has gone through three phases: one of no formal diplomatic exchange at all, one of basic continental coverage and one of limited expansion. Of course, the range of potential bilateral links is quite considerable, so the chapter proceeds by looking in detail at the nature of the bilateral relationship with three countries, India, the Philippines and Egypt. These case studies will look not just at the development of formal diplomatic relations, but also at how bilateral international relations – the economic, social and cultural ties between the countries – have influenced the relationship.

Phases of bilateral diplomacy

The first phase of bilateral Irish diplomacy with the Third World is characterised by an absence of formal contacts. From the establishment of the state in 1922 until after World War Two, there were no Irish Embassies or Consulates in what we now term the Third World. It must be remembered, of course, that there were very few independent states at the time. Almost all of Africa and Asia was still under colonial rule, and in the same way that Irish foreign policy could only begin once functioning self-government had been established, a similar degree of autonomy was needed if that policy was to be reciprocated.

Nonetheless, this phase of no contact does suggest the low priority afforded to the Third World as the Irish Government set about establishing diplomatic relations, because the precedent for setting up links with the independent states of Latin America did exist. Contact had been established with Latin America in 1919 with the appointment of Eamonn Bulfin as representative to Argentina and Frank W. Egan to Chile. This contact had less to do with an Irish interest in Latin America than with the need of the new state which could not yet be described as a functioning self-government to gain recognition internationally. The according of diplomatic status to Ireland from South America assumed great significance for the fledgling first Dáil as Irish diplomats hoped that recognition from Washington might follow.[1] Such links were not established and contact with the South American region was not expanded by the new state until after the Second World War.

The establishment of diplomatic relations at full ambassadorial level with Argentina in 1947 signals the beginning of the second phase of Irish bilateral relations with developing countries. Under the guidance of the Secretary of the Department, Frederick Boland, and the Minister for Foreign Affairs, Seán MacBride, the diplomatic service as a whole was extended. Increased demands were made on the Department through greater involvement in Europe as a result of post-war recovery plans and growing participation in international organisations. Underpinning all this activity was the need to re-establish Ireland's international identity and standing, which had been weakened by the careful neutrality during the Second World War. From 1947 onwards Ireland slowly established and expanded its interest in developing countries. Initially this may not seem to represent any continuity or strategy in overall diplomatic terms. However, each was established with specific aims in mind, although it must be emphasised that the original motivations behind establishing an embassy in a particular country need not by any means be of continuing importance. The relationships are dynamic and changing, and indeed it is probably true that if Ireland were to close all its current embassies and then re-open exactly the same number that a different set of countries would be chosen. However, a pattern does emerge if we examine the original motivations during this phase.

It is not surprising that diplomatic links were established with Argentina given the earlier historical links of the missions from the first Dáil. There was also a substantial community of Irish origin there – between the 1840s and 1860s, 30,000 Irish people emigrated to Argentina, and there are now some 300,000 Argentinians who claim some degree of Irish ancestry and identity.[2] There were significant post-war trading links between the two countries, with Ireland importing Argentine wheat. Finally, the mission acted as an Irish listening post for the entire South American continent, providing Ireland with a toehold there.

The second country that Ireland established relations with in this phase was India. Formal diplomatic ties were established in 1949, shortly after India gained its independence. An Indian Embassy was opened in Dublin in 1951 and an Irish Embassy was opened in New Delhi in 1964. Again, India was chosen for a number of reasons. There were strong historical ties, arising from very similar colonial experiences and this was "one of the original reasons for establishment of [an] Embassy".[3] There was also a large Irish expatriate community in India, consisting of missionaries and of Irish who had been working for the British colonial administration and who opted to remain in India after independence. Finally, India was chosen for more strategic reasons as well. It is the largest democracy in the world and a very important regional, if not global, actor. Once again, therefore, the Irish Embassy was being used as a source of information on the continent in general rather than simply on India. The fact that India was used as the base for the establishment of non-resident relations with Malaysia, Singapore and Thailand in 1974 demonstrates this. These three countries are not only remote from India but also totally distinct political and economic entities and their "coverage" led to no increase in the two-person strength of the New Delhi Embassy.

The third country with which Ireland established diplomatic relations during this phase was Nigeria, in 1960. There had been a long history of association between the two countries with a substantial Irish missionary presence and common colonial experiences. But of greater importance was that during the post-1945 wave of decolonisation Nigeria gained its independence from Britain in 1960 and Ireland could be seen to be fulfilling its anti-imperialist philosophy by establishing contact. Setting up the embassy was seen as being "consonant with Irish support for the ending of colonialism as well as conveying recognition of the importance of the country".[4] The missionary presence posed something of a dilemma for Irish foreign policy during the Biafran War in Nigeria, when the government maintained contact with the Nigerian authorities while a number of Irish missionaries supported the Ibo separatists (see page 53 above).

But in general this first diplomatic step into Africa again gave Ireland a presence in the continent, with the Lagos Embassy playing a continental role. Ireland first attended a meeting of the Organisation for African Unity (OAU) in the 1960s, when the Ambassador to Nigeria made a detour to an OAU summit in Addis Ababa on his way home on leave. This took place on his own initiative rather than the result of a departmental decision, but it demonstrates the type of role that was expected and encouraged.

This phase at least saw the establishment of some ties with Third World countries, compared to the preceding phase when there were none. By 1973, of the 26 formal links existing, four were with Third World countries, one of which was non-residential, indicating the continuing low level of importance of the Third World to successive Irish Governments. The reasons for establishing such contacts can be identified as a mixture of historical, political and strategic. The offices served Ireland's stated alignment in the UN of opposing imperialism and supporting ex-colonies. The development of commercial trade was ancillary to most of the relationships with the exception perhaps of Argentina. The three Embassies were also regarded as 'continental' listening posts with their responsibilities extending beyond the particular country. This is in line with successive governments' need to establish an Irish presence world-wide indicating the independence of the sovereign Irish state. However, not many states would try to cover such extensive areas with so few resources, and if gathering information is one of the important requirements of a diplomatic service and vital to foreign policy formulation, such slender resources may not be sufficient for the task. In the case of the three Embassies, each covered extensive areas with a total staff of two. There was an ambassador and first secretary in both the New Delhi and Lagos Embassies, while in Buenos Aires the ambassador was accompanied by a third secretary.[5]

The rationale behind the final phase of expansion centres on political and economic factors. Community membership marked the widening of Ireland's horizons both in terms of issues and contacts. It was vital for Ireland to be able to adopt stances on matters, particularly of an external nature, from an informed position. Ireland was now participating in the conduct and negotiation of the EC's international trade and political life, providing an impetus to establish relations with many countries for the first time. EC membership also encouraged the Irish Government to establish the Bilateral Aid Programme. Thus, in this third phase of bilateral relations, two features are noticeable: the increased diplomatic network in the Third World, though it is still quite a limited network, and the establishment of a bilateral aid component.

The pattern of expansion of the formal diplomatic network reflects three main concerns. First, the economic aspect of foreign policy is clearly of greater importance with regard to some of the embassies established than was previously the case. For example, trade is clearly regarded as the major reason for establishing an Embassy in Iran, and accounts for roughly half of the work of that Embassy.[6] Of the thirty-six resident and non-resident embassies opened in the Third World in this time, nine were in major oil-producing economies, seven were among the newly-industrialising economies of the Pacific rim, five were in the states of North Africa with which Ireland developed a considerable trade in livestock through the 1970s and 1980s, and three were in the semi-industrialised states of Brazil, Mexico and Venezuela. The second concern evident overlaps with the first to a considerable degree. There was a clear attempt to set up embassies in regionally important political capitals, reflecting the greater foreign policy role being asked of Ireland through the EC. This would explain much of the expansion in the Middle East. The third feature is that, where possible or relevant, relations were being set up with countries where there was an Irish expatriate community. Thus, non-resident links were established with Zimbabwe, a regionally important actor in Southern Africa, but not with Senegal, an equally important actor in West Africa. This has meant a situation where the overall structure of Irish embassies in the Third World reflect important economic powers and important, but predominantly English-speaking, political powers.

The second aspect of this third phase in the evolution of official bilateral relations with the Third World was the establishment of the BAP in 1974. The programme was launched soon after Ireland's accession to the EC and the arrival of Garret FitzGerald as Minister for Foreign Affairs, and these two factors provided the major stimuli behind its establishment. However, it also clearly reflected a deep interest among the Irish public in the area. Indeed, FitzGerald acknowledged these factors when he stated that the aim was "to contribute to the Third World in a manner and to an extent which will meet our obligations, satisfy the desire of the Irish people to play a constructive role in this sphere and add to our moral authority in seeking to influence constructively the policies of other developed countries towards the Third World".[7] He also indicated that Ireland would become involved in projects which would not only benefit the developing country but Ireland also.

Five countries were chosen as "priority countries" in accordance with the above principles: Lesotho, Tanzania, Zambia, Sudan and India. The specific criteria for selection were as follows: (a) relative poverty, (b) ability to absorb and use aid effectively, (c) suitability of structures and policy to facilitate the flow of aid to the most needy, (d) historical, cultural, language and administrative links and (e) special circumstances (for example, the effect of the South African policy of apartheid on Lesotho).[8] All these countries are classed as low income countries. All are ex-colonies, having been part of the British empire at some stage, and so share similar administrative, cultural and linguistic practices with each other and with Ireland. India was dropped as a BAP priority country in 1978 (see pp. 82-90), with Ireland's BAP concentrated thenceforth in Africa. Though it is difficult to identify in any clearer fashion why these specific countries were chosen, it is clear that the concentration of the programme in Africa does allow Ireland a measure of expertise in the area.

The funding and operation of the programme has gone through various stages of evolution. Each year from 1974 to 1980 bilateral aid funds increased as a percentage of GNP, particularly in 1978 and 1979. Development Cooperation Offices (DCOs) were established in Lesotho in 1978, Tanzania in 1979 and Zambia in 1980. The functions of the DCOs are overwhelmingly associated with the development assistance programmes, and the offices spend very little time on consular, political or trade matters.[9] Development workers are also occasionally asked to help out on other tasks. For instance, when an Irish citizen went missing on Lake Tanganyika in 1983, an aid worker employed by the Department of Foreign Affairs who was familiar with the district concerned was sent to the area, and "spent about four weeks almost exclusively engaged in making personal inquiries in the area, checking rumours, and meeting local officials and others".[10] Bilateral funding was reduced in 1981 as a share of GNP but from 1981 to 1986 funding increased again. In the latter period a Development Cooperation Office was opened in Sudan. The present phase in the BAP, starting in 1987, has seen a constant reduction in the total of bilateral aid as a percentage of GNP and total Irish Official Development Assistance (ODA).[11] The level of commitment is also reflected in the closing of the Development Cooperation

Office in Sudan in 1987. Concern was expressed by interested groups about the reduction of the funding of the BAP, particularly as multilateral payments continued to climb after 1986, and about certain structural problems of the programme.

The second report of the Joint Oireachtas Committee on Cooperation with Developing Countries in 1985 indicated concern about the staffing and expertise within the department to efficiently administer the programme. It recommended that the department should apply separate practices to the Development Cooperation Division to enable it to build up a "fund of expertise" which could "shape and administer future programmes". Further, the Division should, it was argued, consult and obtain professional assistance from outside the department when necessary on specific issues, and the report went further to recommend that the advice of returned development and project workers should be sought and incorporated into the decision-making process along with those of NGOs.[12] This point was further developed by ACDC in its final report in 1991. It suggested that "a statutory agency for development cooperation" should be created with responsibility for bilateral aid under the aegis of the Minister for Foreign Affairs but staffed by non-civil servants.[13]

Clearly the Irish BAP has been reduced in priority terms by successive Irish Governments since 1986 and, to re-establish an effective programme, the earlier underlying principles of the programme need reassessment. The decision in 1974 to build up the relative importance of the bilateral side of development aid over the multilateral has clearly been reversed. At present the desire to make a "direct, distinctive and identifiably Irish contribution to development" is more manifest in the multilateral aid component.[14] As a small state Ireland has always been conscious of its lack of both financial resources and political clout but it has tried to act as an "international good citizen" and achieve status and prestige.[15] However, the cuts in bilateral aid are monitored through the OECD's DAC, and cutbacks can only serve to weaken Ireland's international prestige and its reputation as a friend of the Third World, thus diminishing the country's capacity to encourage others, such as its EC partners, to act more altruistically.

The third phase of limited expansion which began in 1973 therefore reaches its limits in the mid-1980s. No more embassies have been set up since then in the Third World. Indeed, the one in Nairobi was shut down, and similarly the bilateral aid budget has contracted rather than expanded. Ireland is currently left with a limited bilateral diplomatic network around the Third World. This applies not just to Ireland's Embassies abroad but also to the embassies established in Ireland by Third World countries. In 1992, 33 countries had permanent resident Embassies in Ireland (see Table 3.1 and Appendix 2), which for the most part reflected Ireland's own diplomatic network. Of course, for a number of countries it is far more convenient to cover Ireland on a non-resident basis, particularly because of the proximity of London, where most countries would maintain a sizeable mission. Two significant discrepancies between Ireland's network and the missions sent to Ireland should be noted. First, most of the oil-exporting countries of the Middle East do not maintain full Embassies in Dublin, preferring to reciprocate the Irish Embassies in their own countries with non-resident accreditation. This suggests that the relationship is much more important to Ireland than it is to the other states. Second, Latin American countries have a much stronger interest in opening or maintaining Embassies in Dublin than Ireland does in that continent. Brazil opened an Embassy in 1991, Mexico, which has consistently been one of the most important export markets for Ireland in the Third World (see Table 3.2), opened an Embassy in the following year, and Chile has sent a number of trade delegations and has also expressed interest in establishing an Embassy in Ireland. The case studies that follow concentrate more on Ireland's diplomatic dealings than those of Third World countries in Ireland. This partly reflects the fact that the relationship is an unbalanced one. Most developed countries do have far greater opportunity for contact with Third World states than vice-versa. The case studies also illustrate the bilateral diplomatic developments that have occurred since 1922, and highlight the limitations of Irish bilateral foreign policy at present.

The Indian case study describes a bilateral relationship which is one of the oldest with a Third World country. It is a traditional one guided by historical ties and common experiences before and during statehood. However, in recent times Ireland has tried to emphasise in the relationship its status as a First World country with the attempt to establish the BAP in India. Both the decision to establish the BAP in India and the decision to discontinue it reveal interesting insights into Iveagh House's priorities. A tie which potentially could have been rewarding for both countries was allowed to atrophy. The relationship with the Philippines was chosen for analysis because the Philippines is an archetypal Third World country with which Ireland has established relations

Table 3.1: Embassies accredited to Ireland, 1991

Resident	Non-resident (accredited from)
Western Europe (16)	**Western Europe (3)**
Austria	Cyprus (Belgium)
Belgium	Iceland (UK)
Denmark	Luxembourg (UK)
Finland	
France	**Eastern Europe (3)**
Germany	Bulgaria (UK)
Greece	Czechoslovakia (UK)
Holy See	Yugoslavia (UK)
Italy	
Netherlands	**other OECD (1)**
Norway	New Zealand (UK)
Portugal	
Spain	**Africa (8)**
Sweden	Algeria (UK)
Switzerland	Kenya (UK)
United Kingdom	Morocco (Belgium)
	Sudan (UK)
Eastern Europe (3)	Tanzania (UK)
Hungary	Tunisia (UK)
Poland	Zambia (UK)
Russia	Zimbabwe (UK)
other OECD (4)	**Latin America (2)**
Australia	Chile (UK)
Canada	Venezuela (Neth.)
Japan	
United States	**Asia (15)**
	Bahrain (UK)
Africa (2)	Brunei (UK)
Egypt	Indonesia (UK)
Nigeria	Iraq (UK)
	Israel (UK)
Latin America (3)	Jordan (UK)
Argentina	Lebanon (UK)
Brazil	Malaysia (UK)
Mexico	Oman (UK)
	Pakistan (France)
Asia (5)	Philippines (UK)
China	Qatar (UK)
India	Saudi Arabia (UK)
Iran	Singapore (UK)
South Korea	Thailand (UK)
Turkey	

Source: derived from IPA (1992)

Ireland, Diplomacy and the Third World

relatively recently. In addition the relationship tests the stated principles of Irish foreign policy while also revealing the role of non-governmental actors, especially missionaries, in foreign policy. The Niall O'Brien case in the Philippines illustrated this, where the Columban Fathers pre-empted government involvement by several months, assuming the role of protecting both an Irish national's and institution's interests. Finally, the bilateral relationship with Egypt is an example of a modern relationship with a Third World country, which was established with little or no particular concern for justice or human rights but instead was influenced by strategic, geo-political and economic concerns.

India

The Irish-Indian relationship is a microcosm of Ireland's relationship with Third World countries. Though there are many cultural ties between the two countries, the starting-point of Irish attitudes towards India is commonly accepted to be their shared colonial status. Both countries were conquered and colonised by Britain; in Ireland's case, from the 1620s onwards and in India from the 1700s. British colonial policies also involved similar harsh economic policies: "India and Ireland were perhaps the worst countries to be a peasant in between 1789 and 1848".[16] Though both countries shared similar experiences, the Irish were also involved in the implementation of colonial rule in India. There were Irish soldiers in the army of the East India Company and, from 1858 onwards, in the British army. Also, one-fifth of the civil servants in the Indian Civil Service before 1914 were of Irish or Scots background.[17]

More important to Irish-Indian relations are the parallel paths to independence. Opposition to colonial rule was perhaps slower to crystallise in India but it is not surprising that independence was achieved in both using similar methods. In an address to the Irish Ambassador in 1964 President Radhakrishnan spoke of "similar experiences – underground movements, imprisonments, ostracism".[18] Ireland's liberation was closely followed by the Indian nationalists. Former President V. V. Giri, who studied for the Bar in Ireland, was friendly with Irish nationalists. Such friendships may have been dangerous to him and he left Ireland when the Rising broke out. Another Indian minister, Krishna Menon, who was External Affairs Minister in the fifties and early sixties, was also a member of the Irish Bar.

Nehru visited Ireland in 1906. He missed the rioting in Belfast and was disappointed that Dublin was quiet, but "he had felt first-hand the force of nationalist agitation and was impressed by the Sinn Féin movement".[19] His visit to Ireland and his understanding of Irish politics further intensified his radical sympathies. His admiration of Irish nationalists, particularly de Valera, continued throughout his life. Both Ireland's path to statehood and the impact which that had on the British empire were of great import to Nehru's India. The Anglo-Irish Treaty in 1921 and movement towards full independence gave Ireland a greater measure of independence than any other Dominion, inevitably nudging others including India to seek it also, thus weakening the Empire. When India was trying to decide on its role in the Commonwealth structure, de Valera's views were greatly welcomed, particularly during a short stop-over visit to India in June 1948. Radhakhrishnan also visited Ireland and, along with de Valera, Lynch and Hillery, visited India. Gandhi, though he never visited Ireland, was influenced by Arthur Griffith and the Sinn Féin idea of non-cooperation.

In the post-independence period parallels continued between Ireland and India: for example religious differences helped lead to partition in both countries. Both inherited a certain nature and form in their institutions: "the old British civil service was maintained intact, the parliamentary judicial and legal systems were modelled on their British predecessors".[20] The 1937 Irish Constitution also provided a precedent for Indian actions. This democratic document, based on the "principles of social policy" and "fundamental rights", provided a model for emerging states and some of these ideas were included in the Indian and Burmese Constitutions.[21] However, a divergence of colonial experience appeared when both countries moved towards complete independence. In Ireland's case the burning desire to establish itself as a republic led Ireland out of the Commonwealth in 1949. For India the need to establish itself as a "republic" but remain within the Commonwealth was acceptable not just to New Delhi but also to London.[22] Two years after the Irish announcement London was more prepared to tolerate a "republic" as long as it remained within the Commonwealth framework. Dublin and New Delhi certainly had differing interpretations of the term "republic".

During the Second World War, when India once again experienced famine and shortages, Nehru criticised American and British help but was laudatory of Irish and Chinese assistance. While Ireland and China were "poor in their own resources, full of their own difficulties ... having had bitter experiences of famine and misery and sensing what ailed the body and spirit of India, gave generous help. India has a long memory, but whatever else she remembers or forgets, she will not forget those gracious and friendly acts".[23] Irish neutrality also "had a tremendous impact on Indian politicians".[24] To them Ireland, though still a member of the Commonwealth, showed independence of action in foreign policy and carved a separate path despite the pressure of its larger neighbour. Irish neutrality succeeded and Ireland emerged unattached which was the path pursued by India and other emerging states in the form of non-alignment on the international stage. But as Keatinge points out, Ireland always "held back from the anti-imperialist collective ... the group of non-aligned states" increasingly led by Nehru.[25] Ireland has not attended any of the non-aligned summits. Irish diplomats in India in the 1970s reported that both countries maintained close contacts in the United Nations and engaged in close cooperation in peacekeeping activities and in working for a global strategy of economic development. There has been little evidence of the realisation of the latter objective, particularly as Ireland turned its attention towards America and Europe from 1972 onwards and India focused on relations with Afro-Asian countries and the Soviet Union. In general the widely recognised mutual understanding and sympathy between Ireland and India has not resulted in extensive ties at national, regional or international levels.

The divergence is particularly evident in the economic development of the two countries and in the trade conducted between them. In 1972, Irish imports from India were valued at IR£5 million and Irish exports were not substantial enough to register in the corresponding official category. In 1990, Irish imports amounted to IR£22.9 million and exports to IR£7.6 million. The bulk of imports in 1990 were in textiles and clothing, which were worth IR£10.2 million, 48 per cent of total Irish imports from India. Irish exports were mostly in electrical machinery, apparatus and appliances and professional, scientific and controlling apparatus.[26] This trade is very small and India does not constitute a significant trading partner.

Irish exports to India peaked in 1983 when manufactured fertilisers comprised 50 per cent of total exports. The Irish Trade Board conducted a market study on the Indian market potential in 1986. It stated that there was "little experience of Irish companies operating in India". Ironically, the Board concluded that because both countries shared "non-aligned status" (*sic*) and were former colonies that India viewed Ireland "with greater warmth than many other countries". In particular, the Board explored the possibilities for Irish telecommunications equipment exports which have since materialised.[27] However, the Trade Board still does not attend Indian industrial exhibitions, unlike the Germans, French and Italians, and has no office or representative in India.

The clothing and textile figures are revealing of the economic relationship in general. Textiles and clothing play an important part in the manufacturing output and exports of developing countries. In the case of India, textiles and clothing accounted for 39 per cent of its manufactured exports in 1981.[28] The corresponding proportion for Ireland was 13 per cent. But while the textiles and clothing industry is more important to India and the other LICs, it has been the industrialised countries which have dominated the trade in absolute terms. Increasing "low cost" competition from the developing countries resulted in the developed world eventually moving to protect its own industries. The first protective legislation was introduced in 1961 under GATT and expanded with the Multi-Fibre Arrangement (MFA) in 1974. This is an international agreement which regulates the imports by western industrialised countries of most textile and clothing products which come from "low cost" sources.[29] The EC is a signatory and in effect, therefore, a ceiling is imposed on the quantity of Irish imports of textiles and clothing from low-cost suppliers. As has been pointed out elsewhere, "in successive revisions of the arrangement its protectionist...role has become uppermost. Today it tightly controls access to developed country markets for textile and clothing exports."[30] Ireland, mindful of its own declining industry, has sought even more stringent import controls cutting across the interests of LIC countries like India when the legislation came up for renewal in 1978, 1982, 1986 and 1991. Though India and other Third World countries have accused the EC of discriminatory action in restricting textile exports it is difficult for the Irish Government to resist pressure from Irish industries to support EC policies to reduce imports from India.

From the above outline of Indo-Irish relations in the pre- and post-independence periods of both countries it becomes clear that the relationship has drifted, with little economic or political cooperation existing at present. The divergent paths of both countries are also clearly visible in the perceptions and identification of the Irish public of India as a Third World country. In 1980, an ACDC survey asked the participants to identify the countries which comprised the Third World. India and Cambodia/Kampuchea were most often cited.[31] Irish popular perceptions were influenced by Irish involvement in India through Gorta projects in the late 1960s and contributions to disaster relief in 1971 during the Bangladesh War. Of greater significance for the Irish public is the Irish missionary presence. Since 1841, Irish priests and nuns worked in India: they were initially concerned with Irish soldiers and their families, though towards the end of the 19th century they extended their activities to non-Catholic communities. However, since independence a policy of "Indianisation" has seen the number of foreign missionaries decline, especially in Indian schools.[32] The missionary element in India has tended to concentrate its activities towards educational, health and economic development due to the small size of the Christian community in India and the multiplicity of religions. However, this has had the positive result that the Irish missionaries have tended to work closely together and is exemplified by the genuinely ecumenical and "Irish" reception given to Dr. Simms, Archbishop of Armagh, when he visited India in 1974. Similarly there were cross-community expressions of sympathy and religious services from Irish people across India on the deaths of Eamon de Valera and Erskine Childers.[33] Both APSO and Goal have personnel there and Gorta, Trócaire and Concern have been involved in aid projects of various kinds in India.

The initial inclusion of India as a priority country therefore in the BAP is not too surprising given the divergent paths of the two countries and the Irish perception of India as a classic Third World country. India had long been accepting external aid in the form of commodities, technical assistance, loans and grants. But in the 1970s western countries increased and co-ordinated the assistance they provided. In 1978, India accepted a pledge of $2 billion from this bloc which was a 12 per cent increase on the previous year. Thus, given the added impetus of international actions and highlighting of India's situation, Ireland identified India as a priority country.

However, the decision to designate India a "priority country" was not taken in consultation with either Irish diplomats in India or with local Indian authorities. The Embassy in New Delhi had made some initial enquiries into the possibilities for Irish assistance, and had suggested that there was some scope for dovetailing any Irish contributions with those of other countries. In particular, it was felt that the Danish and New Zealand bilateral programmes with India might usefully be developed to give a conduit for Irish aid.[34] The expert advice of officials who had immediate experience of the country was not taken into account, with "the basic decisions in question" originating in Dublin.[35] The first aid project involved the donation in March 1974 of £150,000 to the Sophisticated Instrumentation Centre in Madras for the purchase of equipment. The Government intended this action to initiate Ireland's intention to provide India with aid on a regular basis. Unfortunately, "due to the serious budgetary situation in Ireland in 1974 and 1975 over two years passed before we were able to resume aid payments".[36] India did not receive assistance again until late in 1976. The Government's decision in 1977 to set aside further allocations for the following three years was greatly welcomed: "the decision gave our approach to aid in India a coherence which it formerly lacked".[37] However, in 1978 India was abandoned as a priority country, in spite of underspending on the BAP in 1977, 1978 and 1979.[38] The Minister for Foreign Affairs, Michael O'Kennedy, commenting on this decision noted that "it did not prove possible in 1978, for a variety of reasons, to organise a significant programme of development cooperation in India, a priority country from the beginning of our bilateral aid activities". At the same time, the minister believed "that every effort should be made to get a programme off the ground there as soon as possible. A full review is underway at the moment, therefore, to see how this might be achieved".[39]

Spending in India was much less than that on the African countries and the decision to exclude India from the BAP may have been influenced by the need to concentrate Irish resources in one area, Africa. This step reduced costs but also allowed the government to highlight its activities in a more comprehensive way. With over half the BAP funds spent in Lesotho in 1978, Ireland's role as an aid donor assumed greater importance on a national level and also on a European level. Another factor influencing the underspending and problems encountered in BAP in the late 1970s, which O'Brien alluded to in his 1980 report on government aid, was that the Department of Foreign Affairs insisted "that bilateral aid be channelled as far as possible through Irish concerns, guaranteeing the maximum spin-off benefit to Ireland".[40] In the late 1970s, projects were identified for BAP financing generally as a result of an Irish presence on the ground which forwarded a proposal to the Department of Foreign Affairs. The latter then approached the appropriate concern in Ireland best suited to work on the project. Consequently, using these criteria, weak economic links between

Ireland and India contributed to the exclusion. Furthermore, the sums involved were not particularly substantial when compared to sums received by India from elsewhere.

On the Indian side the attendant administrative problems may not have made it worth their while to become involved. Their experience of Ireland's direction of the BAP in their country was not particularly encouraging given the irregularity of funding and the small size of the programme. Irish diplomats in India undertook some preliminary investigations to try to identify a region in which aid could appropriately be concentrated. Their activities however were not supplemented by expertise from Dublin nor indeed from any of the other donor countries already active in India. For example, the Indian Agriculture Ministry suggested to Irish diplomats in 1977 that Ireland should fund a cattle breeding project over the following two years, but that could not be pursued because of the withdrawal of funds. Furthermore, Indian local authorities had not been consulted when Ireland decided to accord "priority status" to India and with the multi-layered nature of the Indian federal union the lack of consultation inhibited the development of the programme.[41]

There were few protestations from the Indian authorities when the Irish programme lapsed. The decision was not queried in the Dáil by Irish politicians, despite the strong historical ties, similarity of experiences and perceptions of India as a Third World country. However, the reinstatement of the BAP to India has since been suggested by Concern and the Joint Oireachtas Committee on Development in 1985.[42] Since the 1978 decision, successive Irish Governments have relied on the work of aid agencies and missionary organisations to continue the tradition of Irish support to India. It is this work which represents the most lasting Irish influence.

The Indian case certainly exposes some of the limitations on the development of Irish foreign policy with Third World countries. The relationship seems to have been founded on a perception of a shared historical background, and there are a number of informal links and ties between the two countries. Such ties can be a useful source of inspiration for drawing two countries into more formal relationships. However, they are not on their own sufficient to maintain a relationship, let alone to allow it to flourish. That depends on a more specifically governmental commitment. The fact that India was the site of Ireland's first Embassy in Asia, and was also chosen as a BAP priority recipient, suggests that at least initially the commitment was present. However, it has since deteriorated.

The reasons for that deterioration are various, and arose despite the initial presence of a number of additional motives necessary for the development of more formal ties. First, India had been seen as being politically a very important country in its own right and in the South Asian region. However, neither the country nor the region have caused any serious or ongoing international problems, of a kind comparable to Southern Africa, Central America or the Middle East. While that may be a source of some pleasure in the region in question, it also goes some way towards explaining why it has faded from the forefront of Irish concerns in the Third World. Irish attention and its limited resources have become concentrated more on what are seen, rightly or wrongly, as more serious international problems.

Second, the existence of reasonably strong economic ties also encouraged the establishment of formal relations between the two countries, but again this aspect of the relationship has stagnated. To some extent, this is due to the path of economic development pursued by India for many years, which was based on domestic industrialisation and import substitution. But trade from India to Ireland has also declined, partially it would seem because of EC membership. India is not a party to the Lomé Convention, which has meant it has had to face rather less favourable conditions in its trading relations with EC states. The Irish Embassy in India places greater emphasis on economic and trade matters in its dealings with Malaysia, Thailand, Singapore and Brunei, which are covered on a non-residential basis from New Delhi. "Economic and commercial relations with those countries are given most emphasis",[43] whereas relations with India are predominantly political and consular.

Third, the attempt to build a relationship based on development assistance foundered. The decision to try to incorporate India among the BAP priority countries is one of the clearer examples of historical and informal links influencing official policy. However, the eventual demise demonstrates how such an influence is not always to be desired. The Irish appear to have entered on the aid programme in India with more enthusiasm than intelligence. India was always likely to prove too vast an arena for Irish aid to have even a minor impact, and furthermore, from an Indian perspective there was likely to be a certain reluctance to accept aid from a small, rural country when India itself has one of the largest scientific research programmes in the world.

Thus, for a number of reasons, the relationship has atrophied. India has much to offer Ireland in terms of its strategic location, political importance and its huge marketing and trading potential. But the relationship has not developed beyond its traditional confines, and it is particularly ironic that although Ireland has invested so much in terms of diplomatic resources, a deeper relationship has not resulted. Undoubtedly, as memories of the common experience of colonialism fade, the existing relationship will be further threatened. Thus, India is an instance of "a bilateral relationship which although historically intense, has never been able to transform itself into meaningful modern links".[44]

The Philippines

Ireland's foreign relations with the Philippines provide us with a good case study of a distant Third World country with which Ireland has few official links but strong informal ties. The Philippines loomed large in Irish foreign policy for a period in 1984 and tested the principles guiding Irish foreign policy and its conduct. Generally, the Philippines had not been central to Irish foreign policy-makers before then, although there were some economic ties.[45] The establishment of non-resident ties with the Philippines from the Embassy in Beijing in 1984 was an acknowledgement, not just of economic ties, but of the significant informal links too. Irish missionary nuns and priests have been working in the Philippines for the past 80 years. The heaviest concentration of Irish Catholic missionaries in Asia-Oceania is in the Philippines where 233 are working. In the Philippines 90 per cent of the population is Catholic, unlike in the rest of Asia where the Catholic Church is in the minority. From the earliest colonial times, the Church identified closely with the state and became a part of the oligarchy. "The wealth of the Dominicans in the Philippines is legendary ... The Jesuits, on the other hand, are the power brokers and they are mainly American: their colleges turn out the ruling castes, the top families".[46]

However, the economic and political direction of the country with attendant widespread poverty, injustice and oppression was a fertile ground for the arrival of the missionary Church. The Sisters of Mercy and the Columban Fathers are "the spiritual workhorses of the Catholic Church in that mission field".[47] They have been highly regarded and welcomed by the Filipinos not just because of their work but because many understand and empathise with problems centring on land issues. In 1990, 12

Irish Churches were operating in the Philippines and informal ties are strengthened by the involvement of two Irish development agencies there.

As elsewhere in the underdeveloped world, two Churches emerged in the Philippines – the Church of the elites and the Church of the poor. This divide became more definite after the issue of Pope Paul VI's encyclical *Populorum Progressio* in 1967, which exhorted Catholics to help the poor worldwide. Throughout the Philippines the native and missionary clergy and nuns expanded their work at parish level, becoming involved in improving the living and working conditions of the poor. But the fight for economic and social reform brought many into conflict with the landowners, the industrialists and politicians. Programmes and projects which "questioned the social system, supported labour unions and raised the awareness of the ordinary people" upset the status quo and were unwelcome.[48] The success of such activity was evident from the campaign launched by elite interests against those involved. The Church of the people was branded communist, enduring personal attack and harassment.

A Filipino-Irish group was established in Dublin in 1975 by Columbans, ex-Columban Fathers and lay people on the occasion of the third year of martial law. They highlighted the increasingly corrupt and abusive nature of the regime. Activities included picketing the American Embassy, marches, public meetings, political lobbying and talks by Filipino guest visitors, "all variously intended to inform, influence and elicit action".[49] The Irish group has been less prominent in Ireland since the O'Brien case (see below) and other cases. However, it has concentrated its activities on highlighting "the economic, political and social realities in the Philippines and to seek support for all groups and movements working for real democracy and peace".[50] This led to criticism of the Irish group by the Philippines Honorary Consul General in Ireland, Michael A. Hennegan. He accused the group of having communist ties and of aiding a propaganda campaign waged by the Philippines Communist Party.[51] In fact the Irish public reacted earlier to, and were more sympathetic to, events in the Philippines than the Government.

One of the foreign companies to get involved in the Philippines under the auspices of the World Bank during the Marcos period was an Irish semi-state body, the Electricity Supply Board (ESB). The ESB had previously refused to become involved in consultancy work in Rhodesia, South Africa or Libya. However, it entered into a management consultancy contract in the Philippines with the National Power Corporation (NPC) in 1978. The ESB made recommendations on the organisation of the NPC itself and on its management of large projects. One of the projects involved building a dam in the Chico River Valley which would have entailed 30,000-40,000 people being relocated. Along with this deleterious aspect of the project, the NPC refused to allow trade unions to work within its structures. This denial of civil rights and unsuitability of the proposed location were not particular to the NPC project. (The building of a nuclear plant costing $2 billion in an earthquake-prone area near Manila provides another example.)

The impact of such policies on Filipino workers and the participation of an Irish semi-state body was soon brought to the attention of the Irish public. Publicity was given in Ireland to a speech delivered by a Filipino Catholic Bishop, Francisco Claver, on the exploitative nature of development projects and he called for the withdrawal of the ESB from the Chico River scheme. He also urged that the Irish Government should take "a moral decision on the Philippines as they had with South Africa".[52] This was echoed by others, including Brian McKeown of Trócaire and Jerome Connolly of the Irish Commission for Justice and Peace, who emphasised the "importance of establishing guide-lines for the general operation of all semi-state bodies and Irish private enterprises in developing countries, to ensure that they comply with the basic values which this country is pursuing in the human rights field".[53] In the case of South Africa, government directives existed banning all economic links, but the Chico River case raised the issue of Ireland aiding other repressive regimes.

The ESB's consultancy role had been developed and expanded following the 1974 oil crisis and was a new important source of income. The Chico River contract was worth IR£400,000 to the ESB and initially was supported by the ESB unions. However, once the exact nature of the Marcos regime and the consequences of the project for the local people became known, all involved on the Irish side were forced to reassess their position. The unions embarked on an 18-day fact-finding trip to the Philippines where they saw the poverty and repression and they immediately banned their workers from co-operating with the project. Opposition was brought to bear by the Columban Fathers missionary order, the ESB Officers Association, the ESB general unions – the AUEW/TASS, Limerick and Dublin Trades' Councils and Dublin City Council. The criticism was refuted by the management of the ESB and P. J. Moriarity, Chief

Executive, said that the ESB was "convinced this development work which is being financed by the bank in all Third World countries is in the present and long-term interest of the people of those countries".[54] But it was the union's ban which prevented any further expansion of the ESB's work there.

The case served to highlight the repressive situation in the Philippines and illustrated the lack of Irish Government interest. The other aspect of the case requiring Government action was on the wider issue of "monitoring and where necessary questioning, the development policies and criteria of the World Bank" of which Ireland was a member.[55] Neither aspect of Ireland's involvement in the Philippines drew Government response or action. The dual nature of Irish involvement in the Third World becomes evident also, with one group of Irish people working with the people while at another level economic interests were involved in perpetuating iniquitous conditions and indirectly propping up the regime responsible. Such weaknesses in Irish foreign policy as were displayed on this occasion were not attended to in subsequent years. Prior to Niall O'Brien's trial in February 1984, the state-sponsored Trade Board was once again criticised by two Philippine support groups for providing training courses for Filipinos. Such activities were seen to provide a cloak of respectability to the Marcos regime. The Trade Board, as with ESB, rejected the criticism saying that it was a matter for government. On this occasion Foreign Affairs stated that aid was not being provided and the question of boycotting the Philippines had not arisen.[56] Ireland's inaction on this issue may be partly explained also by an external factor: the relationship with the United States. The US contributed in no small way to the longevity of the Marcos regime and previous repressive regimes in the Philippines. Marcos was protected by the US from the very beginning of his rule.

In Ireland, the beginning of the end of the Marcos regime is strongly associated with the trial of Fr Niall O'Brien and the Australian Fr Brian Gore. Both were missionaries working in the Philippines who were arrested on 6 May 1983, together with six lay workers, and charged with the murder of a local mayor. Their arrest, detention and trial provides a suitable example of the multi-layered attitudes which exist in official circles towards Third World countries. The Irish Government's response was certainly limited by a lack of resources, particularly as the Irish diplomatic presence was not strong. As the Superior of the Columban Fathers stated, they had no official information and "getting official information is ... difficult for us, because Ireland has no Embassy in the Philippines".[57] At this early stage, O'Brien's supporters and the Irish diplomatic representative do not seem to have liaised. Ireland was represented by an honorary consul, Edgardo Trota, whose main duty was to protect the rights and interests of Irish citizens. But Mr Trota, a wealthy businessman, seemed to have difficulty in obtaining official information and the Department of Foreign Affairs was still trying to get information on the murder charges in November 1983.[58]

However, accepting the lack of structural resources, there is still little evidence of a deep interest among Irish officials in the case following O'Brien's arrest. Despite the immediate involvement of the Catholic Church authorities in the Philippines, trade unions in both countries and aid agencies and other interested groups in Ireland, the Irish Government was slow to get involved. Three months after the arrest the Irish Government had not made any representations to the Filipino authorities and the Irish diplomatic representative was experiencing difficulty in obtaining basic information. There is no doubt that the Government was concerned but when it did get involved it was still very low-key. After a meeting with Irish officials in January 1984, the Superior-elect of the Columban Fathers in the Philippines, Fr Michael Martin, said he "believed they are concerned". But he went on, Ireland had done "sweet damn all" except to send formal protest letters and the Irish Ambassador in Canberra had visited his Philippines counterpart there. Martin said that "the time is over for nice diplomatic letters to be exchanged". He believed that Ireland's low-key response was working against O'Brien's interests but was exactly what the Filipino authorities wanted. He believed the Manila Government had adopted "a policy of delay in order that public interest should wane in the case". Such an approach had been "particularly successful in dealing with the Irish".[59]

Criticism of the inadequacies of the government's role also came from Mrs Olivia O'Brien, Niall O'Brien's mother, who accused the Government of being slow in taking up the case: "it is only because of the efforts of my son and the other priests in custody that they may soon be released".[60] Furthermore, it was undeniable that Ireland had extensive diplomatic contacts which could have been mobilised. Ireland's diplomatic presence in the Philippines may have been limited but Ireland had strong links with major world powers. One commentary noted that "it is now up to the Republic's Department of Foreign Affairs to do everything in its power to secure the release of the two men.

They could make a start by asking the United States Department of State to intervene".[61] Similarly, contacts through EC partners do not seem to have been used up to that stage.

It was the attention given by the Australian Government and the Australian media which kept the case to the fore and ensured that the Filipino authorities were kept in check. The Australian consul was in constant contact with the prisoners. Fr Martin praised the Australian Government whom he felt had not been duped by the Marcos policy of delay. The Irish consul visited O'Brien during the bail hearings, but Trota certainly did not have the same influence as the Australian officials. The Australian media also paid more attention – both of the major television networks frequently interviewed the prisoners and Radio Australia also broadcast items.[62] Indeed it was the actions of the Australian Government in late January 1984 which forced the case along. Bail was denied to the accused and the decision indicated that the death penalty might also be justified. For all concerned the disbelief at the charges was now accompanied by growing fear. The Australian Government responded by suspending a $100 million aid package indicating its unease at the way the case was being handled.

Fr Martin and Fr O'Brien were also bothered at the general lack of interest among the Irish public. In January 1984, O'Brien noted in his diary that he often asked his mother "if particular events which had happened to us in Negros had reached the Irish media. Frequently her answer was No".[63] The priests decided to set up a communications network between the prison and the Columban Headquarters in Navan through which they relayed information to the Irish press. It appears that from May 1983 to January 1984, neither the Irish Government nor the Irish media were overly concerned about the O'Brien case though it encapsulated issues central to the stated principles of Ireland's role abroad, namely concern for ex-colonial countries, human rights abuses and protection of Irish nationals.

It was not until the Irish media realised that they could speak to the prisoners directly by telephone that a surge of interest and attention in the case appeared in Ireland. The Australian media had already realised this – O'Brien related that they "could hardly keep the Aussies off the ... phone".[64] After the bail announcement the Irish radio broadcaster John Bowman got through to O'Brien who explained their situation, and he supported a call from the Columban Fathers to the Government to send a representative to the Philippines to investigate their case: "a person to person approach was more significant than a bureaucratic approach in a country where human relationships are so important".[65] The mobilisation of the Irish media and public gave the prisoners another source of support but in terms of official action, hope was still placed largely in the actions of the Australian authorities. Australian Foreign Minister Hayden was interested in the case and was due to visit in February. As a last resort O'Brien believed that President Reagan's visit to Ireland in June 1984 would assume a greater significance: "the levers of Philippine power lie ultimately not in Manila but in Washington".[66] Clearly this path of action was seen to be the only one where the Irish Government might have some power if it became interested.

By the time the trial opened on 6 February 1984 the Irish Government had come under increasing external pressure to get involved. Pat Gallagher, a Fianna Fáil TD, urged the Government "to launch a world-wide crusade of protest against the Marcos regime" and to instruct all Irish embassies to gather signatures of support. He accused the Government of being slow to get involved – it should, he argued, have sent out a personal representative and it should "stop pussyfooting about the issue".[67] The Irish Catholic hierarchy made representations to President Marcos and prayers were said for O'Brien at Sunday Masses, protests by O'Brien's family and supporters were held outside the American Embassy in Ireland, the media interest increased daily, concerned agencies announced their support, questions about the case were asked in the Dáil and the Seanad, and Amnesty International accorded the detainees prisoner of conscience status. The Irish Government responded finally with the decision to instruct the First Secretary of the Irish Embassy in Canberra, Michael McCluskey, to attend the trial. But the Government did not see the need to send a minister, neither did it deem it necessary to ask Washington to intervene. It was also pointed out that the Honorary Consul would attend, though another Fianna Fáil TD, Noel Treacy, queried his suitability: he said in the Dáil that Trota "was in sympathy with the Philippine regime and was himself a millionaire. He was not suitable to represent Ireland at the trial".[68]

The trial lasted for six months, with some 50 hearings, before the charges were dropped. It was recognised from the start of the ordeal and reiterated again during the trial that Ireland was powerless to influence the judicial process in the Philippines. However, it was also recognised by the Irish media and O'Brien that Ireland's sole weapon was its influence with the US. The Government was unwilling to resort to this action and indeed was inactive and disinterested for a long time. Instead, informal agencies tried to take on the diplomatic mantle. Once the case started, and support for O'Brien rose with awareness of discriminatory judicial practices, the need for the Irish Government to act in some sort of formal manner emerged. The Marcos regime did not want to lose face by dropping the charges but the accused wanted their names cleared. Australian diplomatic pressure was insufficient on its own to solve the impasse; neither were the phone calls from Peter Barry and Garret FitzGerald to O'Brien of much concrete assistance except to bolster personal morale. Likewise, the commitment of McCluskey and Trota held little sway with Filipino authorities.

The Irish Government's concern for the plight of the individuals certainly increased during the period, but until the Reagan visit pressure on the Government resulted only in the above personal contact with O'Brien and the Government finally bringing the case to the attention of the other EC countries. A picture emerges of the limited freedom of action and commitment of Irish foreign policymakers. A small state may be lacking in resources but it should also, when it deems appropriate, be prepared to exercise all aspects of those resources. In Ireland's case, one of the few levers it possesses is its access to a powerful and influential country. It is generally accepted by those who were directly involved in the case from the beginning that it was American pressure which forced the Marcos regime to drop the charges. The American angle had consistently been recognised by O'Brien: "the American dimension in the Philippines is very significant ... It is significant in all that is happening here".[69] Mrs Olivia O'Brien stated in May that all Reagan "has to do is lift the phone to his friend, President Marcos, to secure the release of my son and his companions".[70] Likewise, Seamus Brennan, a Fianna Fáil backbencher, said "that a direct request by Reagan to Marcos would almost certainly succeed".[71] Certainly the course of events after Reagan's visit to Ireland in June speeded up enormously. On the eve of his visit to Ireland, Reagan said that although he "did not know the exact details of the case" his country "had a longstanding relationship with the Philippines, and if there is any way in which we can be of help ... we'd be pleased to do it".[72] Reagan was also experiencing pressure from within his own country – in a pre-election year the American National Conference of Catholic Bishops based in Washington had appealed to George Schulz, Secretary of State, to bring a speedy resolution to the case.[73] Also 52 Congress members signed a petition calling for the release of the prisoners and contacted the Philippines Ambassador in Washington. O'Brien maintained that the pressure on Reagan "was so great that it threatened to overshadow the visit".[74]

In Ireland the Government had to cope with anti-Reagan protests as the visit became a focus for groups opposed to the conduct of American foreign policy, particularly its involvement in El Salvador and Nicaragua. The opportunity was also used by O'Brien's supporters to highlight his case and to illustrate Dublin's inability to influence events in the Philippines. The Irish Government finally bowed to public criticism and concern and Reagan appears to have been asked to intervene. The timing and form of Dublin's request is difficult to ascertain. But given that the Australian Government had been pressing for the dropping of the charges for a number of months it is important that it was from the time of Reagan's visit to Ireland that rumours of the withdrawal of the charges abounded in the Bacolod prison. As O'Brien noted, "there is no question but that things have definitely begun happening in the last few days".[75] He further states that "at almost the same moment as Reagan touched down on the tarmac in Ireland, Bishop Fortich received a telephone call saying that President Ferdinand Marcos was offering us all pardon!".[76] This had been offered to the accused previously and once again all refused to accept a pardon as it implied guilt. However, unlike previous occasions "our refusal of the pardon was not the end of that initiative".[77] Eventually, on 3 July 1984, the charges were dropped. In all, O'Brien had been incarcerated for 17 months. Upon his release he admitted that it was difficult to know the exact reasons for the sudden dropping of the charges but he stated that "the pace of negotiations speeded up after ... Reagan's visit to Ireland with every stage being approved by President Marcos".[78] Undoubtedly, both Dublin and Washington were under pressure from a coalition of groups on the issue. But Peter Barry, Minister for Foreign Affairs, severely criticised the demonstrations and protests during the visit in the Dáil, on 26 June 1984 and suggested that the "significance of President Reagan's visit has not yet been realised" and said that the visit could do "nothing but good for the country".[79]

What does this case study illustrate about the influences on, and conduct of, Irish foreign policy regarding the Third World? The Philippines is a good example of the weakness of Irish foreign policy towards the Third World. The central stated goals are to support humanitarian actions and to promote justice, yet there is little evidence of these in the practice of foreign policy. The lack of a comprehensive foreign policy towards the Third

World and limited diplomatic links make it difficult to adequately protect Irish citizens abroad, one of the principal objectives of the Irish State. The O'Brien case revealed that the Irish public reacted quicker than the Government to the above stated goals and showed its support for O'Brien in a variety of ways, from writing letters of support to him, which numbered around 20,000, to praying and protesting on the streets. The public was, of course, reacting to the increased media attention and, though it was slow to materialise, Irish newspapers, radio and television ultimately gave full and constant publicity. Indeed the advice of one RTE reporter was important during one of the hearings and strengthened the defendant's case.[80] Furthermore, the O'Brien case finally reveals that when the Government's concern emerged after many months of pressure, Dublin viewed the extent of its power as limited to raising the issue with other EC countries, which was more of a lobbying measure than a directive one. But as the pressure increased internally and externally on the Government it found that it did have another option in its range of foreign policy activities. By June 1984, the Government accepted that it was able to exert influence through a third country, possibly resulting in the dropping of the charges. Unfortunately, not all Third World issues attract such a wide range of support from the domestic forces of the Irish public, clergy, hierarchy, politicians and media combined to a unity of forces abroad in the United States, Australia and elsewhere.

Egypt

Ireland's relationship with Egypt only became significant following accession to the EC. The relationship which was non-existent until 1974, was established at full diplomatic level with a resident Ambassador in Cairo from 1976 onwards. Egypt may not be regarded as an archetypal Third World country because of its regional importance and its dominance in the Arab world. The prestige and wealth associated with the ownership of extensive oil resources should be considered as well. But despite the inflow of wealth which accompanies oil production Egypt is a low income country, with a GNP per capita of US$690 in 1991.[81] As early as 1966, Egypt, along with Cuba and Indonesia, were the only countries to default on payments to the IMF. Egypt suffers from the problems of social inequality, poverty, illiteracy, unemployment, urban over-crowding and over-population which are typical of Third World countries.

Up to the 1970s Ireland had only sparse contacts with Egypt. Despite the fact that both countries experienced British colonial administration, this did not promote significant historical connections. Furthermore, missionary contact has been slight with just 20 Irish missionaries in Egypt in 1968 and also in 1990. Similarly, trade links were underdeveloped and it is not regarded as a priority country in terms of aid by either the Irish Churches or development organisations. Even a significant political event such as the Suez Crisis in 1956 aroused little interest in Ireland. Although the Crisis dominated the first UN session that Ireland attended, it did not evoke any independent statement from the Irish delegation. That delegation was "well-prepared, well-phrased and moderate in tone, and its votes on issues of major significance were the same as those of the United States".[82]

However in the early 1970s, it suited the needs of Irish policymakers to establish an Embassy in Egypt. The Government was interested in expanding ties with the region because of the increasing importance of oil to the economy and the desire to extend trade links, particularly in the beef industry. But the specific reasons which account for the establishment of the Cairo Embassy relate to its increasing strategic and regional importance, especially after the Arab-Israeli October War of 1973. From 1973 to 1974 Ireland contributed an infantry force to the Second UN Emergency Force, which had been set up in response to the War. But the oil crisis and the Middle East war of the early 1970s meant that Egypt was of particular importance for the EC agenda, and for Ireland "EC membership was the most pressing reason for opening a mission".[83] Garret FitzGerald stated that Ireland's presidency of the EEC in 1975 would be concerned with improving Euro-Arab Dialogue and the general energy question. He believed that Ireland had a "small reputation as a 'neutral' on the energy question" and on the Euro-Arab dialogue "it could be up to Ireland to find a way out of the present impasse".[84] The increasing importance of the Middle East in Irish affairs was also reflected in the establishment of the Parliamentary Association for Euro-Arab Cooperation in March 1974 and its extension to Ireland in December 1974 with the creation of separate groups in all the Dáil parties. The association hoped to promote greater cooperation and under-standing by both European and Arab states. Irish deputies who participated expressed the hope that a greater awareness of the realities of Arab economic and political life would be developed in Ireland and hoped that the "understanding would extend beyond the area of oil needs and current energy problems".[85]

It was during Ireland's first presidency of the EC that the first joint Euro-Arab meeting within the Euro-Arab Dialogue took place in Cairo, in June 1975. Thus, Ireland played a role in launching this initiative, and as Sharp points out, Ireland has subsequently developed this role. Ireland was credited with skilful handling of the first Euro-Arab Dialogue meetings. An Irish suggestion that there should be no formal national delegations, but rather two composite delegations, one European, the other a pan-Arab one, adroitly steered around problems over recognition of a Palestinian delegation. Ireland was seen as bringing a degree of impartiality to the Dialogue because it had few interests in the Middle East and because of its neutrality,[86] and has established itself as a "useful link between the two groups and as an initiator of policy as an end in itself".[87] Ireland's role was underpinned by the establishment of diplomatic relations with 13 countries in the region between 1974 and 1977 and the creation of resident missions in Lebanon, Egypt, Iran and Saudi Arabia by the end of 1982.[88]

However, EC membership is not the sole focus of Ireland's involvement in the Middle East conflict. Although Irish contingents to UNEF II were withdrawn in 1974, there has been a continuous Irish presence in the Lebanon with UNIFIL, and in Israel, Jordan, Syria, Lebanon and Egypt with the UN Truce Supervision Organisation. The Cairo Embassy is of importance in this context in that it has responsibility for the Gaza Strip dimension of the Middle East conflict.

The development of the Irish-Egyptian relationship through the EC and UN has not precluded its expansion through bilateral channels, particularly the economic. "It cannot be concealed that the Irish interest in relations with the Arab countries is not entirely philanthropic: if the recycling of oil surplus funds earned from oil exports were to mean investment in industry in Ireland, the relief to the Irish economy in the present crisis would be significant".[89] The increasing emphasis on oil made Ireland desirous of securing its own sources of supply and though Ireland in fact reduced its dependence on oil by the late 1970s, the establishment of friendly relations with an Arab oil supplier was not surprising. Trade with Egypt developed considerably in the early 1980s, with Egypt becoming a major market for Irish beef and cattle exports. In 1980, total Irish exports to Egypt were valued at IR£20.6 million, IR£18.8 million consisting of food and live animal products. In 1985, total Irish exports amounted to IR£109 million of which IR£92.2 million was in food and live animal products.[90] This market, however, is very volatile and has not been sustained, having declined steadily through the late 1980s. In 1990 total exports to Egypt amounted to IR£34.4 million, of which food and live animal products accounted for IR£22.6 million. About one quarter of the work of the Cairo Embassy is currently taken up with trade matters and it is regarded as a "very tough environment".[91]

A more recent angle to the bilateral relationship is that in 1991, Ireland gave bilateral aid to Egypt for the first time ever, in the form of IR£3 million worth of milk powder. Up to then neither the Irish Government nor the Irish people considered the Middle East as a major area for bilateral assistance and the aid given in 1991 was directly related to the Gulf War. In general the BAP and relief assistance have been concentrated in countries south of the Sahara "with only marginal interest bilaterally in the aid needs of the Middle East states as such".[92] With the closure of the Embassy in Nairobi and the DCO in Khartoum in 1987, the Embassy in Cairo has assumed non-resident responsibility for dealings with Sudan which once more represents a stretching of resources. Although the Irish Embassy in Cairo has developed an extensive information network of its own with regard to Egyptian affairs, it is far more reliant on information available from Embassies of other EC countries in trying to keep abreast of affairs in Sudan.[93]

EC membership acted as the major catalyst for the establishment of the Embassy, and this marks the principal raison d'etre of the relationship. Ireland has used the contact to develop the bilateral relationship, particularly in the economic sphere, and on the Egyptian side there is a growing attempt to market the country as a tourist destination for Irish sun-seekers.[94] The Cairo Embassy has also served to allow Ireland to develop its Middle Eastern policies in a more comprehensive fashion. The relationship demonstrates the importance of the EC in recent Irish foreign policy, and also highlights the way in which Irish embassies reflect trading links and regional power balances. But once more, resources are strained by having to cover Sudanese affairs as well, and the expertise of Middle Eastern affairs is being stretched to deal with what is really a sub-Saharan state.

Bilateral relations in a broader perspective

It is possible to identify three major reasons to account for establishing foreign relations with Third World countries:

historical, political and economic. Historical factors have certainly played a part in the establishment of the diplomatic network. The Embassy in India, for example, was established because of the strong historical ties, a missionary presence, an emigrant presence through the British administration and, finally, similar statehood experiences. The same features would also be true of the Embassy in Nigeria. However, such informal links are not on their own sufficient reason to establish full diplomatic relations. This is apparent from the Philippines case, where despite a very strong missionary presence, no resident embassy has been set up. Furthermore, the Egyptian case shows that embassies have been set up where no such historical or informal ties exist, and this would apply to other embassies also. Consequently, historical links, though important, are not necessarily the forerunner of formal contact. Furthermore, in more recent years this reason for contact has declined in importance and been superseded by political and economic factors.

Other factors influence the decisions behind Ireland's bilateral diplomatic network. Political reasons have been significant motivations for establishing almost all Irish embassies, certainly in terms of the political importance of the country involved and on occasion the political importance of the region also. This was most apparent with the first three Irish Embassies in the Third World, in Argentina, Nigeria and India. All were important states in their own right, and all were regionally important actors as well. This feature is still apparent, for example in China, where an Embassy was established primarily due to its size, its "political importance as a leader of developing countries, as a regional power and as a permanent member of the Security Council".[95] China is perhaps an exceptional case – not every country is a permanent member of the Security Council, and few come even close to China in terms of population size. But the political significance of countries is an important factor behind the decision to establish and maintain links, and that factor has become even more important since joining the EC. The politically important regions and countries tend to be defined in terms of their importance on the EC's agendas. However, it must be noted that contact is inconsistent. For example, the political importance of Zimbabwe has been recognised by non-resident accreditation, but the political importance of Senegal or Côte d'Ivoire in West Africa has not been acknowledged in similar fashion. An even more glaring example is in Latin America, where very large and politically important countries such as Brazil and Mexico are not covered by resident Irish missions.

The economic reasons behind diplomatic contact are similarly uneven. Trade and business relations have become more prominent, forming one of the principal reasons for links in some cases. This is particularly true of some Middle Eastern embassies, such as Iran, and it is worth noting again that few of the Middle Eastern oil exporting states with which Ireland has established relations have bothered to open reciprocal resident missions in Dublin. However, as Table 3.2 indicates, diplomatic ties with the Third World are by no means accurate reflections of trading links. This is partly due to extraneous political matters – for instance, although Israel and South Africa both feature among the top ten Third World importing and exporting countries, diplomatic relations have been curtailed for political reasons. Table 3.2 also demonstrates the fact that economic links are not always very permanent. The decline in the importance of oil-exporting nations among countries that Ireland imports from is quite marked, and similarly it is unlikely that Trinidad and Tobago will regain its prominence as an exporter to Ireland that it had in 1970. However, one final feature of the Table highlights the disparity between economic contacts and diplomatic ties. South American countries feature prominently on both tables, with for example Brazil being among the top ten Third World exporters to Ireland in each of the three years examined, and Mexico being among the top three Third World importers of Irish exports in each period as well. This makes the absence of more extensive diplomatic relations with Latin America all the more incongruous.

It is difficult to ascertain a single pattern to account for the diplomatic network in the Third World. Some factors are prominent in some periods and not in others, some reasons account for one tie and may not be applied to another. Thus, it appears that contact has been established in an uneven fashion without any overall strategy in mind. Bilateral relations do seem to be more expressive of certain Irish foreign policy goals than others. Sovereignty and security issues play little role, and more emphasis is placed on issues of international justice (particularly in terms of using diplomatic ties to express support for decolonisation) and international order. Potential economic advantages are becoming increasingly significant motivations for diplomatic contact, but that needs to be seen against a background of Irish trade being conducted overwhelmingly and increasingly with Western Europe.

These goals are, however, implemented in an uneven manner, with some active at particular times and then inactive in similar

Table 3.2: Irish trade with the Third World, by country

a. imports (£000)

	1970		1980		1990	
1.	Kuwait	7,030	Saudi Arabia	121,140	Taiwan	90,440
2.	Saudi Arabia	6,876	Iran	39,942	Hong Kong	57,748
3.	Iran	4,743	Kuwait	33,290	Singapore	57,015
4.	Argentina	3,945	Iraq	28,837	China	50,764
5.	India	3,712	Hong Kong	19,693	South Korea	47,979
6.	Morocco	2,734	India	18,168	Guinea	46,848
7.	Israel	2,439	Brazil	17,946	Brazil	41,840
8.	Ghana	2,288	South Korea	16,995	Malaysia	36,000
9.	South Africa	2,099	Israel	15,308	Colombia	29,330
10.	Brazil	1,844	South Africa	11,686	India	22,941

b. exports (£000)

	1970		1980		1990	
1.	South Africa	1,420	Libya	64,122	Mexico	80,341
2.	Mexico	929	Nigeria	37,446	Saudi Arabia	68,929
3.	Trinidad & Tobago	852	Mexico	33,755	Singapore	53,737
4.	Venezuela	839	Egypt	20,652	Iran	46,659
5.	Nigeria	829	Tunisia	17,023	Hong Kong	45,472
6.	Philippines	693	Saudi Arabia	15,273	Nigeria	41,064
7.	Singapore	517	Venezuela	14,629	Egypt	34,454
8.	Morocco	481	Algeria	14,301	Libya	29,647
9.	Sri Lanka	453	Iran	12,526	South Korea	27,781
10.	Malaysia	414	South Africa	11,040	Israel	23,897

Source: Ireland (1971, 1981, 1991) *Trade Statistics.*

situations at other times. This can be related to two connecting factors: resources and policy direction. Embassies are often unable to implement all goals equally. This is due to the limitation on resources, and there is a particular resource limitation imposed in many Third World countries, where less efficient transport and communications facilities necessitate increased administrative duties on the part of Embassy staff. In most cases the administrative work-load has further increased since accession to the EC. For example, in 1986 Ireland introduced a visa requirement for Nigerian citizens as part of an EC move, and this work has become a considerable burden for the staff as no additional staff were allocated.[96] Such work is often regarded as "onerous, difficult and time-consuming", and attention must be directed away from other areas of policy.[97]

The resources allocated to individual Embassies are indicative of the overall foreign policy priority of a country or region, and most Irish embassies in the Third World have made increasing use of contacts available through cooperation and information exchanges with the embassies of other EC countries. This applies especially in cases where Ireland has only non-resident accreditation – although there are honorary consulates in each of those countries, consuls have "no diplomatic or political function",[98] and that makes Irish Embassy staff more reliant on their EC colleagues for such information. In cases where Ireland has no contact, even of a non-resident nature, that reliance is even more pronounced.

Conclusion

The three case studies in this Chapter highlighted certain features of Ireland's bilateral relations, and these have been further borne out by examination of the wider context of bilateral relations. First, it is important to remember that Ireland had virtually no formal bilateral contacts with countries of the Third World until recently, and that membership of the EC was a vital catalyst in encouraging an expansion of those ties. Community membership was also important for having altered the nature of Irish bilateral relations with the Third World. The establishment of an Irish bilateral aid programme is again inextricably linked to membership, and the political and economic interests of the Community also served to provide a particular focus for the expansion of the bilateral diplomatic network.

The Community has also been instrumental in assisting Ireland to develop an expanded diplomatic capability. The exchange of information available through the EPC process has become important both for the Department of Foreign Affairs in Dublin and for Irish embassies abroad, and has reduced the significance of the foreign policy interests of the United States. However, it has also meant that less attention has been paid to other sources of information that are available. In particular, missionaries, aid workers and business people working in the Third World are given little opportunity to feed in their own interpretations and opinions to the foreign policy process.

This is partly a consequence of the operations of the Department of Foreign Affairs, but it must also be borne in mind that at the domestic level, both policy and resources are the product of government decisions. Chapter Two concluded that policy formulation on the Third World is conducted in an elitist and exclusive framework. With little political interest in the broad scope of Third World affairs, the Minister for Foreign Affairs does not consistently accord it the same attention as EC issues or Anglo-Irish relations. Thus, in general the wealth of expertise in the Department makes it the central actor in the process and affords it an exclusivity. But without constant ministerial focus, and with little consultation with NGOs, policy is formulated in a less pro-active fashion and is often reactive to external pressures such as famines, disasters or wars. Accession to the EC has, however, moved towards righting the unevenness in foreign policy by encouraging greater contact with Third World countries and a more planned approach. This latter development is reflected in the increasing and regular contact between Irish embassies and other EPC embassies.[99] However, until there is more widespread political interest and will in improving relations with Third World countries the imbalance will continue.

Footnotes

1   Kirby 1992: 115-6.
2   *Ibid.*: 108.
3   Questionnaire, December 1991.
4   Questionnaire, December 1991.
5   Keatinge 1973: 307.
6   Questionnaire, December 1991.
7   *Dáil debates*, 9 May 1973, 265: 742.
8   Oireachtas 1985: 7.
9   Questionnaire, December 1991.
10 *Dáil debates*, 18 January 1984, 347: 43.

11 ACDC 1991: 52.

12 Oireachtas 1985: 15, 17.

13 ACDC 1991: 10.

14 *Ibid.*: 60.

15 Sharp 1990: 169.

16 Hobsbawn 1978: 202.

17 Potter 1986: 57.

18 Radhakrishnan 1965: 342.

19 Gopal 1975: 22.

20 *The Irish Times*, 22 April 1991.

21 Lyons 1974: 549.

22 Interview, March 1992.

23 Gopal 1975: 22.

24 *The Irish Times*, 23 February 1991.

25 Keatinge 1973: 175.

26 Ireland, *Trade Statistics* 1972: 6; 1990: 12.

27 CTT 1986: 5.

28 Fitzpatrick 1985: 69.

29 Sutton 1989: 270.

30 Matthews 1991: 90.

31 ACDC 1990: 3.

32 In 1990, there were 177 Irish Catholic missionaries, one BCMS Crosslinks missionary, three Methodist missionaries and three Presbyterian missionaries working in India (IMU 1990).

33 Interview, January 1992.

34 Interview, January 1992.

35 Interview, January 1992.

36 Questionnaire, December 1991.

37 Questionnaire, December 1991.

38 ICJP 1980: 30.

39 Ireland 1979.

40 ICJP 1980: 31.

41 Interview, March 1992.

42 Oireachtas 1985: 26.

43 Questionnaire, December 1991.

44 *The Irish Times*, 23 February 1991.

45 Note, though, that the Irish government granted Imelda Marcos permission to stay in Ireland in 1973, following an assassination attempt, and Marcos' daughters attended school in Ireland in the 1970s.

46 *The Irish Times*, 13 August 1986.

47 *Ibid.*

48 O'Brien 1985: 20.

49 *Third World Now*, winter 1991, 46: 9.

50 *Ibid.*

51 Hennegan 1989.

52 *The Irish Times*, 13 December 1978.

53 *The Irish Times*, 26 March 1979.

54 *Irish Press*, 12 February 1978.

55 *The Irish Times*, 26 March 1979.

56 *Irish Press*, 23 February 1984.

57 *Irish Press*, 12 November 1983.

58 *Irish Press*, 12 November 1983.

59 *The Irish Times*, 30 January 1984.

60 *Sunday Independent*, 18 January 1984.

61 *Irish News*, 6 November 1983.

62 O'Brien 1985: 70.

63 *Ibid.*

64 *Ibid.*

65 *Ibid.*: 83.

66 *Ibid.*: 84.

67 *The Irish Times*, 6 February 1984.

68 *The Irish Times*, 8 February 1984.

69 *The Irish Times*, 24 February 1984.

70 *The Irish Times*, 25 May 1984.

71 *Cork Examiner*, 28 May 1984.

72 *Catholic Herald*, 8 June 1984.

73 *Irish Independent*, 31 March 1984.

74 O'Brien 1987: 292.

75 *Irish Independent*, 6 June 1984.

76 O'Brien 1987: 292.

77 *Ibid.*

78 *The Irish Times*, 14 July 1984.

79 *Dáil debates*, 26 June 1984, 348: 695.

80 O'Brien 1985: 104.

81 Sifry and Cerf 1991: 168.

82 O'Brien 1969: 129.

83 Questionnaire, December 1991.

84 *The Irish Times*, 16 December 1974.

85 *The Irish Times*, 18 December 1974.

86 Keatinge 1978: 168.

87 Sharp 1990: 184.

88 *Ibid.*: 183.

89 *The Irish Times*, 18 December 1974.

90 Ireland, *Trade Statistics* 1980, 1985: 8.6, 8.1.

91 Questionnaire, December 1991.

92 Questionnaire, December 1991.

93 Questionnaire, December 1991.

94 *The Irish Times Supplement*, 2 February 1992.

95 Questionnaire, December 1991.

96 Questionnaire, December 1991.

97 Questionnaire, December 1991.

98 *Dáil debates*, 8 December 1981, 331: 1204.

99 Questionnaire, December 1991.

Chapter 4

Ireland, The European Community and the Third World

This Chapter examines how Community membership has affected the development of Ireland's foreign policy, both at the level of policy formulation and more broadly in the conduct of policy towards the Third World. The EC is now an important medium through which Ireland encounters the Third World, both at a political and an economic level, and also offers a means by which the state complements its limited Bilateral Aid Programme. The Chapter examines the significance of the EC as an international actor, and then considers its role in international relations at an economic and political level. We then go on to consider Ireland's position in the European Community in relation to the Third World, and especially the impact of EC membership on Ireland's policies towards the Third World. The latter part of the Chapter focuses on two case studies of the EC's regional links with the Third World, and the possibilities and limitations of Irish involvement through the EC in the Third World. The cases examined are the Lomé Convention (the EC-ACP relationship) and the EC's links with regional groups in Central and South America, especially through the Rio Group and the San José process.

The above cases provide useful insights into how Ireland's membership of the EC has affected the formulation and conduct of its foreign policy towards the Third World. In the first case many of the EC's member states already had long-standing economic and political relationships with the Third World, which provided the initial basis for the establishment of EC-level association agreements. Ireland, on joining the EC, therefore became party to these agreements, and in turn played a role in establishing the first Lomé Convention in 1975. In contrast, the EC's links with Latin America are relatively new, representing a different political direction for the EC, and one that raises questions about its ability as an international actor to affect outcomes in international relations. It also raises the question as to what role a small state such as Ireland can hope to play in such a process, and whether this is the most appropriate level at which Ireland should be involved. In the context of each case we seek to examine Ireland's role in the Community, especially in relation to each of these regional groupings, and in particular in terms of its contribution.

The significance of the EC as an international actor

The European Community has become an important international actor in its own right. The Community has always aspired to play a significant role in international affairs, but was only equipped with a limited legal basis on which to build and develop such an international role. It was initially intended to be principally an economic rather than a political Community, and thus developed a considerable role and presence in international economic matters. It has come to represent a significant trading bloc, and through the establishment of common trade policies towards "third countries", is in a position to regulate the flow of international trade. Nonetheless, it must be remembered that tariff barriers in general have been reduced to negligible proportions through the successive GATT trade negotiations (the standard EC tariff is now approximately 3.5 per cent), and that while many other types of trade barriers still remain the Community's trade regime is quite liberal towards Third World countries, with some notable exceptions.

The Community did not begin to emerge as a significant international political actor until the 1970s. Early attempts at political cooperation, such as the European Defence Community (1954) and the Fouchet proposals (1961-2), failed to win sufficient support from the EC member states and were not acted on.[1] The EC's members did, however, support a new initiative in political cooperation launched at the Hague Conference in 1969 known as European Political Cooperation (EPC). This was to be a limited form of cooperation which was to be conducted at an intergovernmental level, outside the Treaty's normal decision-making rules, and therefore beyond judicial review and distinct from the Community's external economic relations. The objective was "to ensure greater mutual understanding with respect to the major issues of international politics, by exchanging information and consulting regularly; to increase their solidarity by working for a harmonization of views, concertation of attitudes and joint action when it appears feasible and desirable".[2] The EPC procedure was further adapted and consolidated during the 1970s and early 1980s, although the changes were more procedural than qualitative, and it was not until the Single European Act of 1986 that the process was incorporated and institutionalised in the Treaty of Rome. This formalised the existing process, but still maintained the distinction between the work of the foreign affairs ministers meeting under EPC, and the same Ministers meeting as the Council of Ministers. The latest proposals, contained in the Maastricht Treaty on European Union, add new provisions in respect to a "common foreign and security policy", envisaging an even greater degree of foreign policy concertation and the possibility of some defence cooperation, although all this is still to be carried out at an intergovernmental level.[3]

The EC therefore operates under two separate sets of decision-making rules. The first are explicitly laid out in the EC Treaty, and range from rules governing trade through the Common Commercial Policy (Article 113), and association agreements (Article 238) to diplomatic representation in international organisations (Articles 229-231). The second set of rules, referred to as European Political Cooperation, principally provide for intergovernmental cooperation between the member states of the EC in the sphere of foreign policy. The member states' representatives discuss in EPC foreign policy matters which are of common concern but which are not covered under the external economic provisions of the EEC Treaty. In this context the EC's external relations have been a complex affair, leading often to a false distinction between economic and political problems, and the discussion of the same problem in different fora. This was classically the case in respect to the Middle East, where economic and political concerns were difficult to distinguish.

There have been some attempts to remedy this situation. The 1986 Single European Act, for example, provides that "the external policies of the European Community and the policies agreed in EPC must be consistent" (Article 30.5). At a practical level the Commission is now associated with most of what goes on under the guise of European Political Cooperation, and at a functional level it is informed on a day to day basis of what the Presidency and EPC secretariat are doing. However, the divorce of political and economic matters in respect of Community external relations in regions such as Central America, the Middle East and South Africa makes policy-making that much more difficult. The EC is nevertheless seen by many states and international actors as a significant international actor in its own right. This is reinforced by its presence in a variety of fora, such as the UN General Assembly and the GATT. The EC Commission represents the Community in a number of such organisations, and its role is further reinforced by dialogue with a number of regional organisations and groupings such as ASEAN, the Gulf Cooperation Council and the ACP, its missions in particular countries, and its other external relations.

EC external economic relations and the Third World

The EC's external economic relations comprise, as we have seen, a number of elements, ranging from trade to aid, including the Common Commercial Policy, association and cooperation agreements and the Generalised System of Preferences (GSP). First, through the Common Commercial Policy the EC supports the "harmonious development of world trade, the progressive abolition of restrictions on international trade and the lowering of customs barriers" (Article 110). Second, the EC may "conclude with a third country, a union of states or an international organisation, agreements creating an Association embodying reciprocal rights and obligations, joint actions and appropriate forms of procedures" (Article 238, see also Article 113). For example, the Community has developed bilateral and regional cooperation agreements with such states as Brazil and Mexico and regional groupings such as the ACP states, ASEAN, the Gulf States, the Andean Pact and Central America. It has preferential trading agreements with the ACP states, the Mediterranean, the Maghreb (Morocco, Algeria and Tunisia) and the Mashreq (Egypt, Lebanon and Jordan); association agreements with Cyprus, Malta, Turkey and Yugoslavia; and a free trade agreement with Israel. Finally, the EC is also a signatory to the GSP under which "the Community waives customs duties on imports of manufactures from developing countries (with exceptions for so-called 'sensitive products')".[4] There are currently 124 developing and 23 dependent territories covered under the GSP. In its relations with the Third World the Community brings into play all these tools.

The Community is first and foremost a customs union with a well developed set of rules and regulations, which through the Common Commercial Policy have a direct bearing on trade relations with the Third World, governing the conditions under which goods enter the common market. The Community moreover has the sole right of initiative in respect to all areas of trade, from tariff rates and trade agreements to export policy.[5] However, despite the degree of cooperation that exists between member states when its comes to questions of trade policy, it should still be borne in mind that each state has its own economic interests which it can and does protect. This was spelled out by a former British Ambassador to Syria. "The limits on this community of interests should not, however, be ignored. The governments of the EC remain competitors for commercial sales and sometimes for political influence".[6]

The EC's historical economic links with the Third World date from the founding of the European Economic Community in 1957, when the original six members of the Community signed the Treaty of Rome. In the negotiations that preceded the Treaty the French Government insisted that any agreement and hence Treaty must provide for a basis on which it could maintain its colonial relations, so that imports could enter the Community tariff free. This was opposed by the German and Dutch Governments, who did not wish to be seen to be sanctioning French colonial policy. They were, nevertheless, forced to accept the French position or confront the risk of no agreement. The Treaty of Rome therefore provided for the granting of preferences for certain "Overseas Countries and Territories", thereby meeting the French Government's concerns.[7] This meant that products from these countries could be freely imported into the Community, and that in reverse the EC would enjoy similar preferences with respect to the export of products from the EC to these parts of the Third World. The Community also created a European Development Fund (EDF), which was to assist financially the poorest of these states.

The European Community further deepened and broadened its relationship with the Third World in the 1960s and 1970s with the signing of the Yaoundé Convention (1963, 1969) and later the Lomé Convention (1975). The former was a direct response to the independence of colonies in the 1960s creating a free trade area between the EC and 18 African states, and provided a basis on which the French could maintain a preferential trading relationship with their former colonies. In response to the enlargement of the Community in 1973, and particularly the accession of Britain, a new agreement was made, the Lomé Convention. It extended the trading preferences and aid package of the Yaoundé Convention to the African and Caribbean states of the British Commonwealth. The first Lomé Convention, which was signed in Togo in February 1975, included 46 states in Africa, the Caribbean and the Pacific (ACP). Its objective was to "provide for tariff and quota free access for all ACP industrial exports into the EC"[8] and development assistance. It also dropped the requirement that existed under the Yaoundé Convention that Third World states give reciprocal preferences to EC exports in Third World markets, an important concession from the Third World's point of view (see Chapter Five on the GATT case). However, the importance of the ACP states in relation to trade with the EC has been declining – both in terms of imports and exports (Table 4.1). The EC's exports to the ACP as a percentage of its overall trade fell from 9.4 per cent in 1960 to 4.1 per cent in 1987, while imports from the ACP fell from 9.7 per cent to 4.8 per cent over the same period. These figures represent, of course, the percentage share of imports/exports rather than trade in absolute terms, and therefore are only a crude indicator of the importance of such trade. While the ACP may appear less important to the EC – at least in trade terms – the EC still remains an important trade partner for many of the poorer, lesser developed ACP states.

The Community has renewed the Lomé Convention on three occasions – 1980, 1985 and 1990 – which reflects its continuing commitment to the ACP (the details of the most recent Convention, which will operate until the year 2000, are outlined

Table 4.1: The EC's trade relations with the ACP countries (million ECU)

	1960	1970	1975	1980	1982	1985	1987
Exports to ACP	2,392	4,068	8,772	17,048	20,222	19,336	13,843
(% EC total)	9.4	7.5	7.4	7.7	7.1	5.1	4.1
Imports from ACP	2,826	5,472	9,715	20,744	20,140	30,310	16,374
(% EC total)	9.7	8.6	7.3	7.3	6.0	7.5	4.8
EC Trade balance	–434	–1,405	–943	–3,696	+82	–10,974	–2,531

Source: Schmuck (1990: 50)

below and its members are listed in Appendix 3). The Community's commitment to the ACP states has taken a number of specific forms, ranging from financial assistance for structural adjustment, to STABEX and SYSMIN, to support for emergency aid and refugee assistance (see Table 4.2). Notably, in the past, the Community's aid has not been tied, meaning that the states to which aid has been given are not required to meet political or economic criteria. It should be noted, however, that the EC is increasingly working alongside the IMF and World Bank, which means that in the future it is more likely that states which receive assistance will have to comply with externally imposed conditions, such as economic adjustment programmes. Furthermore, it is possible that the European Community will impose its own forms of conditionality distinct from World Bank and IMF criteria in the future. Currently, EC assistance is principally channelled through the European Development Fund, under the auspices of the Commission's Development Cooperation Directorate-General (DG VIII).

By implication these sophisticated trade and aid policies increasingly subsume the activities of many of the EC's own member states' policies towards the Third World. This is particularly the case in Ireland where the total amount of Third World assistance channelled through the EC has had a direct and negative effect on Ireland's own development assistance programme, which has been cut back in recent years. Moreover the appropriateness of the EC's own approach to Third World assistance is questioned in some quarters, where it is seen as an extension of neo-colonialism, perpetuating underdevelopment and economic dependency, while to others it is considered a model policy to be emulated. In Ireland, the EC has certainly been viewed as an increasingly important medium through which development assistance is channelled to the Third World, or rather the ACP states.

In general, the Community's overall range of policies and instruments constitutes a pyramid of preferences in which some states do relatively better than others but all benefit to some degree. On the other hand, those states not fortunate enough to be party to the EC's preference policies are at a disadvantage to those which are. In particular, many Asian and Latin American states which do not have preferential agreements with the EC have been adversely affected, with trade being diverted away from them to the ACP states. The EC has refused to extend preferential treatment to the Asian states fearing that their exports might undercut the prices of domestic producers. There

Table 4.2: Lomé IV: 1990-2000

Membership

12 EC states and 69 ACP states

Financial resources (MECU)

European Development Fund	
Grants for national and	
regional programmes	6,215
Structural adjustment	1,150
Stabex	1,500
Sysmin	480
Emergency aid	250
Refugee aid	100
Interest rate subsidies	280
Risk capital	825
European Investment Bank (EIB)	
Loans for national and	
regional projects	1,200
Total 1900-2000	12,000 (MECU)

EDF Mechanisms

STABEX: created under Lomé I, its purpose is to stabilise the export earnings of the developing states from agricultural commodities.

SYSMIN: created under Lomé II, it is a special financing facility which assists states that are heavily dependent on mining exports to the EC.

Emergency aid: available for disaster relief.

Refugee aid: to assist in the relief of refugee suffering.

European Investment Bank: makes loans out of its own resources, and provides aid in the form of risk capital from the EDF.

Source: Commission of the European Communities (1990)

are also particular concerns about textiles which are covered under the Multi-Fibre Agreement (MFA) (see the Indian case-study in Chapter 3). Nevertheless, under the GSP all the less-developed states have been granted limited preferential access for manufactured and semi-manufactured exports to the Community.

In sum, then, the Community's external economic trade and aid policies present both opportunities and potential threats to the Third World. On the trade side the Community now ensures that most ACP exports enter the EC free of duties and quotas, with some exceptions. The EC also purchases up to 1.3 million tonnes of sugar at EC prices each year. It should, however, be borne in mind that 70 per cent of ACP exports to the EC are of products not currently produced in the EC, and therefore not subject to any form of trade barriers anyway.[9] Furthermore, the Community's market is an extremely important one to the ACP states, particularly to the lesser developed LDCs, who are dependent on the sale of primary products. In this context the Community's aid policies, especially STABEX (and SYSMIN), have been important in stabilising these states' export earnings, and protecting them against undue market fluctuations.[10]

European Political Cooperation (EPC)

In addition to the EC's external trade policies its member states also cooperate through the process of EPC. This provides a limited means by which the member states can coordinate their foreign policy positions, reach agreements and undertake common actions in the foreign policy field, without being unduly bound by the rules of the Treaty of Rome. The members of the EC have striven to coordinate their positions in such fora as the UN and the Conference on Security and Cooperation in Europe (CSCE). They have also attempted to undertake joint action, as in the case of South Africa where the EC states agreed to impose a code of conduct on firms doing business in that country, and in the case of the Falklands war where trade sanctions were imposed on Argentina. EPC is therefore an extremely important process and one that complements and at times impinges on the Commission's own role in international affairs. Whatever its practical effect, it constitutes the principal forum in which EC foreign ministers come together to discuss international issues and crises of common concern to them. It sits at the apex of the Community's member states' diplomatic machines, collecting and processing information from a diverse array of states.

In relation to the Third World the EPC process exemplifies in general the difficulties that the members of the Community experience in making collective decisions in other areas. The differing national experiences, political cultures and national interests make it difficult for the EC to agree on a united response on many Third World issues. As Nicoll and Salmon suggest, "the colonial experience seems to have been particularly significant, with divisions in EPC appearing on Namibia, Rhodesia, apartheid and sanctions, decolonisation, on Third World issues, especially the New International Economic Order".[11] It can therefore be difficult to reach decisions and agree common actions in instances where one or more states' own interests are threatened by common action.

In practical terms, when the states do agree on issues, there are few instruments at their command, in comparison with the powers of the Commission. Lacking the traditional instruments of foreign policy, one of the few means by which the foreign ministers may act is to issue declaratory statements on specific issues, for example, by condemning human rights violations in Nicaragua. But, as one observer has pointed out, "the rhetoric of EPC is crammed with cliches such as "elections should always be 'free and fair' (referring to Nicaragua)" and "political settlements and solutions should always be either 'comprehensive, just and lasting' (on the Middle East) or 'just, stable and lasting' (on Central America)".[12] These declarations are little more than statements of opinion, and have little direct impact on international affairs. They do, however, reflect the EC's views on particular issues, and may lead other states to change their behaviour. It is interesting to note that between 1970 and 1986 over three-quarters of all EPC declarations were concerned with the Third World (Table 4.3). As Pijpers observes, "the Third World in general, and its crises and conflicts in particular were bound to become EPC's major area of interest from the beginning",[13] if for no other reason than because East-West issues were discussed in NATO, the Western European Union (WEU) and elsewhere, and not under EPC, while NATO has avoided discussion of "out of area" topics, thus making the EC one of the few Western fora in which Third World issues can be raised.

In return, the Third World has focused its diplomatic efforts on the European Community and EPC, the principal focus being

Table 4.3: The subject of EPC declarations, 1970-86

	No.	%
Middle East	73	24.4
Asia	43	14.4
Africa	54	18.1
Latin America	39	13.0
CSCE	39	13.0
Cyprus	12	4.0
UN	3	1.0
Terrorism	20	6.7
Human rights	13	4.3
other	3	1.0
Total	299	100.0

Source: Pijpers (1988: 154)

on the President of the European Council, as the representative of the member states, and on the Commission, especially its external DGs. Brussels is now a regular posting for Third World ambassadors, who through their own meetings and fora, press the EC on issues of concern to their countries. For example, the Group of Latin American Ambassadors, or GRULA, attempt to coordinate responses to the EC and present a collective front on certain issues of concern. Similarly, the ACP states through their ambassadors regularly meet with the EC and lobby on specific matters of concern to their states.

Ireland, the EC and the Third World

In relation to the European Community Ireland's Third World policies have been both reinforced and in some areas considerably extended as a result of Community membership. Ireland's bilateral diplomatic links with the Third World were very limited prior to membership, and relations were primarily, although not exclusively, conducted though the UN and its agencies. EC membership marked a significant turning point in Irish foreign policy. Overnight the Irish foreign policy environment had changed dramatically, with Irish officials being involved on a day-to-day basis with the EC's institutions and its officials. The Irish foreign policy process was therefore forced to adapt to the demands which membership imposed on the government, and as in many other departments, there was some restructuring of the Department of Foreign Affairs, with the creation of a European division, an expansion in the number of officials and the substantive broadening of Foreign Affairs' remit. As one Irish official observed, "at the time of entry into the Community the structure of the Political Division at Headquarters in Iveagh House was rudimentary by European standards",[14] but membership led to its expansion and its partial reorganisation on a desk system with a geographical focus. The Department was confronted with new issues and geographical areas on which it had had little or no articulated policy in the past, such as the Middle East, which it was now forced to consider in EC fora (see the case of Egypt in Chapter 3).

Ireland was also obliged to accept the *acquis communautaire*, that is the existing rules and regulations of the EC, especially in respect to the EC's external economic relations, the Common Commercial Policy and EPC. Membership therefore opened up new opportunities to broaden and deepen Ireland's external economic and political relations with other non-EC states, regional groupings and organisations. Realistically, Ireland's role on this new world stage was, as Keatinge suggests, still "to be numbered among the bit players".[15] Its potential influence, as a small state, was bound to be limited both in terms of its formal weight in the EC's institutions, and in relation to its status relative to large states such as Britain, France and Germany. The ability of Irish foreign policy-makers to assert their influence in the Community, and in particular in relation to the Third World, is largely dependent on their diplomatic skills. These skills are, needless to say, largely employed in seeking to secure Ireland's own economic and political interests, and are likely to be only secondarily used on behalf of the Third World, as the following discussion on trade, aid and political issues demonstrates.

(a) Trade and aid

In respect to trade Ireland's principal concerns have been with intra-EC trade rather than with extra-EC trade. Very simply, Ireland's markets were mostly in Britain and Europe, which therefore dictated that Ireland's principal interest would be in maintaining that trade and where possible expanding it. This was particularly the case in agriculture, an area of great domestic political concern, and one which potentially might bring Ireland into conflict with the Third World. The potential threat of Third World imports, and indirectly competition for third markets inside and outside the EC, raised some concerns in both governmental and non-governmental circles. A protectionist attitude prevailed in certain Government departments, such as Agriculture and Industry and Commerce, which were concerned with protecting Irish national economic interests, although the Department of Foreign Affairs was more inclined to avoid a protectionist view. The former departments were therefore keen to support EC-level protectionist measures, especially in the areas of agriculture, textiles and clothing. Garret FitzGerald observed that: "EEC protectionist policies *vis-à-vis* low-cost countries, which have been maintained with strong Irish support, have made the process of development more difficult in a number of countries where a transition towards a manufacturing economy is clearly necessary as part of the process of raising living standards".[16] This implies that Third World products are only welcome in the EC and Ireland under certain conditions, namely those favourable to the Community's member states, and when they are less likely to compete with EC products.

In practice strong Irish views on this subject are tempered by competing images of the Third World and divisions within the policy establishment, and more generally amongst societal interests. Within the government there are three more or less different sets of interests. There is in the Department of Foreign Affairs a strong Third World lobby, mostly in the Development Cooperation Division, which supports the formation of more balanced trade agreements with the Third World, the reduction of trade barriers, and greater overseas aid. However, in economic foreign policy-making matters the Department must first consult and get the agreement of other departments. In contrast the Departments of Industry and Commerce and Agriculture are much more wary of the Third World and trade agreements, and are generally protectionist in their outlook, while Finance is more purely "liberal" in the economic sense. Ireland's position in trade negotiations often represents a compromise between these competing sets of interests, and policy emerges out of consultation between departments. Ireland does not, however, view the Third World as especially important in terms of trade, with a few specific exceptions, and therefore only on particular issues is there debate about the EC's trade policies as they affect the Third World, or alternatively as the Third World affects the EC. Officials at the administrative level are not aware of any specific influence coming from non-governmental sources, be they development activists, business interests or trade unions. The recent Tribunal of Inquiry into the Beef Industry, however, demonstrated that the same does not apply with regard to outside influence on political decision-makers.

Membership has also had a significant impact on Ireland's overseas aid policy. In the first instance it stimulated the development of an official Bilateral Aid Programme. The then Foreign Minister, Garret FitzGerald, was eager to play an active role in all aspects of the EC and its policies and was also committed to developing Ireland's aid contributions. Community membership provided part of the rationale for the establishment of a small Bilateral Aid Programme (1973), as it was considered important that Ireland should be seen to be playing an active role in the Third World.[17] At the same time the EC has become the primary external medium through which government financial assistance is channelled. In 1989 the Irish Government contributed IR£14 million to the EC for Third World assistance: 40.4 per cent of the total ODA budget of IR£34.5 million. Of this, IR£5.5 million, or 0.55 per cent of the total EDF budget of IR£986.2 million, went to the European Development Fund. As a percentage, Ireland's EC contribution is small in comparison with other European states, although it is a significant proportion of the ODA budget, and therefore is important within Ireland. It should also be noted that this contribution is agreed in cooperation with Ireland's EC partners: thus most such expenditures are mandatory, and cannot easily be trimmed. This then has implications for other areas of the development budget which are more vulnerable to changes in the political and economic climate. For example, there has been a steady decline in Ireland's overall financial commitment to the Third World and cut-backs in the Bilateral Aid Programme, which may reflect the feeling in some government circles that the EC, and by extension its richer members, are better placed than Ireland to contribute to the EC's programmes.

(b) Political issues

At a political level the Community impinges on Ireland's foreign and diplomatic relations with the Third World in a variety of ways. Initially, membership of the EC was perceived by some in government as something of a mixed blessing. FitzGerald argued that as a result of membership Ireland had "an input into foreign policy making in disproportion to our size".[18] Nevertheless, the Government also had to persuade the Irish public that membership of the EC, and, in particular, participation in the EPC process, did not threaten Ireland's long cherished position of neutrality. EC membership extended Ireland's interests into a variety of new areas in which the state had in the past little or no interest. For example, during Ireland's first EC Presidency in 1975 the state found itself involved in the Middle East, an area in which it had had no clear policy in the past, but one in which it was now expected to speak for the EC. At the same time EPC was still a fairly new mechanism, having only come into force in 1973, so when Ireland took over the EC Presidency in 1975, this was the first occasion a small and peripheral country was acting as EPC President. Some of the larger and more established foreign policy powers feared that Ireland would be unable to cope with the burdens of the Presidency, and had contingency plans ready to take over the running of EPC in such an eventuality. However, not only did Ireland survive its spell in the spotlight, it is generally interpreted as having prospered, and to have run a very effective Presidency.[19] Irish negotiators have established a good reputation in the Community for their mediating skills, although their ability to put across an Irish interest might be lessened as a result.

In general all political issues and specifically those relating to EPC are handled by the Department of Foreign Affairs. O'Leary notes that "questions which arise in the framework of European Political Cooperation are almost always under the exclusive purview of the Department of Foreign Affairs and, in almost all cases, consultations take place exclusively in that department".[20] Such matters are the prerogative of the Political Director, who in this instance is the head of the Political Division within Foreign Affairs, whereas matters which concern the treaties are often dealt with within the department which has the particular competence for the area under discussion, and are coordinated with the staff on the Permanent Representation. In this bifurcated system Ireland has probably had the most opportunity to influence political issues, especially in relation to the Third World, when it has held the presidency of the European Council, which it did in 1975, 1979, 1984 and 1990. For example, in 1975 Ireland was credited with successfully completing the negotiations with the ACP states leading to the Lomé Convention and in playing a constructive mediating role in the Euro-Arab Dialogue. In general Ireland has tried to play such a role inside EPC, but overall has not been seen by the other states as a significant player in the EPC process. There have, of course, been exceptions when Ireland has taken particularly strong lines on certain issue such as the condemnation of the Reagan administration's policies towards El Salvador in EPC in 1981, and its support of Third

World issues in the UN,[21] where it has tended to be in a progressive minority amongst the other EC states

Most recently, the civil war and consequent famine in Somalia have provided an opportunity for a very strong Irish initiative, aimed at urging an increased aid effort by the UN, the EC and individual member states. David Andrews, Foreign Minister at the time, visited the country in August 1992, which was the first visit by an EC Foreign Minister since the war and famine there came to international attention. The visit was seen as inspirational in securing more extensive EC aid and concessions for Somalia. One newspaper praised Andrews' leading role, taking the view that "the Minister's personal crusade on the Somalian crisis represents the shape of things to come in Irish diplomatic policy. In his view Ireland's proud record of involvement in famine relief and peacekeeping means that we are well placed to exert a real influence on EC policy on Third World and human rights issues".[22] Later on, in October 1992, Andrews accompanied President Mary Robinson on another visit to Somalia, which attracted a great amount of publicity in Ireland. Mrs Robinson travelled on to New York to urge greater action from the UN, and continued to raise the issue on subsequent trips to Singapore and Australia. The visit perhaps accomplished little of immediate practical use for Somalia, but was important both in heightening public awareness in Ireland and in demonstrating Ireland's commitment to the UN and the EC. Both visits showed Ireland taking a very public leading role in expressing concern for Somalia and in exhorting others to show similar concern.

Irish officials have also brought up Third World issues in the more traditional Community decision-making structures, such as the meetings of the General Affairs Council of Ministers and the more specialised councils. These meetings, however, are infrequent, and therefore are not likely to be the occasions at which issues are fully discussed and debated. They are essentially decision points, at which pre-agreed policies are for the most part "rubber-stamped". For example, in 1989 the member states' development ministers met twice. The agenda of each of the Development Council's meetings was far-reaching but the discussions were of a general nature, the detailed work having already been undertaken in the member states' Permanent Representations[23] and in the Commission's Development DG. Ireland was responsible, along with a number of other states, particularly Denmark, for placing a number of issues on the table for discussion in these meetings, especially the issue of women in development. Irish Ministers also acted on behalf of the EC in a number of other ways. For example, in 1984 Jim O'Keeffe, the then Minister for Overseas Development, visited Kenya and Ethiopia to assess the famine situation on the EC's behalf.

There have also been extensive daily contacts between Department of Foreign Affairs officials in Dublin and the Commission in relation to the Third World. In particular, this involves primarily, but not exclusively, the Directorate-General for Development (DG VIII) and the Directorate-General for External Relations (DG I). The exchanges between these DGs and the member states' foreign ministries comprise at one level simply information-sharing, but also, and more importantly, the discussion of difficult issues and preparation of proposals for the Ministerial Councils takes place at this level. Such dialogue and exchange contributes to a better understanding of issues on the Irish side, and also provides a means of reaching consensus in preparation for further action.

In summary, Ireland's general stances on Third World trade, aid and political issues broadly reflect Ireland's piecemeal, if progressive, position towards the Third World at other levels of Irish foreign policy. On economic issues Ireland is conservative and principally concerned with protecting its own markets, as and when they are perceived to be threatened by external competitors. The Third World, however, does not pose particular threats to Irish producers who for the most part are not in competition with many of these states. On aid Ireland has tended to take a positive stance, having developed a limited Bilateral Aid Programme, but lacking the larger development budgets of many other European states, it has tended to place its emphasis on the contribution of Irish knowledge and skills to the Third World, which is primarily undertaken at a bilateral level. Finally, Irish support for the Third World on political issues in the EC tends to be based on the principles of Irish foreign policy first enunciated in the UN in the 1950s. In adopting positions based on the principles of international justice and order, Ireland's moralistic position is often in conflict with other EC states such as France and Britain as EC voting in the UN illustrates. It is, however, more difficult to judge whether this has any practical effect on the EC's policies and in EPC declarations, and to what extent Irish foreign policy-makers actively pursue their policies in EC fora. This will be examined in the two case studies which follow on the Lomé negotiations and Central and South American relations with the EC.

Ireland and the Lomé negotiations

The Lomé Conventions have been regarded by the EC as the show-piece of its policies for Third World development, exhibiting a progressive and constructive attitude to Third World trade and development issues. The Third World has, however, viewed the conventions and the Community's trade and aid policies more sceptically. This divergence of views provides an opportunity to examine Ireland's own commitment to Third World development and highlights its own competing interests in relation to Lomé states. Ireland's principled and often moralistic attitude on Third World issues has not always translated into support for and concrete action on behalf of the ACP states in the European Community. This in part reflects the overall limitations of the Irish foreign policy-making which is often piecemeal and reactive to events, rather than pro-active and constructive, in its approach to formulating responses to Third World issues. It also more generally reflects the unwillingness of politicians and the public to substantially support expanded foreign policy action in the Third World.

The limits of Irish foreign policy are illustrated by Ireland's role in the most recent round of Lomé negotiations, which began in October 1988 and were completed in December 1990. While in the past Ireland appeared to play an important role in the final stages of the last three rounds of negotiations, partly because it held the EC Presidency at the time, its role in the most recent negotiations seems to have been quite slight. The negotiations were dogged by a variety of problems which in part explains Ireland's own silence and ambiguous attitude to what was going on. The West European states were largely uninterested in the negotiations and defensive in their attitudes, and at times even hostile towards the demands of the ACP states. On the other side, the ACP states were concerned about their own economic position and changes in the EC's internal market and were fearful that aid might be diverted to Eastern Europe. In addition to these problems, the heterogeneous nature of the ACP bloc, with its geographical and economic disparities, made it difficult for the ACP to reach agreement on common interests and to advance a united front to the EC. The negotiations were also being conducted during a period of great turmoil and political change in Europe and the Community, and therefore took a back-seat to these other more momentous developments in Europe. The ACP representatives were very aware that international change had placed them in a relatively weak position in relation to the EC, and were anxious to remind the North that they should not lose sight of their problems relative to those of Eastern Europe.

The negotiations brought to the fore fundamental disagreements between the EC and the ACP over financial resources, access to EC markets, commodities and debt issues.[24] For Ireland, of course, many of these issues had little significance in terms of the Irish economy with the exception of the beef issue. Ireland could therefore afford to be broadly progressive in its stance being neither a staunch advocate of free trade, such as Britain, nor a supporter of protectionism, such as Italy and the other Mediterranean states. This was reflected at the governmental level in the views of the different departments. The principal Government actors concerned with the negotiations were the Departments of Foreign Affairs, Agriculture and, to a lesser extent, Industry and Commerce. Foreign Affairs was chiefly responsible for articulating Ireland's views in the EC's fora, principally through the Permanent Representation in Brussels and the ACP ad hoc working group in the Council. This, however, required something of a balancing act on the part of Foreign Affairs, which had to take account of the interests of the Departments of Agriculture and Industry and Commerce in protecting Irish producers, while wanting to articulate its own broader agenda. Agriculture's principal concern was to protect Irish beef and sheep meat exports from Third World competitors, while Industry and Commerce was concerned with the "rules of origin"[25] on manufactured products originating in ACP countries. In contrast the Department of Foreign Affairs' interests were far more political: for example, it supported concessions which would lead to increased beef exports from Namibia to the EC. The Department of Foreign Affairs convinced the Department of Agriculture to accept concessions on Namibia. There was an explicit feeling in Foreign Affairs that such a policy was necessary, that Ireland would have to back up a rhetorical commitment to Namibia with practical support in this fashion.[26]

In general, Ireland's policy and positions during the negotiations reflected the general principles of Irish foreign policy articulated in the UN in the 1950s: support for humanitarian principles, international justice and order. It therefore supported the reference to human rights made in the preamble to the new Convention. At a less abstract level, Foreign Affairs supported measures for structural adjustment and low levels of aid conditionality for states seeking assistance. Other more explicit humanitarian concerns included support for improved primary health care and education. In particular, Foreign Affairs supported the inclusion of a social chapter in the Lomé Convention, and intervened when it felt that there was insufficient attention being paid to the role of women in development. It also successfully opposed proposals to place strict new conditions on aid, which were proposed by some of the other EC member states. Ireland was, therefore, generally on the more progressive side amongst the EC states, but the extent to which this met the preferences of Third World countries is harder to judge, since it is difficult to distinguish a single set of Third World interests within the ACP grouping.

Beyond the executive branch of government there was little public interest in the negotiations, and very little media coverage of what was happening. There was little debate in the Dáil, with the exception of questions from Nora Owen and Michael D. Higgins. Otherwise, it was simply not a newsworthy item. There was no real Irish angle, and there were few general or sectoral interests in the negotiations: some newspapers were more interested in criticising an Irish MEP for participating in an EP-ACP parliamentary meeting in Barbados, which was seen as an unnecessary junket. The negotiations were for the most part conducted through the Department of Foreign Affairs and the Permanent Representation in Brussels. The negotiations were therefore carried on at both a geographically distant location and at a technical, bureaucratic level, which discouraged public participation and yielded little opportunity for public comment. The fact that Irish economic interests did not appear to be at stake further diminished the importance of the negotiations in the eyes of the traditional sectoral interest groups – the farmers, trade unions and employers' organisations – which might otherwise have expressed more interest. The Lomé negotiations inspired little interest among the non-governmental organised interest groups, who did not actively lobby the Department of Foreign Affairs on any sustained basis. In general, while the negotiations failed to arouse much governmental or public debate in Ireland the Government and the Department of Foreign Affairs did consistently pursue the type of interests expressed in the Bilateral Aid Programme, that is, they tended to be humanitarian, and focused on concern for the poorest countries in the Third World, predominantly Africa.

Overall, involvement in Lomé has had a positive effect on the Department of Foreign Affairs' understanding of the Third World, at least in the sense that officials have come into contact with a wide range of Third World states. It has furthermore played a constructive if limited role in pursuing certain issues on behalf of the Third World in the EC's decision-making fora with some degree of success. This has earned Ireland a good reputation in the Third World, in contrast with some other European states which are still perceived as former colonial masters. It has enjoyed an especially good relationship with the ACP member states, leading one Ghanaian envoy, during a visit to Ireland, to describe Ireland as the "EC's moral conscience".[27] Irish ministers are seen as having been supportive of Third World concerns in the first three rounds of the Lomé negotiations and having helped to bring the negotiations to a successful conclusion. As *The Irish Times* noted, commenting on the first Lomé Convention, "Irish diplomats found themselves leading the Community side in an area that, to say the least, has not traditionally been an obsession of Iveagh House, and at the final delicate stage of those negotiations".[28] This was not purely an honorific position. Sutton comments that "the sensitivity and efficiency of the Irish Presidency in overcoming last minute problems, and the fellow feeling of the African, Caribbean and Pacific Group with Ireland as a small country that struggled for independence has often been noted by the African, Caribbean and Pacific partners".[29]

In this context, Ireland's foreign policy-makers have played an important if still limited role in the EC in supporting the ACP's interests, provided that they did not come into conflict with Ireland's own political and economic interests, while at the same time being seen to be an impartial mediator. This view, however, has to be offset against the broader public indifference to Lomé, perhaps reflecting Ireland's overall limited interest in the Third World. It also must be borne in mind that beyond the actual negotiations Foreign Affairs has maintained little interest in the EC's day-to-day involvement in the Third World. If anything it may have even shed some of its own existing bilateral aid obligations on the grounds that it has to contribute to the EC's European Development Fund, over which it has little say about how the money is spent. There have been cut-backs in the Bilateral Aid Programme perhaps reflecting the view that Ireland's own financial resources preclude further development of the programme, and that the Community now is seen as the principal medium through which Ireland contributes to the Third World. Such cut-backs may also reflect the low priority accorded to Third World issues in Irish political circles, both within government and more broadly in Irish political culture. Seldom have foreign policy issues, especially Third World issues, been important during election campaigns in Ireland. Indeed, given the parochial nature of the Irish political system, political support for Third World issues is not high on the agenda of most politicians since it does not win votes and might even lose them votes if they are perceived to be over-concerned with external interests.

Ireland, the EC and regional dialogue in Central and South America

In contrast to its relationship with the ACP states, the EC had little direct involvement in Central and South America until the late 1980s. It was only following the third enlargement of the Community in 1986, to include Spain and Portugal, that the region was brought into sharper focus. At a political level the EC-Latin American relationship was strengthened by Spain's commitment to the region, and specifically by its support for the establishment of democratic regimes. The EC has therefore developed an interest in and sought to promote greater intra-regional cooperation and dialogue as a means to resolving conflict in the region

Prior to Spain's membership of the Community the EC's relationship with the region was limited to several trade agreements and more general support for Latin American integration. The EC has in recent times continued to foster bilateral trade agreements and has also sought to develop a dialogue through regional organisations (see Table 4.4). These economic bilateral links were established on the basis of a number of trade agreements provided for under Articles 113 and 228 of the EEC Treaty. The EC's economic links with the region have, however, steadily declined, with exports from the EC to Latin America falling from a high of 7.2 per cent of the EC total in 1970 to 3.8 per cent in 1988, reflecting partly the impact of austerity policies in the region.[30] The European states with the greatest trade links with the region have been Germany, France and Italy – surprisingly, all have greater interests than Spain – and most European investment has been concentrated in a few states – Brazil, Argentina and Mexico.

At a political level the Community has developed a particular interest in supporting greater political dialogue in the region

Table 4.4: EC-Central and South American Links

Bilateral:

EC-Argentina Non-Preferential Trade Accord	1971
EC-Uruguay Non-Preferential Trade Accord	1974
EC-Brazil Non-Preferential Trade Accord (also 1980, 1982)	1974
EC-Mexico Non-Preferential Trade Accord	1975

Interregional:

EC-Latin American States Dialogue	1971, 1981
Consultations with Contadora Group	1983
EC-Andean Pact Cooperation Accord	1983
Cartagena Agreement	1983
San José Ministerial Conference	1984
EC-Central American Cooperation Accord	1985

Source: Ginsberg (1989: 90-105)

through its links to regional groupings in Central and South America. These have ranged from support for Latin American integration, the origins of which lie in the 1950s with the attempt to promote economic development through economic integration, to the more recent regional groupings which have been established to support both the establishment of democratic regimes in Latin America, and especially to end the violence in Central America. Table 4.5 highlights both the past and more recent attempts at regional integration, cooperation and regional groupings.

The EC has developed its most extensive range of contacts through the two dominant regional groupings: the Rio Group and the San José Process.[31] The issues discussed in the Rio Group have included the economic crisis in Latin America, foreign debt, and the drugs problem, while with the Central American states the dialogue seeks to "reinforce the efforts of the countries of Central America themselves, with the support of the Contadora States, to bring an end to violence and instability in Central America and to promote social justice, economic development and respect for human rights and democratic liberties in that region".[32] The Community's contacts, therefore, with these regional groupings have principally been at a political level, whereas the economic relationship between the EC and the region has been far less developed. It has supported the peace process and sought wherever possible to reinforce it through dialogue. Moreover, while it is concerned to develop a broader

Table 4.5: Central and South American Regional Groupings

Latin American Free Trade Association – Mexico, Colombia, Venezuela, Ecuador, Peru, Brazil, Bolivia, Paraguay, Chile, Argentina, Uruguay	1960
Central American Common Market – Costa Rica, El Salvador, Guatemala, Honduras, Nicaragua	1960

Caribbean Free Trade Agreement
– Antigua, Barbuda, Bahamas, Barbados, Belize,
  Dominica, Grenada, Guyana, Jamaica, Montserrat,
  St Kitts-Nevis, St Lucia, St Vincent, Trinidad
  and Tobago
	1968

Andean Pact – Bolivia, Ecuador, Colombia, Peru, Venezuela	1969
Caribbean Community – Same countries as Caribbean Free Trade Agreement	1973
Sistema Económico de Latinoamérica (SELA) – 26 countries of Latin America and the Caribbean	1975
Southern Cone Common Market (MERCOSUR) – Peru, Uruguay, Argentina, Brazil	1985
Latin American Integration Association – Same countries as Latin American Free Trade Association	1980
Contadora Group – Colombia, Mexico, Venezuela, Panama (Support Group: Uruguay, Argentina, Brazil, Peru)	1983

Rio Group
– Argentina, Brazil, Peru, Uruguay and the
  Contadora Group (joined in 1990 by Chile,
  Ecuador, Bolivia, Paraguay)
	1986

San José Process – Central American states	1985

Sources: Ginsberg (1989), Grabendorff (1990)

relationship with the region, such a relationship will depend on the continuing move to democracy and respect for fundamental human rights. It will also depend in part on the further development of economic relations and the willingness of the Community to open its markets to Latin American goods, to assist with the debt problem and to invest in the region. While the Community has expanded its representation in the region from initially one office, in Caracas, to new offices in Brasilia, Santiago de Chile, San José, Mexico City and Montevideo, the development of further relations is probably unlikely at the present time.

Ireland's links with the region have tended to be at a non-governmental level, principally through missionaries, trade and development agencies.[33] It has had few formal diplomatic contacts with the region, and even less of an economic relationship, with some important exceptions (see Chapter 3). This reflects Ireland's status as a small state, and one that must therefore focus its diplomatic links on areas and countries that are most likely to be important to Irish national interests. Certainly, prior to EC membership Irish interests and concerns with Latin America were mediated through the UN which provided the principal forum in which Irish foreign policy interests and concerns were articulated. Ireland in many instances strongly supported UN resolutions on human rights, democratisation and economic prosperity in the General Assembly, and similarly supported human rights issues in the UN Commission on Human Rights of which it was a member between 1983 and 1988. Its diplomatic links with Latin America prior to membership had been with Argentina but after 1973 it further expanded its links with non-resident missions to Mexico (1977), Brazil (1978) and Venezuela (1980).

In this context Ireland's diplomatic interests in the region have grown in recent years although it remains largely distant from becoming actively involved on a daily basis in the region. Its principal concerns in the region, which are of a political rather than an economic nature, are mediated through the European Community, European Political Cooperation and the United Nations. In this sphere the UN remains an important arena in which Ireland, in conjunction with its European partners, can raise issues concerning the region and in respect to US involvement. A select number of Irish officials and politicians now have a detailed understanding of the problems of the region, and can contribute to discussions in the EC and in EPC on the region. Irish officials participate in the Council's two working groups on Latin America, one of which is concerned with trade and aid and the other with EPC matters, a number have also travelled to the region as part of national and EC delegations and have participated in the regional dialogue that the EC has established through the San José process and the Rio Group. Irish officials were even instrumental during Ireland's EC Presidency in 1984 in institutionalising the regional dialogue with Central America through the San José process. Ireland is perceived in a very good light by Latin American states: the Mexican Ambassador to Ireland commented that "not only with the Contadora process and the San José group but also when we established the Rio Group we always found the Irish Government very supportive".[34]

At the governmental level the Department of Foreign Affairs is the principal department concerned with Latin American issues, and within it these issues are handled in the Political and Development Cooperation divisions. Within Foreign Affairs the region is covered by two individuals of whom one is the regional officer, while the other covers Latin America as one of several other EC interests. There is, of course, a high degree of overlap between the two individuals' functions, and they spend considerable time exchanging information on what is going on in the region. In particular, much of what they are doing is digesting information from Brussels and elsewhere, and then determining what the implications of the EC's actions are for Ireland, and whether Ireland should support the Community in its declarations and actions. They are also engaged in a process of consultation with colleagues in other departments, such as Agriculture and Industry and Commerce, and with the Permanent Representation in Brussels. One example which illustrates both the work of Foreign Affairs and Ireland's interests in the region was the UN Conference on Environment and Development held in Rio de Janeiro in 1992. Most of the issues on the conference agenda affected Ireland only indirectly, such as whether the European Investment Bank should lend money to the region, and the appropriate level at which to transfer science and technology. These are issues that concern the EC, and therefore issues on which Ireland as a member of the EC is expected to be aware of, especially as they impact generally on the Community's economy, but they are not for the most part of great interest to the Irish Government. Ireland has tended to adopt similar positions to those of Spain, Portugal, Italy, Greece and France with which Ireland usually finds itself in agreement on Latin American issues.

In contrast to these types of issues the problems of Central America have proven particularly difficult, requiring a balancing act on the part of the Department of Foreign Affairs. Its political masters have at a rhetorical level strongly condemned the violence in Central America, but have not supported any particularly Irish approach to the problem. For example, in April 1983 during the Dáil debate on Central America Peter Barry, then Foreign Minister, suggested that "the Government's policy in relation to Central America has three main objectives: (1) the furtherance of respect for human rights, (2) the promotion of essential social and economic reforms, (3) support for the creation of the necessary political and diplomatic basis for a peaceful settlement to the conflict and tensions in the area".[35] He also suggested that "even though geographically Central America is distant from this country, this does not mean that we can be indifferent to its fate. We all have a role to play encouraging a dialogue both between and within the countries of Central America which will serve as a basis for the establishment of a permanent peace in the area".[36] During the same debate Niall Andrews stated that "we have here in Ireland a special interest in the region because of the vital and courageous work which our missionaries are carrying out".[37] A number of TDs have also visited the region and voiced concern over human rights violations and US involvement in the region.[38]

In general, however, while the Government has acknowledged the problems of the region, and has condemned human rights violations it has done little more. In particular, it has studiously avoided openly criticising the United States on its policy towards Central America, fearing that this might damage relations. The Government has supported the Community's actions and declarations inside EPC, and is regarded as having given very clear and straightforward support compared to other EC states. A Mexican Ambassador to Ireland noted that "the fact is that we have the sympathy of Ireland in creating these mechanisms of dialogue between Latin America and the European Community".[39] However, these sympathetic statements have often not been backed up with effective action. As Kirby notes, "many active on Central American issues believe Ireland is not forceful enough in putting its point of view forward in the EC and the UN".[40] Overall, Ireland's participation in the region has remained limited and largely symbolic with less consistent public interest in Central and South America than in Africa. What this demonstrates is both the failure of Irish foreign policy-makers to actively pursue these issues at any level in Irish foreign policy. It moreover demonstrates the weakness of relying on the regional level for action – the EC is not always either the most appropriate or necessarily the most useful forum in which to pursue Irish foreign policy interests.

Conclusion

The two cases examined in this chapter offer various insights into Ireland's relationship with the European Community, and especially how that relationship affects Ireland's links with the Third World. Membership of the EC had an important and dramatic impact on the formulation and conduct of Irish foreign policy towards the Third World, leading to an expansion of Ireland's contacts to many new Third World states in different regions of the world. The regional dimension to Irish foreign policy has therefore in many areas replaced and supplanted the UN and bilateral levels as the most important level at which Ireland comes into contact with the Third World. Nevertheless, it is not always the most appropriate level nor necessarily the most effective level at which Irish foreign policy-makers can make an impact, as the two cases suggest.

While the European Community has taken on new significance as an international actor, forging an array of economic and political links with the Third World, there are still many limits as to the role it can play in international relations. Its historical links and more recent association with the Third World have added an important dimension to Irish foreign policy. The range of its links, which include a comprehensive economic relationship with the ACP states and more fragmentary political links with Central and South America, have brought Irish foreign policy-makers into contact with many new states and particular problems they had not faced in the past. As a member of this Community, with its wide range of links with the Third World, Ireland is in a position to attempt to influence EC policy on the Third World. From the Third World's perspective the EC is an important international actor, and one whose influence has been growing in recent years, and therefore they are concerned to influence its policies. In this context Ireland is seen as both more sympathetic to and supportive of Third World interests and is thus considered a useful friend and mediator in EC fora.

The European Community therefore offers an important forum and medium through which Ireland may play a role in the Third World. As an international actor, however, the

Community is limited in what it can do in international relations. On an economic level it can, as we have seen, act for its member states in a variety of ways. In the first instance, it establishes the parameters within which trade is conducted under the terms of the Common Commercial Policy. Second, it has established a number of cooperation and association agreements with different states and regional groupings. Finally, on a political level the EC's members work together within EPC to coordinate their foreign policies. Nevertheless, in this arena cooperation is entirely dependent on the willingness of the member states to agree and then act together. It is, however, difficult to arrive at such agreements and even more difficult to maintain joint action, as demonstrated by the Falklands case, when both the Irish and the Italian Governments withdrew from common sanctions on Argentina after having first agreed to impose them.

The role the Community therefore plays in international affairs tends to vary according to the issue and area under discussion. Its particular responses to emerging problems in the world, especially in relation to the Third World, have been inconsistent and fragmentary, reflecting the Community's own slow development in this field. The EC is not a state, and does not always have the right to speak for its members. Moreover, it lacks the traditional tools of diplomacy and military force to influence outcomes. Its influence is in many ways far more subtle and dependent on the perception of other states, who see it as a powerful force in international affairs. In practical terms, this means that the Community's external relations have developed in response to both the different demands of the member states, such as the British and the French Governments' concerns over their former colonial interests, and, equally importantly, in reaction to specific events, such as the oil crises of the 1970s, which had a direct bearing on the member states' economies. Only in the 1970s and perhaps more particularly the 1980s did the EC begin to develop its relations with other more distant states and regions of the world on a more pro-active basis.

From the Irish perspective the EC has been perceived as a medium through which Ireland can play an active role in world affairs, and indeed Ireland's contacts with other states, especially in the Third World, have expanded greatly since membership. It has developed a Bilateral Aid Programme and fostered further formal diplomatic links with a number of Third World states. The Community has also become the principal forum through which Ireland articulates its interests and concerns with respect to the Third World, thereby replacing in part the UN as the most important international forum for Irish foreign policy-makers.

There is, however, a risk that those in high office and especially within the Department of Foreign Affairs will view the Community as the best means by which to pursue Irish foreign policy goals. These goals which may vary from concern over particular national economic and political interests to the more general principles of Irish foreign policy such as justice, morality and international order, are not always compatible with EC membership. The Community's interests and those of the larger EC member states are sometimes different from those of Ireland. There are, for example, as Chapter 5 demonstrates, a number of instances in which Ireland has found itself in a "progressive" minority bloc during voting on Third World issues in the UN and in opposition to the larger EC states such as Britain, Germany and France.

These types of problems and dilemmas are highlighted in the two cases we have examined. In the Lomé negotiations, the Department of Foreign Affairs attempted to balance Ireland's own national economic concerns against a genuine desire to promote and support Third World interests. In general, the Department struck a reasonable balance between maintaining Ireland's interests while, at the same time, promoting those of the Third World. Nevertheless, the Department has not consistently supported Third World interests, and seems relatively content to leave many issues to the EC. Irish ministers and civil servants could seek to play a greater role in both the formulation and conduct of EC policy than they currently do. Similar criticisms may be levelled at Ireland's interest in Latin American affairs. While Irish ministers have supported EC and EPC declarations on Central America, there has been little concerted and sustained action. This is despite the fact that there is no particular clash with domestic Irish economic interests, though there have been times when the Government has sought to steer clear of coming into conflict with the United States.

This raises a further issue concerning Ireland's overall influence and role on Third World matters in the EC. As a small state with few formal historical links with the Third World it finds itself both better informed and more involved than in the past *vis-à-vis* the Third World. Yet, it is questionable whether such involvement has led to any extended influence over what the EC does in the Third World. In the Lomé case, for example, Irish officials and politicians did play an initially constructive role in the negotiations of the first three Lomé conventions, but during the most recent round Ireland played a less prominent role in the

EC-ACP negotiations. Ireland was more involved in intra-Community discussions, which reflects both the fact that unlike previously Ireland did not hold the Presidency and so was less prominent in the final stages, and that because the earlier Conventions had agreed a considerable range of concessions for ACP states already, Ireland had little scope to champion further concessions. It did pursue a limited number of objectives which were seen as important in development terms but it was no more an active proponent of Third World interests on this occasion than any other state.

Ireland's interest in Lomé was considerably greater, however, than its interest in Latin America, where in the past it had relatively few links and interests. Within the Community, therefore, Ireland's active interest in Latin American policy was quite limited. While undoubtedly Irish officials are now better informed and aware of developments in the region, this has not had any particular impact on Irish policy. In general Ireland's stance in the EC with respect to Latin America has been based on the fundamental principles initially expressed in the UN, and now more widely articulated as the principles of Irish foreign policy (see Chapter 5). While involvement in the EC has broadened the scope of Irish foreign policy to now include Latin America, no further formal diplomatic missions have been established in the region, and Irish economic interests remain limited.

What these cases demonstrate are the constraints and limitations of relying on the EC to make and implement foreign policy. Even when the EC is actively involved in a region, either at an economic level, as in Lomé, or at a political level, as in Latin America, there is still a role for independent state action. Individual EC states may also prefer to choose and pursue alternative courses of action. Such action may not necessarily conflict with EC policy but may in fact complement it. For example, a number of the EC states already have extremely active aid policies above and beyond their commitments to the EC. The influence, then, of any one state in the Community, especially a small one, is limited and there may therefore be times in which such states will seek to implement alternative policies that satisfy their own particular objectives in foreign policy. In this context Ireland should not relinquish responsibility for the formulation and conduct of its own foreign policies towards the Third World. There is a risk that both Irish politicians and foreign policy officials will hide behind the EC claiming both that the Community is the principal medium through which it must act while at the same time using the EC as an excuse for inaction.

Footnotes

1 Pryce 1987.

2 Holland 1988: 13.

3 Keatinge 1991b.

4 Matthews 1991: 76.

5 Molle 1990: 442.

6 Tomkys 1987: 435.

7 Part IV, Articles 131-6. In 1958 over a fifth of the African population was covered under the EC's Associate Members status: French West and Equatorial Africa, Madagascar, French Somaliland, the French Cameroons and Togoland, the Belgian Congo, Ruanda-Urundi, and Italian Somaliland.

8 Molle 1990: 442.

9 Mahler 1990: 4.

10 Needless to say, the manner in which these mechanisms have operated has been the source of considerable controversy in the ACP, where the EC's actions are not always viewed as benevolent.

11 1990: 124.

12 Dinan 1991: 403.

13 1988: 154-5.

14 MacKernan 1984: 17.

15 1978: 137.

16 FitzGerald 1988: 339.

17 O'Neill 1982: 130.

18 Sharp 1990: 127.

19 Wallace 1982: 50.

20 1985: 148.

21 Keatinge 1983: 144; Holmes, Rees, Whelan 1992.

22 *The Irish Times*, 14 September 1992.

23 The Community and national levels are formally linked through the Permanent Representation of each state to the EC. In the Irish case three members of the Permanent Representation spend most of their time on EC trade and aid matters. They collect and collate information, passing it on to Foreign Affairs, and especially the Development Cooperation Division, as well as to other government departments. They also advise the Irish Permanent Representation in Brussels on Irish interests in the meetings of Coreper (the Committee of Permanent Representatives of the member states).

24 Flaesch-Mougin and Raux 1991: 343-4.

25 The term "rules of origin" is used to refer to the issue concerning what percentage of a product's parts are manufactured in the country from which the product originates.

26 Interview, Department of Foreign Affairs, March 1992.

27 *Irish Press*, 25 November 1978.

28 31 December 1975.

29 1989: 266.

30 Montecinos 1991: 3.

Chapter 5

Ireland, the United Nations and the Third World

The multilateral aspect of foreign policy does not just encompass relations within and between regions. As the worldwide nature of economic structures, environmental issues and communication networks has become ever more pronounced, states have sought a global dimension to their foreign policies, and there are a number of foreign policy fora which reflect the growing importance of the inter-relationships of all states. Most of these are associated to some degree with the UN, which makes it by far the most significant global organisation, but other organisations need to be looked at also. This Chapter examines Irish foreign policy as it is expressed through the UN and other global fora, and will focus on three case studies: Ireland's contribution to the UN's peacekeeping operations in the Congo, Ireland's voting record in the UN General Assembly and the stance adopted by Ireland in the Uruguay round of the General Agreement on Tariffs and Trade (GATT) negotiations.

Ireland's involvement in global organisations can be considered to have begun with membership of the Commonwealth. The Third World dimension of this organisation was never very apparent during Ireland's membership, which was ended in 1948. Ireland's work in the Commonwealth was largely devoted to establishing the constitutional freedom and sovereignty of the "white" Dominions, and Ireland worked most closely with the Canadian and South African Governments.[1] The continuing colonialism of the British Empire that was represented by the Commonwealth was not an issue for the Irish representatives. However, the way in which Ireland used the Commonwealth to help establish independence and sovereignty served as a model for the emerging Third World states in the postwar era. "By 1937 Ireland's main work had been done, but even its latter demonstrations of independent action had their importance, studied as they were in India, where they created the basis for the acceptance by India and Pakistan of continued Commonwealth membership after independence ... That so many new African states have since felt able to remain Commonwealth partners must, in some considerable measure, be due to the conscious work of transformation undertaken in the Cosgrave period and to the admittedly more negative decisions of de Valera".[2]

In 1923 the Irish Free State was admitted to the League of Nations. Membership entailed the young Irish state coming into contact with problems and issues of what was to become the Third World, even if that area was still largely under colonial rule. The initial Irish response was not overwhelmingly impressive, but a number of important features of the country's dealings with Third World states today were evident in the League. The negative aspect was largely due to the general lack of interest in the League itself, or in any foreign policy activity other than Anglo-Irish relations. One study of Irish foreign policy at the League of Nations concludes that "it is probably more accurate to speak of Irish 'activity' rather than 'policy', and to keep in mind the extent to which it was the activity not of Ireland but of a few individuals who happened to be Irish".[3] This was particularly so with regard to Third World affairs. Barcroft notes that the Irish representative to the League of Nations was left to make his own policy on a number of occasions, such as on the Manchurian crisis of 1931-36, "because direct Irish interests in the Far East were negligible",[4] and over two South American border disputes, "obscure enough in themselves and obviously of less than no concern to Irish public opinion".[5]

The only issue to generate much interest or discussion in Ireland was the Ethiopian crisis in 1935-6. This seemed a clear-cut case of imperialist aggression, but "opinion was in fact divided".[6] When the Taoiseach, de Valera, sought to commit Ireland to supporting the League against Italy, a range of opposition emerged in the Dáil. Some were opposed because Ireland would find itself on the same side as Britain, others feared it might lead to conscription. There was also a strong pro-Italian lobby, led by Fine Gael TD Sir Osmond Esmonde, who had been a Dáil emissary to the USA, Canada, Australia and Spain, had worked for the Department of External Affairs, and had been a delegate to the League of Nations.[7] He declared that "I am in sympathy with the Italian people, as I believe that this is a just war on their behalf" while denouncing the Ethiopian emperor, Haile Selassie, and praising the Italian fascist leader – "Mussolini is the Abraham Lincoln of Africa, out to abolish the slave trade".[8] Finally, there was opposition from the far right. Fine Gael TD Paddy Belton expressed sympathy with "civilised, Christian" Italy's need for land, voiced his suspicion about the USSR having imposed sanctions on Italy and stated "I daresay there are Jews there or thereabouts in Ethiopia".[9] De Valera succeeded in securing Irish support for the League, but the degree of opposition was remarkable.

However, the policy which developed was still one which saw Ireland emerge as something of a leader for small nations. This came about particularly through the efforts by the Irish Government to secure important posts in the League. Irish representatives were elected to the Council of the League, Ireland's permanent representative to Geneva, Seán Lester, was the first small-state national to be Deputy Secretary-General, and de Valera was elected President of the League's Assembly in 1938. From these positions, Ireland did not simply establish that small states had a role to play, but also worked to protect small state interests. De Valera "became a recognised spokesman for the smaller powers" and acted as "one of the League's uncomfortable consciences".[10] Two strands are evident: first, a tendency to identify with other small states rather than larger powers; second, as an expression of how a small state can best defend its interests in the world, an interest in encouraging all states to obey certain rules of international behaviour. The first could not be specifically identified as a liaison or association with Third World states simply because most had yet to gain independence and were therefore unrepresented in the League of Nations. The second was of necessity curtailed when it became evident that the League of Nations had no will to enforce such rules, but it was to re-emerge later on. The global outlook seen embryonically in Ireland's foreign policy in the League of Nations was reborn with Irish membership of the United Nations in 1955.

Since its inception, the UN has both expanded and evolved considerably. The expansion has seen the accession of most of the states of the world, including of course the many newly-independent states of the Third World. Evolution has entailed either establishing a wide variety of subordinate or affiliated agencies, or incorporating existing agencies into its framework. The Irish response has varied according to the different UN bodies Ireland has joined. Membership of the UN is a starting point from which states can build up a wide range of global contacts, and by examining these we can begin to draw an overall picture of Irish policies at this level. Membership can cover four main areas of activity. First, it allows states to participate in some of the institutions of the UN, either permanently as with the General Assembly, or in rotation as with most members of the Security Council. Second, it allows states the option of participating in other UN activities should they so choose, such as involvement in peacekeeping activities. Third, states can choose to contribute financially to a number of UN-sponsored bodies which are run as NGOs such as the United Nations Development Programme, the United Nations Children's Fund (UNICEF) and the World Health Organisation. Finally, certain organisations, most notably GATT, are only under the most tenuous of UN auspices, so that the decision to join does not depend on being members of the UN and can be made separately.

The principal institutions of the UN, of which all states are automatically members and in which they automatically take part, are the UN General Assembly and the UN Security Council. Ireland has of course participated fully in the work of the General Assembly since accession. Of the two Irish Permanent Representations to the UN, in New York and Geneva, it is the New York mission which deals most with General Assembly matters. This goes beyond the meetings of the General Assembly itself to the meetings of the seven committees which prepare much of the material that goes before the Assembly. The annual opening sessions of the General Assembly (which usually meets for three to four months a year) have also been graced regularly by an address from the Irish Minister for Foreign Affairs and, on occasion, an address from the Taoiseach.[11] Membership of the Security Council is more limited: there are fifteen members, five of whom (USA, USSR/Russia, Britain, France and China) are permanent members, leaving ten seats to be filled among the other states. Ireland served as a Security Council member twice, for a half-term of one year in 1962 and a full two-year term in 1981-82.[12]

Of greater moment are the peacekeeping operations that Ireland has opted to join. The Security Council has established 26 missions up to 1992 and Ireland has contributed to 20 of them (see Table 5.1). The forces themselves have ranged from unarmed observer forces to armed peacekeeping ones, and have varied considerably in size and in duration of operation. The Irish contribution has also varied, from a handful of officers to large army contingents and from brief bouts of activity to protracted engagements. What is of particular note is that all but two of these UN missions have been in what is, broadly speaking, the Third World. This has had a number of consequences for Irish foreign policy. It gave Ireland practical interests in parts of the world it had previously had little contact with, at least during the time each force was deployed. This in turn meant that such parts of the world have a slightly greater awareness than would otherwise have been the case of Ireland and things Irish. From the nature of the exercises, a profession which would otherwise have little to do directly with the Third World has developed greater links there, and the army personnel on such missions have been a regular source of information for Foreign Affairs. In general, Irish involvement in this sphere has percolated beyond those directly involved in a way that usual foreign policy activities would not: peacekeeping activities are more in the public eye, and generate greater awareness, even down to the level of colouring Irish idioms at times.[13]

Ireland's commitment to UN peacekeeping activities has even meant extending regular credit to the UN, and in one case footing the bill for Irish involvement entirely.[14] In some areas of UN activity Ireland's contribution is purely financial, apart from some supervision largely by the Geneva Mission. There are some external organisations affiliated to the UN which are funded in this way, as well as a number of trusts, funds and committee programmes run by the UN's central authorities. Most of Ireland's contributions are channelled through the Department of Foreign Affairs, but other Departments are involved as well, notably Agriculture and Health (see Table 5.2). Most of this expenditure is classified as direct aid, and this accounted for, on average, about four per cent of the whole development aid budget of Foreign Affairs in the period 1974-89 (see Table 5.3). However, in overall terms the Irish contribution is slight. For example, the total budget of UNICEF in 1990 was US$821 million, of which US$608 million was contributed by Governments and international organisations and US$213 million came from non-governmental sources. The Irish Government contributed US$357,500 or 0.06 per cent of the governmental share and non-governmental contributions from Ireland accounted for US$490,000, or 0.23 per cent, of the latter share. The total Irish contribution came to 0.1 per cent of the total UNICEF budget for the year.[15]

Finally, there are those bodies associated with the UN but which are autonomous and have distinct memberships. Agencies such as the International Meteorological Union and the

Table 5.1: Ireland and UN peacekeeping missions, 1948-92

title[a]	years	type	Irish	years	type
UNTSO	1948-date	OM	Y	1958-date	obs.
UNMOGIP	1949-date	OM	Y	1987	obs.
UNEF I	1956-57	PK	N		
UNOGIL	1958	OM	Y	1958	obs.
ONUC	1960-64	PK	Y	1960-64	inf.
UNTEA	1962	OM	Y	1962	obs.
UNSF	1962-63	PK	N		
UNYOM	1963-64	OM	N		
UNFICYP	1964-date	PK	Y	1964-date	inf.[b]
DOMREP	1965-66	OM	N		
UNIPOM	1965-66	OM	Y	1965-66	obs.
UNEF II	1973-79	PK	Y	1973-74	inf.
UNDOF	1974-date	PK	N		
UNIFIL	1978-date	PK	Y	1978-date	inf
UNGOMAP	1988-90	OM	Y	1988-90	obs
UNIIMOG	1988-91	OM	Y	1988-91	obs.
UNAVEM I	1989-91	OM	N		
UNTAG	1989-90	PK	Y	1989-90	obs.
ONUCA	1989-92	OM	Y	1989-92	obs.
UNIKOM	1991-date	OM	Y	1991-date	obs.
UNAVEM II	1991-date	OM	Y	1991-date	obs.
ONUSAL	1991-date	OM	Y	1992-date	obs.
UNAMIC	1991-92	OM	Y	1991-92	obs.
MINURSO	1991-date	OM	Y	1991-date	obs.
UNTAC	1992-date	OM	Y	1992-date	obs.
UNPROFOR	1992-date	OM	Y	1992-date	obs.

Key: OM: observer mission. PK: peacekeeping force. Obs: military observers. Inf: infantry

Notes: (a) Appendix 4 contains a key explaining the mission titles.
(b) Irish infantry force with UNFICYP withdrawn in 1973. A number of officers remain.

Sources: United Nations (1990, 1992); and information supplied by the Department of Defence, 1992.

Table 5.2: UN organisations contributed to by Ireland, 1984-89

Department of Foreign Affairs:
UN general budget
UN Children's Fund (UNICEF)
UN Development Programme (UNDP)
UN High Commissioner for Refugees (UNHCR)
UN Relief and Works Agency (UNRWA)
UN Trust Fund for South Africa (UNTFSA)
UN Educational and Training Programme for South Africa (UNETPSA)
UN Fund for Namibia (UNFN)
UN Institute for Training and Research (UNITAR)
UN Fund for the Victims of Torture (UNFVT)
UN Publicity Fund against Apartheid (UNPFAA)
UN Voluntary Fund for Women's Development (UNIFEM)
UN Emergency Organisation (UNEO)
UN Industrial Development Organisation (UNIDO)
World Bank (a.k.a. International Bank for Reconstruction and Development,
    IBRD), and World Bank affiliates:
International Development Association (IDA)
International Finance Corporation (IFC)
Multilateral Investment Guarantee Agency (MIGA)
Food and Agricultural Organisation (FAO), and other agricultural agencies
    and funds:
World Food Programme (WFP)
International Fertiliser Supply Scheme (IFSS)
Food Aid Convention (FAC)
International Fund for Agricultural Development (IFAD)

Department of Agriculture:
Food and Agriculture Organisation (FAO)
International Seed Testing Association (ISTA)

Department of Defence:
International Committee for the Red Cross (ICRC)

Department of Health:
World Health Organisation (WHO)
UN Fund for Drug Abuse Control (UNFDAC)

Department of Energy:
International Atomic Energy Agency (IAEA)

Department of Industry and Commerce:
World Intellectual Property Organisation (WIPO)

Department of the Environment:
UN Environmental Programme Voluntary Fund (UNEPVF)
UN Centre for Human Settlements (Habitat)

Department of Education:
UN Educational, Scientific and Cultural Organisation (UNESCO)
International Institute for Educational Planning (IIEP)

Department of Labour:
International Labour Organisation (ILO)

Department of Communications:
International Telecomunications Union (ITU)
Universal Postal Union (UPU)
International Civil Aviation Organisation (ICAO)
World Meteorological Organisation (WMO)

Office of Public Works:
International Union for the Conservation of Nature and Natural Resources
    (IUCNNR)

Source: Ireland (1985-90)

Table 5.3: ODA contributions to UN agencies by Ireland, IR£'000s, 1974-89

	1974	1975	1976	1977	1978	1979	1980	1981	1982	1983	1984	1985	1986	1987	1988	1989
UNICEF	75	75	105	122	160	250	200	266	225	330	330	380	420	320	105	118
UNDP	238	238	290	340	415	720	659	800	690	895	930	1070	1175	900	295	325
UNHCR	11	12	15	—	19	104	75	150	100	200	220	250	275	210	85	95
UNRWA	43	40	50	57	70	115	100	175	120	240	260	300	330	250	65	72
UNTFSA	3	3	3	3	6	14	13	28	15	20	21	25	27	20	6	7
UNETPSA	5	5	6	7	9	13	13	28	15	20	21	25	27	20	6	7
UNFN	1	1	1	3	6	9	9	25	11	15	16	21	23	17	6	7
UNITAR	4	8	5	5	5	5	5	11	4	9	11	11	12	9	—	—
UNFVT	—	—	—	—	—	—	—	—	—	—	5	7	8	6	2	2
UNPFAA	—	—	—	—	—	—	1	5	1	1	1	—	1	1	1	1
UNIFEM	—	—	—	—	—	—	—	—	—	—	—	20	30	25	7	7
UNU	—	200	—	—	—	—	—	—	—	—	—	—	—	—	—	—
UNEO	—	—	—	—	—	—	—	—	—	232	—	—	—	—	—	—
UNIDO	—	—	—	—	—	—	—	—	—	—	—	—	83	80	90	97
IBRD	390	850	848	665	812	647	1,179	1,407	789	1,400	1,400	2,918	1,597	1,557	956	1,000
IDA	—	—	—	987	818	582	—	—	1,659	1,904	2,254	1,724	2,187	2,969	3,103	2,940
IFC	—	—	—	—	—	—	—	—	—	—	—	—	—	—	50	55
FAO	30	17	36	50	36	34	16	80	100	55	58	61	60	54	34	20
WFP	260	328	516	561	489	519	739	636	817	897	697	1,247	1,370	1,355	—	—
IFSS	—	—	—	—	—	—	207	268	287	317	342	360	377	383	—	—
FAC	—	—	—	—	—	—	—	—	—	—	—	—	207	721	518	1,012
IFAD	—	—	—	—	—	—	—	—	—	—	—	—	300	235	—	172
MIGA	—	—	—	—	—	—	—	—	—	—	—	—	—	—	283	283
Misc.	71	66	120	200	208	258	300	350	474	465	454	444	587	1,124	824	882
TOTAL	1,131	1,843	1,995	3,000	3,053	3,270	3,516	4,229	5,307	7,000	7,020	8,864	9,096	10,360	6,153	7,102
% GNP	.031	.048	.044	.056	.047	.044	.041	.040	.046	.052	.048	.057	.056	.058	.033	.035

Notes: Payments actually made. Does not include all contributions to UN agencies, only contributions recognised as development assistance by the OECD. Does not include disaster relief payments, some of which have been made to UN agencies such as UNICEF, UNDP and UNDRO (UN Disaster Relief Organisation).

Source: Ireland, (1982–90).

Universal Postal Union are largely technical. They are administered by the relevant departments in Ireland, which are responsible for paying affiliation fees. The most significant autonomous body is the General Agreement on Tariffs and Trade, which Ireland has adhered to since 1967. GATT negotiations are primarily concerned with securing open markets and fair competition in international trade, but the application of these procedures recognises a need for special consideration of the trading problems faced by less-developed countries.[16] The Irish involvement includes an affiliation payment each year,[17] which comes out of the budget of the Department of Foreign Affairs, but is not classified as development assistance.

Ireland's position in the GATT negotiations will be examined in more detail later, but the discussion so far serves to introduce two features of Ireland's relationships through the UN. First, they encompass a very wide range of foreign policy methods. Ireland is involved through classical foreign policy means of resident missions and participates in many UN fora through the time-honoured techniques of diplomatic exchange and consultation. At the pinnacle of this process are the sessions of the UN General Assembly, where policy is openly declared through votes. Although much of international politics is declaratory in nature, it is nevertheless still rare for a country's policy to be thus expressed so openly. But those votes can lead to the country being drawn into further action, normally beyond the practices of Irish foreign policy. The UN can and has imposed economic sanctions on countries, in which Ireland has participated. The UN has also imposed military sanctions in certain cases, and although Ireland took part only in peacekeeping activities rather than the more aggressive interventions in Korea in 1950-51 and Kuwait in 1991,[18] those activities have been Ireland's only military commitments abroad. Finally, the work of UN-sponsored agencies has drawn a wide range of additional activities into the Irish foreign policy sphere, such as economic agreements, social and human rights matters and cultural issues.

Second, although there is considerable breadth to the type of activities engaged in, the range of actors involved is more limited. It does not extend much beyond the various civil service departments concerned. The Department of Foreign Affairs clearly has the lion's share of responsibility for UN affairs, but on particular issues there is substantial input and even leadership from other Departments such as Defence in connection with peacekeeping activities, Industry and Commerce in GATT negotiations, or Justice on refugees. What is noteworthy is the dearth of input from non-governmental actors. Very little direct lobbying at the UN can be seen at all, with virtually all attempts to influence policy taking place domestically. This activity takes place largely through interest groups, as the UN receives relatively little attention in Dáil proceedings. Of course, this situation reflects an important feature of the UN as a foreign policy forum. It is rarely a place where policy is made, rather it is where policies already formulated are expressed. The strong campaign run by a number of agencies including Trócaire and Oxfam on the issue of accreditation of Cambodia to the UN was the exception rather than the rule.

These features will emerge in more detail from the case studies that follow. The first looks at Ireland's contribution to peacekeeping activities, and concentrates on the Congo operation of 1960-64. It can be argued that the Congo represents a somewhat untypical operation, where the UN force was drawn into the conflict to an unusual extent. But it also represents one of the most extensive Irish commitments, and although the Irish approach to subsequent operations was changed, much of that is due to the lessons learned in the Congo. The second study looks at the Irish voting record in the roll-call votes in the UN General Assembly. Here, there might have been certain advantages in concentrating on the votes on one issue, such as Cambodia, but the approach adopted gives a better general picture of Irish foreign policy. Finally, Ireland's contribution to global economic discussions, and particularly the Uruguay Round of GATT negotiations, will be examined. There are several economic fora that could have been chosen as case studies, but GATT underlines the limits of formal UN control and the involvement of a number of Irish actors who would normally be outside the foreign policy sphere. The three studies give a good idea of the breadth and the variation of Irish foreign policy as expressed through the UN and other global fora.

The Congo peacekeeping operation

The first case study concentrates on what is probably the most distinctive feature of Irish involvement in the UN, its contribution to peacekeeping forces. Within two years of being accepted as a member, Irish officers went to serve with UNOGIL

(UN Observer Group in Lebanon), and since that time Irish Army personnel have seen continuous service with the various UN forces. One of the most extensive instances of involvement was during the Congo Civil War in the early 1960s, when a total of 5,300 Irish soldiers served with ONUC, the UN operation in the Congo.[19] At one time, there were nearly 1,400 Irish soldiers in the Congo, and the average strength of the Irish contingent was maintained at between 700 and 800 from 1960 to 1964.[20] The Civil War had developed shortly after the Congo, now Zaire, had gained its independence from Belgium, when separatist tendencies in a number of regions of the new state led eventually to the Belgian-assisted secession of the province of Katanga. The UN intervened because of the danger that major powers would be drawn into the conflict, and the original UN emergency force gradually became increasingly embroiled in the conflict.

Ireland's decision to get involved had been presaged by Seán Lemass' assertion in 1960 that small states such as Ireland could exert authority and influence in the General Assembly well beyond their objective capacity to do so. "With her anti-colonial record and her neutral status he [Lemass] thought Ireland well fitted to attract support and possibly to lead the new nations".[21] However, this ambition soon ran into problems. Domestically, there were divisions and doubts among the different political parties about participating, and even within the cabinet itself where views ranged from the enthusiasm of the Department of Defence to "the usual Finance fears of extra financial burdens".[22] A second problem emerged from Ireland's attitude to the origins of the conflict. The Government followed the interpretation of the Secretary-General and of other Western states that the new Congolese Government was unable to cope with internal problems and the Belgian Government had no option but to intervene to protect its nationals. This ran directly counter to the African view that Belgian intervention itself was the major problem.[23]

Finally, there was a degree of controversy over the composition of the UN force. The Africans had wanted an all-African UN force but the Belgians had insisted on European contingents. Ireland agreed to participate only after another European state, Sweden, had done so, but both had to face a degree of antagonism. This was most evident in August 1961, when the Congolese Prime Minister, Patrice Lumumba, criticised the presence of Irish and Swedish troops in Katanga and called for them to be withdrawn and replaced by African contingents.[24] The hostility appears to have been motivated partly for racial reasons, as non-white, non-African contingents were not thus singled out, and the European troops were accused of being biased in favour of protecting whites in the Congo. But there was also a political basis for the hostility. African states suspected the European contingents of being biased towards Belgium, and they were supported in this by the USSR, which sought an all-African or an all-Afro-Asian force.

Irish involvement in the Congo took three distinct paths. There was the direct contribution of troops to ONUC, which began in the summer of 1960. There was also Ireland's political contribution to finding a solution to the conflict. And a further complicating factor emerged: Ireland agreed that one of its diplomatic representatives at the UN, Conor Cruise O'Brien, be seconded to work for the UN in the Congo. He became the representative of the Secretary-General in Stanleyville, capital of Katanga, and played a controversial role in the conflict. Militarily, Ireland, along with all UN forces, became more entangled in the Congo, culminating particularly in the deaths of nine Irish soldiers at Niemba in 1960. Ultimately, 26 Irish soldiers were to lose their lives in the Congo, of whom 14 died in combat, the heaviest toll Ireland has yet suffered on UN duties. The deaths began to weaken Irish enthusiasm for participation.[25] Politically, reservations became more pronounced also as the nature of the UN action in Katanga changed. Keatinge has noted that some of Ireland's support for participation was fired by a desire to prevent Communist infiltration or take-over in the Congo. "Initially, support had been based on the theoretical impartiality of the UN, but in the case of the Congo UN intervention was tacitly assumed by the western powers to be a means of keeping the Soviet Union out of Africa".[26] But as ONUC began to use more and more force against the Katangese secessionists, western powers became far less enthusiastic about events. Ireland began to find itself in an invidious position, caught between commitments to the UN and to friendly western states. It was nevertheless in a position to express its concerns as a member of the UN's Advisory Committee, and was not therefore powerless to act. It might, for example, have withdrawn its forces from the auspices of the UN as a number of other countries did,[27] but in fact chose not to do so.

The Government's discomfort was heightened by the presence of Conor Cruise O'Brien in Katanga, a very visible symbol of Ireland's participation in the UN. O'Brien was centrally involved in implementing a UN resolution which allowed ONUC to become much more active in pursuing a settlement of the conflict. His interpretation took a maximalist view, and led eventually to his being removed from the Congo. Whatever his effect on UN policy, O'Brien had a clear impact on Irish foreign policy. His statements while in the Congo, his subsequent newspaper articles in *The Observer*, and a later book on the subject[28] were highly critical of the roles of certain western states in the Congo, and this caused some disquiet back in Dublin. The timing is important: "In view of impending negotiations with the EEC the ex-diplomat scarcely endeared himself to the Irish leaders by his public allegations that Britain, France and Belgium had actively been sabotaging the UN effort".[29] However, continuing US support for UN efforts to resolve the conflict assuaged Irish opinion and kept the country involved until the conflict ended.

The Congo case reveals a number of features about Ireland's UN policies. In particular, the ambition of asserting a leadership role in the non-aligned world was sorely dented if not completely destroyed. The Congo demonstrated that however impeccable Ireland's anti-colonialist credentials might be, they still could not overcome a barrier that was to some extent racial. It also showed that there was a clear limit to Ireland's support for the Afro-Asian countries, and that Ireland identified more closely with its western neighbours. Foreign Minister Frank Aiken "recognised Ireland's ideological affinity with the West – during the Congo crisis her policies often diverged from those of the more radical nations of the non-aligned world".[30] This applied not just to the government but extensively through the political parties. James Dillon of Fine Gael still argued that in Ireland's desire to become "the acceptable spearhead of moderate opinion in Africa",[31] it had "kicked France in the teeth, stabbed America in the back, and kicked Belgium in the stomach".[32] But in reality the only TDs to openly advocate that Ireland should align itself far more strongly with the Afro-Asian position were the two National Progressive Democrat[33] deputies, Noel Browne and Jack McQuillan. The Dáil for the most part proved ill-informed, and that in turn encouraged the Government to keep from discussing the Congo question in the Dáil too often.[34]

The Congo affair also suggested the impending domination of the Irish foreign policy agenda by the EC. Heathcote again notes that in the aftermath of the conflict, the Dáil showed little interest in assessing the operation or its implications, concentrating instead on the Irish application for Community membership.[35] The Congo certainly exposed the gap between principle and practice in Irish foreign policy. "Among those Dáil parties that appeared unanimous in their belief that Ireland's historical experience and tradition of neutrality had qualified her uniquely to lead emergent states, unanimity vanished whenever concrete foreign policy issues were debated".[36] The fall-out was not all negative: despite the losses suffered, Ireland maintained its commitment to peacekeeping, even if the scope of such activities was far more closely scrutinised after the Congo.[37] It is also noticeable that Ireland's involvement generated far greater interest in and awareness of faraway places and events.[38] Heathcote comments: "it is startling that the Dáil should have held heated debates about the distant Congo and that Irishmen should take sides in the Congolese faction struggle".[39] But the same author provides the best postscript to the affair: "Because of her ideological sympathy with the Western world and because of the strained race relations in the Congo, Ireland's expectations of leading the non-aligned world were disappointed".[40]

Since the end of the UN operation, Ireland has had very few further dealings with the Congo, or Zaire as it is now known. However, an interesting development took place in the late 1970s. In 1977, a force of mercenaries and ex-Katangese secessionists invaded Zaire. France assisted Morocco and Senegal in sending a force to support the Zairean government of President Mobutu, but a year later fighting flared again. This time French troops intervened directly, with support from some Belgian troops.[41] Such French adventurism creates huge problems within the Community, because EPC procedures suggest that all states should endeavour to support the unilateral actions of their colleagues.[42] With regard to the Zairean case, Foreign Minister Michael O'Kennedy said that Ireland had not been consulted or informed in advance but would not protest to France about the action. In the face of criticism in the Dáil, he admitted that "our sources of information are necessarily limited. In these circumstances I do not believe that it would be appropriate to issue a statement as suggested" [i.e. a formal protest].[43] Other unilateral actions have created further awkward situations, such as the French military intervention in Chad in the 1970s[44] the French attack on a Greenpeace ship in New Zealand in 1985, French delays in recognising Angolan independence[45] and of course the Falklands War of 1982.[46]

Nonetheless, the experience in the Congo did not deter Ireland from continuing to support UN peacekeeping activities. Certainly, governments probably have taken greater care to avoid committing forces in cases where the UN risks becoming part of the problem rather than the solution. However, the UN itself has also been more careful in deciding where, and more importantly how, it commits itself. Irish involvement has normally been limited to relatively small officer contingents, thereby avoiding the situation that occurred in 1964 in which one-sixth of the Army was overseas and involved in peacekeeping operations in the Congo and Cyprus. Sizeable numbers of troops have however served with UNEF II in Egypt-Israel in 1973-74, and currently with UNIFIL in South Lebanon. Such service is viewed very positively within the Army and has certainly given the Irish public greater interest in those conflicts.

In the case of UNIFIL, there has been a direct political spillover – relations with Israel have been strained because of incidents that have occurred in South Lebanon. This was by no means peculiar to Ireland's relations with Israel. It applies to all troop-contributing countries, and particularly to the Netherlands and Norway, where there were noticeable shifts in policies that had previously been very sympathetic to Israel.[47] But the harassment and attacks on Irish soldiers serving with UNIFIL by local Israeli-backed militias[48] have certainly contributed to continuing reluctance on the part of the Irish Government to establish resident diplomatic links with Israel, and has also led Ireland to seek EC support on occasion. Perhaps the most significant example of the latter came in early 1980, when the Israeli-backed "de facto forces" of Major Haddad launched an extensive campaign of harassment of UN forces. During this campaign three Irish soldiers were kidnapped and two of them murdered. This incident led to an Irish initiative for a meeting of troop-contributing nations, held in Dublin on 2 May 1980. The meeting led to combined diplomatic approaches by the troop-contributing countries to the Governments of Israel, the US and the Lebanon,[49] but the Irish also mobilised support among their Community partners. The issue was raised both in EPC and in the Community framework, and culminated in statements by the European Council (i.e. the heads of government) in April and June 1980 condemning the attacks.[50]

Interestingly, this period corresponds with a key period in the development of Irish and European policies towards the Middle East issue in general. Early Irish policy had been rather disjointed and disinterested, but in the late 1970s, the Irish Government began to give more explicit support to the Palestinian cause. This culminated in the Bahrain Declaration of then Foreign Minister Brian Lenihan in February 1980, where Ireland recognised Palestinian rights to statehood, not merely a homeland, and accepted a negotiating role for the PLO. But the Bahrain

Declaration was watered down over the year, particularly after Fine Gael claimed that "Ireland had been thrust into a dangerously exposed position for short-term economic gain or out of incompetence".[51] Ireland had no difficulty in fitting in with the Venice Declaration of June 1980, which remains the cornerstone of the EC's policy on the Middle East. The Venice Declaration steered clear of mentioning Palestinian statehood and referred obliquely to the PLO being "associated with negotiations". Ireland has not attempted any further national initiatives, but it remains "clearly on the pro-Arab side of the European norm, along with Italy and France",[52] and although Ireland has conceded somewhat in order to fit in to a European consensus, the same is true to a much greater extent of EC members which had traditionally been much more pro-Israeli, most notably the Netherlands and Germany.

Of course, Irish involvement in peacekeeping activities in the region is only one of the factors which explains overall Irish policy towards the Middle East,[53] but it is an important concern. Normally, peacekeeping forces would not generate such a high political profile. That UNIFIL has done so is partly explained by the nature of the mission. "UNIFIL is generally held to be the most complex and difficult UN peacekeeping operation ever, with the possible exception of the Congo operation",[54] and by comparison Ireland's other peacekeeping adventures have been far more politically sedate. Nonetheless, there is a perceptible foreign policy component in all peacekeeping activities. First, the presence of Irish soldiers in a foreign country and in a zone of at very least potential danger creates foreign policy considerations, as the government will inevitably wish to protect its citizens even when on UN duty. Second, although Irish troops remain fundamentally part of a UN force, they can also contribute to the information available to the Irish Government with respect to particular conflicts. Finally, peacekeeping operations influence the general tenor of Irish foreign policy in that they allow the country to build a role and an image as a good international citizen, and furthermore create a demand that the country maintains that role and image to a degree.

In general, although peacekeeping activities have not given Ireland the authority and influence that was once imagined, they remain an important and useful aspect of the country's foreign activities. This is not solely tied to the country's neutral status, as a number of countries which are members of military alliances have contributed to UN peacekeeping forces (see Appendix 4). In that context, closer military integration in the EC need not necessarily compromise Ireland's participation in peacekeeping activities. It is also possible that Ireland's peacekeeping activities need not remain within a purely UN aegis. Attempts have already been made to portray the involvement of Ireland, France and the Netherlands in the UNIFIL force as an EC contribution,[55] with the one-time British Ambassador to Syria stating "EC contingents participated in the United Nations Interim Force in Lebanon".[56] The breakup of the Yugoslav Federation in 1991-92 saw a more genuine EC peacekeeping force being deployed. But successful participation in peacekeeping by Ireland, whether with UN or any other forces, will depend on the Community adopting a generally non-aggressive, non-assertive foreign policy. Peacekeepers need not declare formal, principled neutrality, but it helps to be seen as, at very least, unbiased in practice if you wish to be an acceptable peacekeeping agent.

Voting in the General Assembly

The case study above dealt with very particular aspects of Ireland's international relations which, as we have seen, offer departments other than Foreign Affairs a significant input. This has its own foreign policy implications, but in a secondary manner. The UN is also a forum where foreign policy positions are displayed directly, and nowhere is this more apparent than in the votes of the General Assembly. Not only do these provide clear statements of position on a range of issues, they also indicate how the votes of one country match up with another. This is particularly significant in Ireland's case because of membership of the EC and the consequent coordination of foreign policies through EPC. The votes at the General Assembly are a manifestation of foreign policy stances which EPC has explicitly sought to manage.

A study by Hurwitz (1976) concentrated solely on EC performance with respect to decolonisation issues, although the author notes that these accounted for nearly 44 per cent of all resolutions from 1946 to 1974 and he suggests that the decolonisation issue was "highly representative of all EEC voting in the United Nations".[57] He found that the EC showed quite a high degree of voting cohesion overall, but that this masked some differences. Denmark and Ireland were slightly more liberal, France and the UK slightly less so than the average of the Community of Nine. These differences, however, were not very marked, and Hurwitz notes that "the EEC is a grouping of white post-industrial states who seek to maintain the status quo in this area of United Nations policy".[58] But Hurwitz does devote a little more time to the Irish case, stating that "the Irish Republic must be excluded from this comment. Its score ... demonstrates a very strong commitment to self-determination".[59] He puts forward two possible explanations: that Ireland feels a sense of identification with Third World countries because it has similar problems of economic development, and/or because of a shared experience of colonialism.

Hurwitz's study examined the Community up to 1974, a period which covers only two years of an enlarged EC and only one year where a political cooperation mechanism was operating. He suggests that Ireland became marginally less supportive of decolonisation issues after accession, but notes that no definitive assessment could yet be put forward.[60] Foot's analysis of the voting record from 1975 to 1977 goes some of the way into this area. She notes a relatively stable voting consensus at around 60 per cent, and that cooperation was improving on other fronts, such as allowing the EC Presidency to speak on behalf of all states.[61] She identifies two blocs within the EC, a conservative one led by Britain and Germany, with the French displaying quite maverick behaviour, especially on nuclear issues and the Middle East, and a progressive one led by Denmark and Ireland. "Denmark and Ireland often join together and vote differently from the other member states on many Third World issues. On a number of occasions these two states are joined by the Netherlands and Italy to form what may be called a 'progressive' minority voting bloc".[62]

The main points in both of the above analyses are reinforced by Lindemann's two studies of the Community's votes. She identifies a clear degree of solidarity among the Nine in issuing joint statements, but that voting cohesion is far from perfect, at around the 60 per cent mark noted by Foot.[63] Furthermore, the lack of cohesion was particularly evident on important issues: "one diplomat from the Third World characterised the common voting behaviour of the Nine as being uniform on unimportant questions and divergent on important ones, whereas the opposite held for the countries of the Third World".[64] Again, Ireland's position merits special comment: "On many issues Ireland feels closer to the developing nations than to the industrialised world because of her not so distant colonial past and her agrarian economy".[65] However, this comment is extended to just three of the four issue areas examined in detail, the Middle East, decolonisation and disarmament. In the fourth area, economic support for the Third World, Ireland is not singled out.[66]

Lindemann again includes Denmark alongside Ireland, noting the Nordic links once more, and also identifies the Netherlands as having a particularly progressive record on economic and disarmament issues.[67]

A further study by Laffan provides a detailed analysis of how Ireland's UN votes are decided upon in connection with votes on the issue of South Africa from 1980 to 1986.[68] She notes that "agreement among Member States on 'apartheid' resolutions is not prevalent"[69] with joint voting only occurring on seven out of seventy occasions in that period. This is partly explained by the accession of Greece to the Community as that country has a distinctive foreign policy on many issues. But Laffan also notes that the most striking feature is the difference between the Community's four largest states and all others. Britain, Germany, France and Italy have consistently adopted a far more negative stance than their partners, especially the former two.[70] Although Ireland is by no means the most positive, "Ireland rarely votes with the larger EC states on South Africa and is willing to go it alone or to vote in the minority voting block".[71] That voting bloc includes Denmark, Greece and the Netherlands, and Laffan also notes that Spain, which was to join the Community in 1986, and Sweden, Finland and Norway, were all voting in more or less the same way.[72]

A study by Holmes, Rees and Whelan covers the 1980s in general rather than purely from the perspective of the South African issue. Overall during the period the proportion of uniform EPC votes showed a clear decline in comparison with Lindemann's study, stabilising around the 40 per cent mark. One analysis links that decline with the problems of accommodating Greek foreign policy after that country's accession, but also notes that the Greek position became somewhat more quiescent in the latter part of the decade.[73] This is borne out by the frequency with which Greece was prepared to vote in isolation from its Community partners up to 1986.[74] Again, two clear blocs are in evidence. The UK leads a conservative one which includes France and Germany. Greece and Spain lead a progressive one, with Ireland and Denmark. Ireland is consistently prepared to vote in isolation in EPC, particularly on issues of disarmament. It is also just as consistently part of a progressive minority on general Third World issues, though this is more pronounced on political issues than economic ones, where Irish support for issues such as the NIEO has been less forthcoming. But in general, as has been pointed out, Irish adhesion to an EPC consensus has by no means distanced it from the foreign policies of other West

European neutrals, with whom Ireland has a consistently very high degree of voting correlation.[75]

If we try to draw these various different strands together, a clear overall picture of Ireland's voting at the UN emerges. There is no evidence of any dramatic shift as a consequence of EC membership. On the contrary, the Community has often failed to translate improvements in cooperation into voting cohesion. This is partly due to the problems of acclimatising new member states to the process, but even so Ireland, along with other states, has very consistently demonstrated its foreign policy independence. This has been expressed regularly by votes in isolation, but far more frequently by votes as part of a minority bloc within EPC. All the studies cited above identify that bloc as being progressive and favourably disposed towards Third World countries. Only two limitations to that can be noted. First, Ireland does not tend to vote in isolation in favour of Third World issues. Votes in isolation are nearly all to do with disarmament issues, indicating the continuing strength of, and attachment to, neutrality in Ireland. But this could simply be because other countries are more willing to support Ireland in a minority position on Third World issues. Second, as has been noted above, there is a tendency to be less supportive on Third World economic issues, reflecting perhaps Ireland's own economic problems and self-interests. But that slight blemish cannot detract from a generally strong and enthusiastic level of support for the Third World in the UN.

It can be supposed that Ireland and the other progressive states "will continue to form a minority voting group unless special efforts are made to develop a European foreign policy on certain North-South issues".[76] Any such effort is likely to favour the progressive camp, which has grown stronger with Greek and Spanish accession and which promises to be strengthened again should countries such as Sweden, Austria and Norway join the Community. This would reinforce Ireland's own foreign policy position in the UN, as it is clear that even if only by chance rather than design, it finds itself more in consensus with a general category of small Western European states than with any overall EPC position.

This was also evident during Ireland's two-year period on the Security Council from 1981. The Security Council is a rather unusual forum from the perspective of EC cooperation. Both France and the UK are permanent members of the Council, and they have discouraged any Community cooperation at this level, fearing it might weaken their claims to permanency. This gave the Irish Government a little more room for manoeuvre, and the Minister for Foreign Affairs started by announcing that "Ireland will bring an independent voice and judgement to the Council".[77] The main foreign policy issue of the period was the Falklands War of 1982, where the Irish Government found itself "in the uncomfortable position of pursuing a middle power approach to the dispute in one international arena, the UN, while actively siding with one of the belligerents in another, the EEC".[78] Sharp goes on to say that "initially, the response of the Irish Government to these difficulties was to ignore them",[79] but once the dispute escalated with the sinking of two Argentine warships, Ireland sought to distance itself from the EC sanctions. It also called a Security Council meeting after the sinkings, but this initiative was widely regarded, domestically and internationally, as ill-advised, and was dropped. Other negotiating channels, less formal than the Security Council, were felt to have a better chance of producing a positive outcome, and the Irish initiative was dropped.[80] On the more usual matters before the UN, Ireland kept generally to the lines of its General Assembly policy, for instance in voting against the US, UK and France when they vetoed four resolutions on South Africa during Ireland's presidency of the Security Council in April 1981.[81]

The Uruguay Round of GATT negotiations

A very different perspective on Irish activity within global fora is given by the current round of GATT negotiations. The GATT is not a UN body, as although it was established from UN origins, it is organised and administered quite autonomously and is not subject to UN supervision. It came into operation in 1948 to try to expand world trade and reduce or remove trade barriers, and has pursued those goals through a succession of multilateral negotiating conferences, the most significant of which have been the Dillon Round (1960-62), the Kennedy Round (1963-67), and the Tokyo Round (1975-79). The idea of multilateral trade negotiations was inspired by the Americans, who wished to replace their existing bilateral agreements with an all-encompassing multilateral trade framework. The latest negotiations, known as the Uruguay Round, are currently being held, and they indicate accurately the concerns of GATT, the interests of Ireland at the negotiations, and how Ireland responds to the economic interests of Third World countries.

The most recent GATT negotiations began in Punta del Este, Uruguay, in September 1986. The negotiations, which involve over 100 states,[82] are extremely complex and are made more so by the fact that they are being conducted on four different levels. The highest level negotiations are conducted at the ministerial level, and have been the most publicised aspect of the whole process with the particular splits and divisions being aired in public. At a functional level the negotiations are conducted through a Trade Negotiating Committee, and then at a lower level through two groups of negotiators focused on goods and services respectively. Below these three levels a myriad of technical negotiating groups are at work. There are also informal talks that take place, and these are a particular source of worry for Third World states, because deals are quite likely to be struck in such talks without their involvement.

In these discussions Ireland's interests are very much bound up with those of the European Community. In the negotiations the EC acts for its member states, all of whom are party to GATT, and is empowered to do so under Article 113 of the EEC Treaty which concerns the Common Commercial Policy. The Community's interests are therefore represented by the Commission, and especially the Directorates General for External Relations and Agriculture, and the Article 113 Committee, made up of representatives of the member states. On the one hand, these arrangements strengthen the Irish position. The EC's voice is clearly stronger than that of Ireland and therefore there is a greater opportunity to favourably influence the outcome of these negotiations. On the other hand, Ireland's own influence is also only in proportion to its own size and standing in the EC. However, the EC's negotiating stance has generally been very acceptable from an Irish perspective, particularly with regard to agricultural issues.

In the current round of negotiations, attention has shifted from discussion of tariff reductions on industrial goods to a variety of new areas, of which the most prominent and controversial have been agriculture, trade in services, non-tariff barriers and intellectual property rights. For example, of the fifteen original items listed on the Punta del Este declaration for discussion, interim agreement was reached on all but four by December 1988. The four outstanding issues included agriculture, protection of intellectual property rights, textiles and the reform of the safeguards system. Of all these issues it was agriculture that proved the most recalcitrant problem and brought the GATT states into direct conflict. On this issue the US and the Cairns Group, led by Australia, opposed the EC's existing Common Agricultural Policy, which they contended was excessively protectionist. It was this issue that attracted most media attention. It provided a good newsworthy event in which two economic titans – the US and the EC – were set to do battle, and in which individual negotiators on both the US and EC side found themselves in the world spotlight: on the EC side, Frans Andriessen, the EC's Commissioner for External Affairs and Ray MacSharry, the Agricultural Commissioner, and on the American side Clayton Yeutter, the US Trade Representative, and Carla Hills, the chief American negotiator, all achieved media prominence.

While the EC was prepared to accept some degree of reform and liberalisation of agriculture, and was indeed pursuing its own internal CAP reform plans, a primary objective remained to preserve key CAP elements of producer support. However, the Community's attempt to present a united front in the negotiations was fraught with internal difficulties at two levels. First, within the Commission the DGs for External Relations and Agriculture were themselves divided on the issue. The External Affairs DG supported more liberal reform proposals, being principally concerned with negotiating an overall package of proposals acceptable to all EC states and likely to gain wider acceptance. The agricultural DG's interests were more selective and narrowly defined, being principally to preserve as much of the CAP's subsidy system as possible. They also had to ensure that any proposals put forward for the reform of the CAP would be acceptable to the Council of Ministers. In particular, this faced opposition from Germany and France, and without their support it was unlikely that a comprehensive reform package could be introduced. At the same time, it should be remembered that MacSharry was the Irish Government's appointee on the Commission, and although he was supposed to show no national bias, Irish agricultural interests and the Irish Farmers Association could not have been far from his mind. At home in Ireland his early proposals were greeted with strong opposition and farm protests, leading to street rallies and a poster campaign opposing his proposed reforms.

Within Ireland the Government's interests were very similar to those of many of the other EC states. In particular, on the subject of agriculture the Government supported maintaining the maximum degree of producer support consistent with the need to reform the CAP, and because it shares many agricultural interests with France, it has been able to hide behind the larger state to a degree and let it take the criticism. The Irish position on GATT is led by the Department of Industry and Commerce, with Agriculture also being a significant actor. The Department of Foreign Affairs is thus reduced to a secondary role on GATT negotiations. It acts as more of a mediator between the interests of other Government departments. Foreign Affairs does try to promote what it sees as the interests of the Third World, but these have been given less prominence than Ireland's own economic interests. Foreign Affairs is not faced by a united front among the other departments: for instance, Industry and Commerce is probably more free-trade oriented than the more protectionist Agriculture. But its success in promoting a more progressive stance towards the Third World has been minimal. The Department of Industry and Commerce has stated that "Ireland takes a conservative view of the need for reform of agricultural trade ... Ireland has a conservative stance on some of the other issues in the Uruguay Round",[83] citing particularly the textile and clothing sector and general industrial subsidies.

The fault is therefore not with the Department of Foreign Affairs, nor is Ireland by any means the only country adopting such conservative positions. In general, the Third World's interests, both generally in GATT and specifically in the EC, tended to take back-stage and were accorded a very low priority within the trade negotiations. In this forum they were very much the bit actors. As Matthews notes, "the original text of the General Agreement gave no explicit recognition to the special trade problems of the less developed countries",[84] although in practice they have received "differential and more favourable treatment".[85] The Punta del Este Declaration at the opening of the negotiations made a number of concessions to the less developed states. While the negotiations have been dominated by the US-EC agricultural dispute a number of Third World issues have come to the fore. These have tended to be focused on market access with the Third World states arguing for a reduction of tariffs and other barriers on their exports. In particular, discussions have focussed on the Multifibre Arrangement, tropical fruits and agricultural products: all of which constitute the basis for continuing disputes between the Third World and the EC.

In general the Third World states were also concerned that trade liberalisation might have further adverse effects on their own domestic industries with the threat of Northern products being dumped on their markets such as had been the case with the EC and sugar. However, Third World states also stood to gain from some aspects of the negotiations. For example, the draft Final Act of the Uruguay Round includes proposed concessions to allow more successful marketing of tropical products in processed or semi-processed form; easing of the kind of trading difficulties associated with natural resources products are also expected to be part of the final agreement. The concept of special and differential treatment of less-developed countries, to take account of their economic and financial state, is carried into the draft final text in a number of commitments, obligations and concessions.

While there do exist potential gains for the Third World, and while it would also be wrong to view the Third World as anything like a homogeneous bloc in the negotiations, it can be said that the different interests of the Third World have all received only secondary attention.[86] The problems over agriculture dominated the Round, and affected negotiations on other topics. When one agricultural session broke down, an American representative commented that "the sharpest words came from some of our Latin trading partners, the Brazilians and Argentines in the lead, but also the Chileans, Colombians, Uruguayans all being harshly critical of the European position. And the Brazilian and Argentine ministers got up and left the room ... and went around to some of the other negotiating sessions that were still going on ... [they] interrupted the proceedings, and took their delegations out of the room on the spot, saying that if the agriculture negotiations are not to proceed forward, i.e., if the principal interest of many of the developing countries of the world is not addressed in this negotiation, there is no benefit for us in proceeding with any of the negotiations and we are not going to leave our negotiators in the room to make any concessions at all on ... other major areas".[87] While the US clearly has its own agenda to pursue, and the comments above must be read as part of an ongoing EC-US public relations battle, nevertheless a reform of agricultural practices would also be in the interests of many developing countries.[88] But such dramatic acts as that described above have still produced no major concessions for them.

Third World countries made some attempt to lobby Ireland on GATT issues, both through Irish Embassies and directly to the Department of Foreign Affairs in Dublin.[89] But despite the Department's efforts, their interests went largely unheeded in the overall Irish stance. Irish political interests in GATT focussed on the country's own economic interests, and the Department of

Agriculture, in particular, was concerned that Irish representatives should, wherever possible, defend the EC's agricultural policies. Foreign Affairs was unable to put across the broader impact of such policies on the Third World. Irish interests in GATT were principally of an economic nature, and were easily identifiable. The pursuit of these interests consumed the time and energy of all Irish officials engaged in or proximate to the negotiations both within the EC and in GATT itself. There was little time left for consideration of other issues, and the Third World's interests were secondary to Ireland's own national interests. Whereas it might have been possible to partially reconcile these two sets of potentially conflicting interests, nothing appeared to be done to achieve this. In general when Ireland's own economic interests come into opposition to its more generally expressed humanitarian interests, it is the latter that lose out. The political will to confront some domestic economic lobbies is lacking.

Of course, in other arenas Irish economic interests are less directly at stake, and here Ireland has maintained a more progressive stance. One example is the UNCTAD conference held in Nairobi in 1976. West Germany sought to prevent the establishment of a Common Fund for Commodities, but Ireland opposed this negative stance. "The Irish delegation was one of a group of sixteen industrialised states which worked for a compromise position on the commodities fund proposed by the Third World governments".[90] But that is also a reflection of the relative importance of such fora: although the significance of fora such as UNCTAD should not be trivialised, nonetheless the major economic decisions are taken elsewhere. The decision by the US and UK to withdraw from UNESCO in 1984 and 1985 respectively indicates how economic powers evade the UN's slightly more democratic fora and rely instead on ones where their power can be fully exercised. The two withdrawals also left UNESCO without 30 per cent of its member states' income.

The development of Ireland's Third World policies in the UN

The three case studies examined above provide useful insights into Ireland's relationship with the UN system and the ways in which this affects and alters the country's relations with the Third World. What is most immediately evident is the importance of the UN system in expanding the horizons of Irish foreign policy. Prior to membership, Irish foreign policy was largely confined to a limited circle of bilateral relations and some relatively inconsequential regional links with bodies such as the Council of Europe. This was not just a limitation in terms of where Ireland was represented: it also affected the range of issues that Ireland was expected to have an interest in. The scope of foreign policy was geographically constrained and the foreign policy actions taken were similarly limited.

The UN system offered Ireland greater breadth and intensity of involvement in international affairs, and this was felt most strongly with regard to the Third World. First, Ireland was now being brought into contact with Third World issues to a far greater extent than hitherto. Second, the UN was becoming increasingly dominated by the foreign policy concerns of the Third World nations.[91] The system also offered involvement in foreign policy matters for a wider range of actors. The assortment of UN agencies, conferences and affiliated bodies have drawn in other government departments besides Foreign Affairs, although it must be remembered that this has been largely confined to governmental actors. Non-governmental groups are not as active in lobbying at the UN or on UN issues as they are in other fora. The UN system has furthermore expanded the nature of Irish foreign policy. Irish delegations were being asked to attend more conferences and meetings on a broadening agenda of issues, and Ireland was also being involved in peacekeeping activities. Nevertheless, the Irish Government avoided membership of the non-aligned movement. It was "both too neutral and too militant for the Irish Government", which was for the most part very much in the Western camp.[92] The nature of Irish foreign policy was altered in another important way, because the practice of the General Assembly in holding public votes on foreign policy questions made Ireland's stance on such matters far less secret and contributed to an idea of openness with regard to foreign policy.

However, all of these developments, while important and worthy, constitute little more than the medium for expression of policy. The development of Irish policy and how it has been applied to the Third World in particular are distinct issues. In this regard, the openness of the expressions of policy at the UN are of considerable assistance, because clear statements of policy principle are available. When Ireland joined the UN, the then Foreign Minister Liam Cosgrave enunciated three principles of foreign policy:

(a) that Ireland would support and respect the obligations of the UN Charter;

(b) that Ireland would try to maintain a position of independence on all issues, judging them on their merits;

(c) that Ireland would be committed to support Christian and western ideals and values.[93]

Clearly the three principles are not entirely concordant with each other, and in particular there is potential for difficulty in reconciling the two latter ones. Indeed, Cosgrave himself noted as much in that same Dáil speech when he emphasised that Irish support for self-determination and decolonisation would have to take precedence over its western friendships. But rather than that being the pattern of emphasis adopted, each of the two principles has had its own periods of ascendence and decline, and neither has ever been pursued to the abandonment of the other.

Initially, despite Cosgrave's comments, precedence seems to have gone more to the western stance, but following a change of government in 1957, the principle of independence was pursued for a while "with considerable courage and pertinacity".[94] This period has acquired a distinct gloss in retrospect, as people have touted it as a golden age of Irish foreign policy to which the country ought to return forthwith. Such an acclamation is too uncritical. First, Ireland's assertions of independence were only evident in certain selected issue-areas, notably nuclear non-proliferation and disarmament. Otherwise, policy continued much as before, which is not to say that those policies were not always independent or worthy. Second, the policies of this supposed "golden age" need to be seen as a product of their time. The late 1950s and early 1960s presented a window of opportunity, where Ireland was participating in international affairs to a far greater extent than before without yet having developed an open economy. This meant that direct material interests in international dealings were few, which in turn allowed greater flexibility in foreign policy positions. Finally, the policies were not pursued with any great consistency. The conviction to carry through decisions is not much in evidence, as can be seen in the case of the vote over Chinese representation – Ireland voted in favour of discussing the accreditation of China, but then voted against allowing them into the UN.[95]

In general, Irish policy at the UN has attempted to combine an independent approach with a leaning towards the west. It is a balancing act which has been maintained throughout Ireland's career at this level. It is in this light that the impact of EC membership on Irish involvement in the UN needs to be seen.

There can be no doubt that membership has seriously altered the style of Ireland's foreign policy. The Community in all its guises is the agency through which Irish foreign policy is mediated. However, whether or not it has affected the substance as well as the style in the UN is less certain. The process of foreign policy concertation can be seen as a formal re-statement of the third principle, that Ireland identifies with and aligns itself towards its Western partners, but it does not mean that the second principle, of independence, has been abandoned.

EPC has served to make the relationship with the West more open and explicit. It has also made it a more purely European rather than Western commitment, which has given Ireland greater freedom from American interests and pressures. The process has also secured certain practical advantages for Ireland. One of the key features of EPC is the exchange of information which takes place among the foreign ministries. This is clearly of benefit to Ireland given its limited overseas representation. Furthermore, the quality of this greatly expanded quantity of information can also be assessed with more ease, because EPC cooperation has led to a much keener understanding of the motivations behind partners' foreign policies, creating what has been termed more "transparent" foreign ministries.

Again, this should be contrasted with what was the case previously, where Ireland still had to depend on friendly Western states to fill out information on issues, but was in a much weaker position to judge and interpret the information being received. EPC has not created constraints for Irish foreign policy, it has made them more explicit. At the same time, it is important to note that Ireland's UN voting record has not become noticeably different from that of other European neutrals.[96] Ireland might align itself with other non-Community European states, but to assume that Europe is a monolithic bloc pursuing interests that are inimical to Ireland's traditional foreign policy concerns is utterly false. There are clearly some European states that are more conservative, some that are more progressive, and Ireland seems to stand much more with the latter, with states such as Denmark, Greece, Spain, Sweden, Norway and Austria. Nevertheless, EC membership has had a very direct impact on the way Irish officials work in the UN. For example, there are daily meetings of the member states' delegations while the UN General Assembly is in session between September and December, and there are also weekly meetings of the Permanent Representatives or their deputies. While such cooperation and dialogue does not always translate into voting together, it does present to the outside world a very cohesive front which is potentially a very influential force.

In general, Ireland continues to strike a balance between its commitment to an independent stance and its commitment to friendly states, which means that the country still adopts principled positions at the UN. Given the number of issues before that body, Ireland has tended to concentrate time and effort on selected topics rather than devote equal attention to all subjects, but the selection of topics is an explicit statement of foreign policy priorities. The issue-areas currently singled out are disarmament, human rights, apartheid and peacekeeping.[97] The thinking behind this choice reflects the historical experience of colonialism in Ireland and the current practice of neutrality. This might be expected to create a set of circumstances generally favourable to the promotion of Third World issues in Irish foreign policy, so it is worth examining how the balance of UN principles has affected the Third World relationship in particular. Certainly, the issue-areas that Ireland has focussed its attention on include a number which are directed at the Third World, such as its anti-apartheid stance and general commitment to support decolonisation. Initially, Ireland's attempts to implement a principled policy were somewhat ad hoc and uninformed. Faced with issues in countries where Ireland had no material interests to protect and little contact in general, it was easier to respond by reference to a few vague general principles.

Despite erstwhile notions of grandeur, of Ireland as a leader of developing nations, it has proved slightly less easy to translate principles into policies. Nevertheless, Ireland has consistently been identified as a progressive state among the Europeans in the UN, particularly with regard to Third World questions, and that identification has survived joining the European Community. Indeed, it is possible to argue that EC membership has heightened the importance of the country in the UN and in other fora. Irish foreign policy is now under greater scrutiny and attention because it is part of a Community position, whereas previously it was just one small state among many. However, although Ireland must be seen as generally and genuinely supportive of the Third World, a number of provisos need to be attached which serve to weaken the relationship.

First, the principles expressed are those of the Department of Foreign Affairs, and while that Department exercises an important role in UN matters, it does not control all aspects of the relationship. Particularly when dealing with economic issues, other departments have a stronger role, and in most instances (the notable exception being the Department of Defence) this means a certain abandoning of the more ethical approach. Economic self-interest makes Ireland adopt policies much more in line with a generally conservative Western position. There is plenty of scope for a number of Government departments to adopt a more progressive line on issues relating to the Third World.

Second, decolonisation as an issue is becoming much less relevant. It is a welcome victim of its own success, because at this stage very few colonies remain. Ireland's commitment to opposing apartheid and its contributions to the UN peacekeeping force in Namibia show that the country's anti-colonial stance is still strong, but once apartheid is finally defeated there will be precious few decolonisation causes to be fought for. That is not to say that colonialism in all its forms has ended. However, Ireland's policy has always concentrated on the aspect of formal sovereignty being achieved in decolonisation issues, rather than on, say, economic independence. Ireland's tepid support for the NIEO shows that the country is less enthusiastic when it comes to issues of de-neo-colonisation, to coin an ugly phrase. There is a clear reluctance to commit Ireland too much in support of demands for the NIEO, but this is born out of Ireland's economic self-interest, not Community imposition. As has been noted above, the Netherlands has been free to pursue a much more progressive line on this issue.

Third, Ireland's support for Third World issues in the UN has to date emerged largely in a reactive fashion. In itself, that is no particular problem – much of foreign policy is reactive by its very nature. What is distinctive about the Irish case is that there is an absence of forethought about the type of issues it might be suddenly confronted with. Although foreign policy must often react to events, it is feasible to try to plan ahead to deal with possible eventualities. Ireland has a set of principles through which to interpret events that have occurred, but does not seem to be trying to initiate events in order to further those principles in practice. This was most in evidence in the case of Community attempts to impose a sanctions package on South Africa. Although Ireland favoured more stringent measures against the apartheid regime in South Africa, the Government was very reluctant to embark on any Irish initiative without Community agreement.

Conclusion

In sum, the UN system demonstrates a number of features of Irish foreign policy towards the Third World. First of all, the UN reinforces the fact that Irish foreign policy is increasingly channelled through the European Community. Once again, it is more accurate to talk of policies than a single policy. The Irish stance in GATT negotiations is distinct from the approach being adopted towards the Middle East; policies towards UNCTAD and towards peacekeeping are different in nature. There are, however, certain general principles which underlie Ireland's overall foreign policy, principles which can generally be termed progressive. The problem for Irish foreign policy at the UN has been to try to translate ideals into actions. Implementation of principles has exposed weaknesses in Ireland's foreign policy and contradictions between some of the goals the country is trying to achieve. Finally, the UN shows most strongly the extent to which Irish foreign policy is the preserve of a very limited group of actors. The nature of the UN is less likely to expose the weaknesses engendered by the exclusiveness of the Irish foreign policy system, because activities tend to be concentrated in one or two venues. But the absence of more general participation, consultation and supervision is notable.

Footnotes

1   Sharp 1990: 4.

2   Harkness 1970: 252.

3   Barcroft 1979: 20.

4   *Ibid.*: 26.

5   *Ibid.*: 28.

6   *Ibid.*: 27.

7   Browne 1981: 338.

8   *Dáil debates,* 6 November 1935, 59: 531.

9   *Ibid.*: 522.

10 Keatinge 1970: 142.

11 Seán Lemass in 1963, Jack Lynch in 1970 and 1978, Charles Haughey in 1982, and Garret FitzGerald in 1985. On two further occasions the Taoiseach has met with the UN Secretary General while on an official visit to the USA: Liam Cosgrave in 1976 and FitzGerald again in 1984.

12 Dorr 1986: 13.

13 O'Brien (1962: 292 fn.1) notes the term "bloody Baluba" becoming a popular term of abuse in Dublin for a while in the wake of the Congo crisis.

14 This was the case in Cyprus (Sharp 1990: 57-62). Ireland was owed roughly IR£15 million in December 1991 by the UN, with IR£14 million of that arising from peacekeeping work.

15 UNICEF 1991.

16 Matthews 1991: 42.

17 Affiliation payments are worked out according to a percentage of each country's world trade. In 1992, the Irish contribution came to 576,543 Swiss francs.

18 Note, however, that although Ireland was not a direct military participant, it did support the interventions.

19 Fabian 1971: 158.

20 Sharp 1990: 50-51.

21 Heathcote 1971: 881.

22 Farrell 1983: 118.

23 Heathcote 1971: 883.

24 Higgins 1980: 133-36.

25 Heathcote 1971: 890-891.

26 Keatinge 1978: 161.

27 Higgins 1980: 95.

28 O'Brien 1962.

29 Heathcote 1971: 896.

30 *Ibid.*: 897.

31 *Dáil debates*, 5 April 1962, 194: 1387.

32 *Ibid.*: 1411-1412; attributed to Dillon by Frank Aiken in the Dáil.

33 A small short-lived left wing party not to be confused with the conservative Progressive Democrats founded in the 1980s.

34 Heathcote 1971: 893.

35 *Ibid.*: 897.

36 *Ibid.*

37 Keatinge 1978: 161.

38 Note, though, that Ireland did claim a historical connection with the Congo: "Sir Roger Casement, an Irishman, had exposed serious abuse around the turn of the Century. By a quirk of history, his fellow countrymen, from the independent Ireland he had not lived to see, also played a notable role in the history of that distant land" (*Ireland Today*, March 1980, 1026: 5).

39 Heathcote 1971: 900.

40 *Ibid.*: 901.

41 Farrands 1985: 84-85.

42 Sharp 1990: 206.

43 *Dáil debates*, 14 June 1978, 307: 1104.

44 Farrands 1985: 81-84.

45 Holland 1988: 30.

46 Keatinge 1991a: 162.

47 Skogmo 1989: 144.

48 Though note that attacks on UNIFIL came from both the Israeli and the Arab sides (Skogmo 1989: 54-55).

49 Skogmo 1989: 148-9.

50 Keatinge 1983: 145.

51.Sharp 1990: 185.

52 Keatinge 1984b: 26.

53 *Ibid.*: 19.

54 Skogmo 1989: 1.

55 Rummel 1988: 128.

56 Tomkys 1987: 430.

57 Hurwitz 1976: 443 fn1.

58 *Ibid.:* 441.

59 *Ibid.*

60 *Ibid.:* 445.

61 Foot 1979: 360.

62 *Ibid.:* 358.

63 Lindemann 1982: 121.

64 Lindemann 1976: 264.

65 *Ibid.:* 266.

66 *Ibid.:* 122-129.

67 Lindemann 1976: 266.

68 Laffan 1988: 32-42.

69 *Ibid.:* 69.

70 *Ibid.:* 42-44.

71 *Ibid.:* 71.

72 *Ibid.:* 44.

73 Regelsberger in Pijpers (ed.) 1988: 35.

74 Holmes, Rees, Whelan 1992: 72.

75 *Ibid.:* 77.

76 Foot 1979: 358.

77 *Ireland Today*, December 1980/January 1981, 972: 6.

78 Sharp 1990: 219.

79 *Ibid.*

80 *Ibid.:* 224-26.

81 *Ireland Today*, June 1981, 997: 14.

82 There were 103 states affiliated to GATT in April 1992.

83 Press release, Department of Industry and Commerce, 2 November 1989.

84 1991: 42.

85 *Ibid.:* 47-8.

86 Indeed, many LDCs are principally concerned with ensuring that their earning from primary products, such as tropical fruits, are not adversely affected by EC protectionist trade barriers. They are therefore "concerned to defend the principle of differential and more favourable treatment as essential for their growth and oppose suggestions that might erode their special treatment" (Matthews 1991: 56).

87 National Press Club briefing, 14 December 1990: 3-4.

88 Matthews 1985.

89 Interview, Department of Foreign Affairs, June 1992.

90 Keatinge 1978: 186.

91 Lindemann 1982: 111.

92 Sharp 1990: 63.

93 *Dáil debates*, 3 July 1956, 159: 142-145.

94 O'Brien 1969: 130.

95 *Ibid.:* 132.

96 Holmes, Rees, Whelan 1992: 72.

97 Interview, Department of Foreign Affairs, November 1991.

Chapter 6

Evaluating Irish Foreign Policy

At the outset of this book we pointed out that there are competing perceptions of the position Ireland occupies in the world. Some have been prepared to accept that Ireland occupies a peripheral position in the world, both geographically and politically. Others have challenged the notion that an island must inevitably be insular and isolated, and have forged considerable links between Ireland and the rest of the world. The book has attempted to describe in more detail the links that have emerged between Ireland and the countries of Africa, Asia, Central and South America and the Pacific region, and has then tried to analyse the formal governmental links that have emerged between Ireland and the Third World.

In this concluding chapter, we will examine to what extent the contacts and relationships that exist between Ireland and the Third World, and indeed the perception among some that Ireland could and should have such contacts, spills over into the foreign policy carried out by the Irish Government. Foreign policy is not constituted by the sum of all the international contacts that exist for a country. Foreign policy links can exist between countries that have no other links, and it is also possible that non-governmental ties do not always entail formal foreign policy links. But although foreign policy is something distinct, nevertheless there is an overlap between it and the broader scope of economic, cultural and private ties which we have termed international relations. International relations form the broad backdrop for foreign policy in many instances, so it is worth starting by re-emphasising the extent of that role, and the ways in which such wider contacts do and do not influence policy. In Ireland's case, the broad context of international relations affects foreign policy in two distinct ways. First, there is a historical background of contacts between Ireland and countries of the Third World which still contributes to how both sides view each other in foreign policy terms. Second, there are the current ties, economic and personal links, which provide a more direct input into foreign policy affairs.

The influence of the historical background

The historical background of relations centres very strongly on the impact of Ireland's own experience of colonialism. The fact that Ireland was itself part of the British Empire has provided a number of sources which continue to influence the relationship between Ireland and the countries of the Third World today. There was a level of direct contact and involvement. Irish people worked within the British colonial services, as administrators and as soldiers. But the experience of British colonialism created an indirect impact on Ireland as well, which manifested itself as contacts with the Third World in a number of ways. First, although the mass emigration from Ireland largely compelled by the great famine of the 1840s was directed overwhelmingly towards the USA and Australia, a small group settled in Argentina and have maintained a sense of Irishness there to this day.[1] Second, Britain's control of the Irish economy again had indirect consequences for relations with the Third World, though in this instance more because of what they prevented rather than what they provoked. Irish trade was curtailed and subjected to British trading interests, and Ireland's own economic development was inhibited by Britain.

The impact that carries through to influence present-day policies is somewhat paradoxical. Although Ireland shares the experience of having been a British colony, the experience is not equally shared. Ireland was something of a privileged colony. But nevertheless Ireland seems to have escaped very lightly from its somewhat compromised position. Third World states have been far readier to remember Ireland's example in breaking away from British rule than its being implicated in the maintenance of colonialism, and Ireland has gained a certain stature as a consequence. Furthermore, people within Ireland have also preferred to recall the country's anti-colonialism rather than its collaboration with Britain. This has given a basis for government policy, and a number of non-governmental organisations have attempted to build campaigns around the parallels between Ireland's experience under Britain and current-day events in the Third World, most notably the Famine Programme run by

Action From Ireland (AFrI). Finally, the fact that some Irish people, who had been working in British colonies in the Third World, stayed on when those colonies won their independence has had some impact, though only in a marginal way. The experience gained by Irish people in British service was not made use of by the new Irish state, and even the Irish community in Argentina is little more than something to be mentioned in polite speeches. Although Ireland withdrew from EC sanctions against Argentina during the Falklands war, this was defended on grounds of neutrality.[2] The Irish-origin community in Argentina was barely mentioned, unlike the references to the large Italian community there when Italy too withdrew its support from EC sanctions.

It would be inaccurate to suggest that all of Ireland's relations during the colonial era were channelled through Britain and the British Empire. Although the other major colonising powers were not nearly as significant to Ireland, they were responsible for initiating what has remained a major Irish contact with the Third World to this day. The initial demand for Irish missionaries came not from Britain but through French missionary organis-ations, anxious to extend a Catholic presence into English-speaking colonies.[3] This perhaps represents one of the earlier examples of European influence over Ireland's international relations. The impact of the missionary connections was slightly different to that of other links dating from colonial times. Although they originally replicated the geographical spread of Ireland's other colonial contacts, being concentrated in the English-speaking world, the missionary links survived into the post-colonial era. Thus, their impact is not solely that of an historical memory, but as part of a current-day set of circumstances.

International contacts in the present day

The main influence on foreign policy exerted by such contacts is that of creating an Irish presence abroad. In the case of missionaries there are still large numbers working in the Third World, over 5,000 in 1990, and their presence has expanded well beyond the English-speaking world. Indeed, the only major growth area for Irish missionaries is in South America. But missionaries do not just constitute an Irish presence in the Third

World. They have a wider impact than that. In a number of Third World countries Irish missionaries have played an important role in educating the political and administrative elites of the newly-emerging states. Julius Nyerere of Tanzania and Robert Mugabe of Zimbabwe are perhaps the most widely-known examples. Within Ireland the missionary movement and the Church in general have served to channel information and knowledge about the Third World back to the Irish people, through publications, pulpits and schools.

To some extent missionaries can also lay claim to initiating a further range of contacts with the Third World, this time through non-governmental aid agencies. However, although a number of these agencies have their roots in various churches, they have developed in their own directions and have also been joined by a number of secular-based aid agencies. Given Ireland's reputation as a supplier of volunteers and personnel to work in the Third World, it is somewhat surprising to find relatively few Irish aid workers abroad. In 1991, there were 2,500 development workers working abroad, 2,000 of whom were missionaries.[4] Most of the non-missionaries are on government-funded contracts or are working with Concern, who have the largest number of overseas volunteers of the Irish NGOs.

A third major source of contact between Ireland and the Third World today comes through economic ties. Although Irish economic interests as a whole have never had significant trading links with the Third World, certain firms and industries have substantial Third World interests to protect. In many instances, official visits to Third World countries are based first and foremost on trade interests, and embassies are increasingly involved in support of economic activities. This was most in evidence during a public inquiry into irregularities in one of Ireland's major beef exporting operations, where it emerged that the Irish Embassy in Iraq had appeared to favour the Goodman Company over other Irish firms. "When it came to selling beef to Saddam Hussein, the interests of Larry Goodman were indistinguishable from the interests of the Irish State", is how one Irish paper interpreted the evidence given by the Irish Ambassador to Iraq to the inquiry.[5] The newspaper also published what it termed "an extraordinary 'begging bowl' letter"[6] sent by the then Taoiseach Charles Haughey to Saddam Hussein in 1989, in which he personally requested that Iraqi monies due to Irish companies be paid. More generally, embassies are expected to work for export trade creation. A Fianna Fáil TD, Jim Leonard, argued in the Dáil that "the day of social graces and social functions for diplomats should take second place to industrial promotion work", to which Foreign Minister Peter Barry replied that "one of their prime functions is the selling of goods and the promotion of Irish trade".[7] The impact of economic links extends beyond the direct effect of an Irish presence in the Third World and material interests there. There is an additional factor created by Third World countries' trade with Ireland, because the relationship is not just in one direction. Although Ireland is not an important market in its own right, the import of goods from the Third World has pushed some trading links onto the domestic economic agenda. Although trade unions have at an official level been highly supportive of Third World interests, certain Irish sectors have supported EC trade restrictions.[8]

In general, there are two features to note with respect to the impact of the background factors on Ireland and on Irish foreign policy. First, the links that have been established, be they missionary, non-governmental, or economic, are spread widely across the world. There used to be a concentration of the Irish presence towards the English-speaking world, but that is now much less pronounced. Second, the links that exist are virtually wholly unidirectional. Third World countries have very few comparable links with Ireland. How these factors affect foreign policy will now be examined.

Phases of Irish foreign policy

During the course of this study, Irish foreign policy has been examined at three different levels, the bilateral, the regional and the global. These three have not always co-existed and have not been of equal importance at times when they have. Irish foreign policy towards the Third World has developed through a number of phases, which reflect the changing balance and importance of each of the levels as well as the changing nature of Irish policy. These phases may be summarised as follows:

(a) Sporadic globalism, 1922-39
(b) Effective isolation, 1939-48
(c) Limited bilateralism, 1948-73, overlapping with
(d) Active globalism, 1956-73
(e) Regional dominance, 1973 to date

The first phase stretches from the founding of an Irish Department of External Affairs in 1922 through the interwar period to 1939. It is characterised by very sporadic official contact with the Third World and most of that contact came about through Ireland's involvement in global-level international organisations. Bilateral links were non-existent. Although the First Dáil had established unofficial missions in Chile and Argentina, these were not maintained after independence, and Ireland had no embassies in Africa, Asia or Latin America. Of course, it should be borne in mind that there were very few independent countries there at this time. But in the one forum where the interests of still-colonised countries could be raised at that time, the British Commonwealth, Ireland was far more concerned in asserting its own independence and sovereignty. These were the watchwords of Irish foreign policy during this phase. Even the earlier unofficial missions in South America were intended primarily to canvass support for Irish independence and these issues dominated Ireland's activity in the main global organisation of the time, the League of Nations. But the League also allowed Ireland the best opportunity of the time for involvement in issues affecting Third World regions. As we have seen, many of the incidents which came before the League evoked no particular Irish response. However, Ireland did play a significant part in establishing a role for small states, and one issue did excite a great deal more attention, the Italian invasion of Ethiopia (see pp. 146-7).

The second phase covers the period of the Second World War. Although the League of Nations was not formally discontinued until after the war, it fell into disuse after its failure to respond to the Italian aggression and generally to the growing threat of conflict. Ireland thus lost the one channel for contact with the Third World it had, and this second period is one of isolation from Third World concerns almost entirely. Foreign policy was concentrated on the hazardous task of maintaining neutrality during the war. Ireland remained a nominal member of the League throughout the period, but was prevented from transferring its involvement to the new global organisation, the United Nations, so that Ireland's lack of opportunity for contact with the Third World through multilateral organisations continued.

The third phase saw Ireland making up for its previous lack of opportunity to some small degree. The first Irish Embassy in the Third World was established in Argentina in 1948, and this was followed in the early 1960s by Embassies in Nigeria and in India. In each of these cases a reciprocal mission was also established in Dublin. This was the first time that Ireland had such formal diplomatic links with Third World countries. The exchange of embassies indicates a growing Irish interest in affairs and events of the Third World. However, this should be set against a general expansion of the Irish diplomatic network, as the country gradually emerged from isolation. The reasons for establishing the embassies were those of traditional diplomacy. Each of the three countries was an important state in its own right. Each also had particular Irish links and contacts – missionaries in Nigeria and India, the Irish-origin community in Argentina, and historical links with India. But there was an additional factor to the work required of the embassies. Each one reported not simply on the affairs and events of the host country, but also acted as a continent-wide listening-post. This emphasises the growing Irish interest at an official level in contacts with the Third World, but also demonstrates the limited resources available to try to put it into practice. Each of these embassies had only two staff, who were required to cover huge areas.

This third phase of tentative bilateral links overlaps with the fourth phase to an extent. There was no increase in Ireland's bilateral diplomatic representation until the 1970s, but in the meantime another strand of Irish foreign policy became active again. In 1955 Ireland was finally admitted to the United Nations, so that contacts at a multilateral level with Third World countries could be resumed. In comparison with Ireland's involvement through the League of Nations there was a far more active involvement with the Third World through the UN. This was partly due to the changing nature of international political structures. Ireland joined the UN just as waves of decolonisation created a huge increase in the number of independent Third World states, which in turn made global political structures such as the UN much more sensitive to the interests of the newly-emerging states.

However, the more active Irish involvement in Third World affairs in the UN is also evidence of the country's own commitment and interest. Perhaps as a reflection of the country's increasing sense of self-confidence and self-assuredness in its own independence, more time was devoted to supporting the demands for independence of others. The UN provided the ideal forum for Ireland. Since much of the work of the General Assembly was taken up with declarations of policy, this allowed Ireland to exhibit its concern and commitment without requiring very much in the way of more practical support. This phase of active global involvement fitted in quite well with the rest of Ireland's links with the Third World at the time. The limited bilateral links which preceded UN membership continued through this period as well, but despite the country not having the resources to build a more comprehensive diplomatic network beyond its three continental listening posts, a fairly extensive range of contact was available through the UN.

This dual-level situation of limited bilateral contacts coupled with more extensive and more active involvement at the global level persisted through to the early 1970s. The next phase of the development of Irish foreign policy towards the Third World began with EC membership in 1973. For the first time, Ireland now had the opportunity of involvement with the Third World at all three levels, bilateral, regional and global. However, the new element in this equation, the regional dimension provided by the EC, began rapidly to exercise a strong influence on the other areas as well. In this fifth phase, Irish policy has been characterised by a very strong degree of Europeanisation. The regional dimension has become the most significant for Irish foreign policy, and at the same time has had a considerable impact on the bilateral and global levels also.

At the bilateral level, the diplomatic network has expanded quite considerably since Community membership. Two major trends can be discerned within that. First, part of the expansion can be explained by the establishment of Ireland's own Bilateral Aid Programme in 1973. Prior to that time, Irish aid contributions were either voluntary and non-governmental or else were passed on through multilateral agencies. Not only did the Community require additional multilateral contributions from Ireland, it also helped encourage the establishment of the BAP. Second, Ireland's increased political importance as a member of the EC encouraged an expansion of the diplomatic network to include certain regionally important states, though the selection also reveals much about Ireland's trade interests since the 1970s. At the global level, the EC sought to exercise a greater role in coordinating the foreign policies of all member states, and in a more general sense Irish Governments now had less time and fewer resources to devote to pursuing foreign policy goals through the UN, because the EC was taking up much more time and effort.

This phase has continued through to the present day. The Community has clearly emerged as the main forum for Irish foreign policy concerns, and much of Ireland's involvement with the Third World is channelled directly through the EC. However, the UN remains another forum where Ireland has significant opportunity for contact with the countries of the

Third World, even if there is a greater degree of coordination through European Political Cooperation now. Finally, a bilateral level also exists, and although there is once more a strong degree of convergence with European partners, a separate Irish contact remains. What needs to be examined next is the actual policy that emerges from these various levels of Irish foreign policy.

Third World policies: goals and principles

One point which emerges clearly from the discussion so far is that a number of different and quite disparate issues seem to be involved. A distinction was made earlier between five different goals which underpin Irish foreign policy: the goals of sovereignty, security, economic well-being, international order and international justice. If each is examined, the diversity of Irish Government contacts with the Third World becomes fully apparent.

The goal of justice in the international arena is the one which would seem to have the greatest relevance to contacts with the Third World, and certainly the conception of international justice espoused by successive Irish Governments seems to bear this out. The Irish BAP is built upon this ideal, and again many of the issues that Ireland has taken an interest in and which have emerged in the Third World include these sort of ideals of justice, for instance Ireland's support of decolonisation and its support for human rights issues. These have been expressed quite broadly at all three levels, although action to back up rhetorical support might not be equally forthcoming.

The second goal is that of pursuing some conception of order in the international milieu. As has already been noted, a small country like Ireland is most likely to support some principle based on international rules and international fora. Ireland has certainly pursued that type of line quite consistently, and again there are clear implications for policy towards the Third World. Irish policy has frequently supported the rights of other small states, and this has included most Third World countries. Although this sort of stance is perhaps best suited to expression in a global forum such as the UN, it also appears at the regional level, where Ireland is clearly identified with a number of other small states in the European Community, and indeed in Western Europe in general, as pursuing a more progressive line of policy.

The goal of economic well-being has been the motivation for a range of contacts at the official level. The state has increasingly become involved in trade promotion activities, international trade negotiations, support for commercial activities and the like. This perhaps plays an even more significant role in Third World countries, where contacts with local governments through embassies can be much more necessary to securing contracts. Official relations with a number of Third World countries are based on the trading relationships involved, especially with the oil-exporting countries of the Middle East and the NICs of the Pacific rim. However, in this context it is slightly strange that relations with Central and Latin America (particularly Mexico, which has been a significant trading partner for a number of years) have not been formalised to a greater extent.

The fourth goal, that of security, has had a similar "inspirational" effect. Ireland's policy of military neutrality is echoed by the non-alignment of many Third World states, and again Ireland is seen as having contributed to the idea that neutrality or non-alignment is a proper policy for a newly-independent state. But it has also created a rather more indirect spillover for dealings with the Third World. Rather than marginalising Ireland on the world stage, neutrality has been an important factor in giving Ireland a military role abroad. Since 1958, the country has contributed contingents to UN peacekeeping operations, and these have been important in extending Irish interest and attention around the world. It should be noted that neutrality is by no means a *sine qua non* of peacekeepers. Countries from many military alliances have contributed to UN forces, and for example, Canada and Norway have records similar to Ireland's, even though they are both members of NATO. The important requirement for peace-keepers is not being neutral, but being acceptable to the parties involved, but in this respect Ireland has built a good reputation in many parts of the Third World, and this is clearly related to its neutral status.

The goal of sovereignty is perhaps the one which has had least to do with Ireland's Third World relations, but even it has had some bearing on the development of relations. The pursuit of sovereignty in Ireland has meant two things. In the initial period after independence, it meant asserting that independence and trying to establish the rights and the role of the Irish Free State. And on a more continual basis, it has meant following the goal of a united Ireland, even if only rhetorically. Both approaches have influenced dealings with the Third World, as has been seen.

Ireland's efforts to mark out its independence served as an example for other countries when emerging from the British Empire, and not just in a vague sense. Most notably in the case of India, those countries have been prepared to pay due credit to Ireland for that pioneering role. The influence of Northern Ireland is somewhat more paradoxical. Although Ireland's own irredentist claim has made successive governments more accepting of other liberation movements, at the same time there is an evident reluctance to identify too strongly with political violence in pursuit of such aims. This has clearly limited policy, for instance towards the African National Congress (ANC) and the Palestine Liberation Organisation (PLO).

Irish policies towards the Third World

The overall picture is one of foreign policy towards the Third World being drawn from a number of different sources, two of which can be singled out as having particular relevance. The attempt to pursue some form of international justice through foreign policy is clearly an important factor in policy towards the Third World. Generally, it has encouraged Ireland to take a progressive stance on issues such as decolonisation and aid (if not necessarily to back it up with money). The second factor which figures more prominently in Third World affairs is the economic element. Trade links between Ireland and the Third World are becoming increasingly significant, and give a very different perspective on relations, as Ireland's progressive record is far less evident here. Trade links have also created a rather more balanced relationship, because there is a substantial degree of Third World economic activity with Ireland to be considered as well as Ireland's own activities.

However, although drawing attention to the importance of the goals of international justice and economic well-being, it should be stressed again that different aspects of Irish policy towards the Third World can be associated with all of the general goals Ireland is pursuing. This has two significant consequences. First, it seems clear that there is no such thing as a single Irish foreign policy towards the Third World. Rather, there are a host of different policies dealing with various aspects of the Third World. These can be divided geographically and functionally. In geographic terms, it is reasonable to talk in terms of a Middle

Eastern policy or a policy towards Central America. In functional terms, there are identifiable policies connected with trade or human rights. Of course, there is a degree of overlap between these two categories as well. For example, policy towards the Middle East is intertwined with policy designed to secure access to oil supplies. But in no case is the overlap sufficiently extensive to warrant application throughout the Third World. There is no single, cohesive foreign policy aim in Ireland's dealings with the Third World.

It is worth digressing briefly to ask whether a single policy should be expected or desired. Certainly, the palpable diversity among the countries here defined as Third World suggests that a variegated set of policies is far more suitable. However, as was stated at the outset of this book, there are common features and problems among the countries of the Third World, and if another country wishes seriously to assist in addressing these problems, then it ought to espouse some notion of a progressive foreign policy towards the Third World. This need not be a clearly articulated set of aims and objectives, but can be a more general commitment underlying the other types of foreign policy goals dealt with above.

It is here that the second significant consequence of the diversity of Irish dealings with the Third World becomes apparent. There is a notable gap between how different strands of policy are expressed. At one level, there are a number of policies which are articulated largely as principles and as values to be sought. These would include policies derived from the goals of international justice and international order, which are expressed in rhetorical form for the most part. At another level, there are policies which have a far more concrete, substantive base in activity, particularly those developed from goals of economic well-being. This may be put another way. Some of Ireland's foreign policy towards the Third World might be termed morally-inspired. It is this area that tends more towards accepting the notion that there should be an underlying commitment to progressiveness in dealings with the Third World. However, it remains a largely rhetorical strand of policy. The second element of policy towards the Third World could be termed materially-inspired, which tends to be more concerned with economic self-interest than magnanimity. These distinctions should not be read too simplistically. Not all policies that could be described as morally inspired have such pure motivations – for example, a proportion of Ireland's aid contributions are tied to employing Irish aid workers. APSO employs 450 Irish people which may have been influential in the decision to maintain its funding when other areas of bilateral assistance were cut by up to 80 per cent.[9] Similarly, material motivations need not necessarily be antithetical to Third World interests – certain trade links could be mutually beneficial. But the distinction is worth making, as the two different motivations have contrasting effects on the implementation and the evaluation of policy.

Actors and formulation

Before examining implementation and evaluation of policy in more detail, it is worthwhile drawing together the influence of the various actors involved in policy formation. The roles that they play in the formulation of policy provide a basis for assessing the effect of the policy. At the outset, we identified three types of actors involved in the policy process – governmental actors, non-governmental organisations and the non-organised non-governmental sphere.

At the governmental level, the primary role of the Department of Foreign Affairs is clearly in evidence. It is the major agency through which relations with the Third World are mediated. The executive is involved with Third World affairs only marginally, primarily in support of trading links if the pattern of official visits is considered. Other government departments have only incidental, though concentrated, Third World involvement. The involvement of semi-state agencies attached to government departments is similarly limited. For the Department of Foreign Affairs, relations with the Third World are not seen as being of primary importance in the way that relations with the EC or with the United Kingdom would be, but they are accepted as being a significant secondary strand of foreign policy. However, a number of points need to be borne in mind when considering the role of the Department of Foreign Affairs.

First, there is an historical factor to be considered. The attention given by the Department to the Third World has only recently become organised. Up to the 1970s, Ireland had very few embassies or other formal links with Third World countries, and contact with, or information about, other states was even harder to come by. Since that time, diplomatic coverage of the Third World has become much more comprehensive and structured. There are more embassies and other offices, information sources on other countries have improved markedly through EPC and the Department has been restructured to reflect the expansion of interests. However, there remains a problem of catching up for the earlier years. The Department of Foreign Affairs is still learning about the foreign policy interests and the foreign policy requirements of much of the Third World.

That learning process is inhibited by the second factor, the size of the Department. Compared to other West European countries, Ireland has far fewer embassies and staff, and in the battle for the allocation of these scarce resources it is the Third World which fares the worst. Links with Third World countries are the weakest in the Department. To some extent, the small size can be portrayed as an advantage in terms of allowing for easy exchange and consultation within the Department and also generating opportunities for all diplomats to gain a wide and diverse range of experiences. However, it also means that the advantages that accrue from specialisation are not available, and that the Department is unable to fully devote the time and resources that are warranted to the Third World.

A third factor concerns relations with other government departments. Although, as has been said, these departments are not as involved with the Third World in an overall sense, they do have a considerable degree of involvement in specific areas. This is most noticeable with the GATT negotiations, where the role of the Department of Foreign Affairs has become that of a mediator between the Departments of Industry and Commerce, Agriculture and Finance, all of whom are pushing their own particular lines. This indicates how the foreign policy establishment takes a back seat on occasions when another department has very specific interests to pursue or protect, and the kinds of policies being pursued by other departments are by no means as progressive towards the Third World as those of Foreign Affairs. This is not true in all cases: the peacekeeping activities of the Department of Defence give it a more progressive hue, for example. But in other instances the opposite holds true, and this applies most particularly when economic issues are being considered.

The final factor concerns the role of the semi-state agencies. Although a considerable number have been established which have particular involvement in Third World affairs, they have been limited to the role of consultative agencies. The Department of Foreign Affairs has been reluctant to devolve too much authority to them and governments have sought to minimise their influence. This has been most in evidence in relation to the attempts to establish a national council to consider and advise upon development issues. Not only has the creation of such a body been resisted, but the less powerful Advisory Council on Development Cooperation (ACDC) was itself disbanded in 1991, shortly after producing a report which was quite critical of aspects of the Government's aid effort. The implication for foreign policy has been that the governmental sector has so far failed to provide itself with an adequate mechanism for objective self-appraisal and independent assessment, functions that semi-state or fully independent agencies could provide.

In their potential to act as detached commentators on the foreign policy process, semi-state agencies are similar to a number of actors in the non-governmental sector. There is a wide range of actors within the non-governmental category, with a common feature that they all to some extent act as lobby and advice groups. This is probably least apparent with political parties, which occupy a unique position half in the governmental structure and half outside it. Their policies reiterate the progressive Third World stances on many issues, such as aid and human rights, and at least in their official pronouncements all the parties seem to be quite sympathetic to Third World interests. However, two factors contribute to a lessening of the impact of political parties. First, the majority of party members pay little or no attention to foreign policy or aid matters, so that party policies on the issues remain pious aspirations, not matters of political urgency. The second factor weakening their involvement is the institutional structure of the Oireachtas. There are very few effective parliamentary mechanisms available to debate or discuss foreign policy issues of any kind. A committee on foreign policy is to be established, but none has previously existed. Furthermore, a committee on development cooperation was disbanded in 1987, and the Joint Committee on Secondary Legislation of the European Community has little time available to discuss the EC's foreign policy implications.

What remains for political parties are activities such as raising questions in the Dáil, lobbying ministers, and attending political briefings of the Department of Foreign Affairs. In this respect, their activities are little different from those of pressure groups. Pressure group actors can be divided into two types, single-issue and multiple-issue groups. The former include solidarity groups and aid agencies, which pursue only Third World issues. The latter includes a wider range for which Third World or foreign policy issues are one among many, for example trade unions and environmental groups. Although single-issue groups are more continuously active on Third World issues, both face similar problems in trying to influence the formulation process. They do so in two ways. First, they run public campaigns designed to stimulate greater awareness of Third World countries in the population generally. Second, they lobby politicians, Foreign Affairs and other relevant government departments on specific issues. Evidence suggests that they have not yet achieved a primary formative role in public opinion, although there has been a notable confluence of public and pressure group opinion on some issues, such as Central America. Their direct influence at governmental level is hard to judge. Certainly, the Department of Foreign Affairs is very open and arranges meetings easily, and the Third World lobby is probably the most firmly established foreign policy lobby as well as being regarded as the most effective.[10] But pressure group activists are uncertain about the impact achieved by such meetings.

However, within Foreign Affairs the view is slightly different. Foreign Affairs does not seem to regard pressure groups as a significant source of information or influence on decision-making activities. This applies generally, not just to aid or solidarity groups but also to business and agricultural interests. The relationship seems to be based on politeness rather than genuine exchange. Pressure groups are tolerated, but the Department prefers to rely on diplomatic networks for information, and this once again underscores the importance of EPC as an information resource in Ireland. This was demonstrated by the Irish delegation that attended the Earth Summit in Rio de Janeiro in 1992. Although the Government provided £20,000 to fund a delegation from NGOs, the latter were not included in the official Government party which travelled, unlike the practice adopted by most other EC member-state delegations.[11] This applies not just to the lobbying and influence of pressure groups within Ireland, but also within Third World countries. Embassies and other offices do not regard Irish aid workers or business people stationed in the same country as significant sources of information.[12]

Finally, the impact of non-governmental non-organised actors on policy formulation should be assessed. The media is the most important single contributing factor behind public opinion, and as was evident from the BBC's coverage of the Ethiopian famine of 1985 it can inspire not just public reaction but governmental response as well. However, both the media and public opinion fall prey to two weaknesses. First, Third World or foreign policy issues are only two among many issues occupying their minds, and this raises questions about the balance and consistency of their attention. As was noted with regard to the now famous BBC reports from Ethiopia, it is possible that if, for instance,

Indira Ghandhi had been assassinated one week earlier those reports might not have been transmitted and there might never have been any Live Aid. Second, the attention of both the media and the public tends to concentrate on "newsworthy" or "interesting" situations. This means that the more mundane, day-to-day foreign policy questions (in other words, the great bulk of such activity) are not given much scrutiny or attention, again freeing the hands of governmental actors.

Implementing policy

Irish policy towards the Third World has developed from rather inauspicious beginnings to become relatively comprehensive and well-informed. This reflects a growing awareness of the Third World in Ireland, at a number of levels. At the level of what we have termed international relations, there is an increasing amount of commercial exchange; Irish aid agencies are becoming increasingly well established; there is even the prospect of a greater degree of Irish tourism to the Third World, as venues in Thailand, the Caribbean and Egypt become more accessible. The only strand of informal links that is declining is the missionary presence in the Third World. And at the level of official government policy, relations with the Third World have expanded considerably in the past twenty years.

It would be wrong to ascribe this growing awareness totally to a single cause. Changes in communications and transport technologies, the increasingly global nature of economic activities and the increased affluence of Irish society all play a part. However, one factor which deserves special consideration is the EC. The Community has been a major inspiration behind the development of diplomatic ties. An improvement in the scope, structure and organisation of relations with the Third World only came about with EC membership, and the EC has significantly altered Ireland's aid, trade and political relations with the Third World. This does not mean that a sovereign Irish position has been abandoned, rather that it has been expanded and is now channelled through a very different and far more important medium.

Thus, there is a clear Europeanisation of the implementation of Irish foreign policy, not just towards the Third World but in general. Ireland decides on policy stances in conjunction with its European partners; it issues statements and declarations of policy with them; it participates in fact-finding missions, international conferences and, occasionally, sanctions as part of the Community. Although individual decisions, statements and actions are by no means unheard of, they now constitute the exception rather than the rule of Irish foreign policy behaviour. In this respect, it is worth noting that there is no single European policy towards the Third World either. A range of different policies is evident across the member states. France and Belgium have both been involved in military interventions in Africa, and France has jealously guarded its one-time African colonies as a *domaine reservée*, a sphere restricted to French influence. Britain and Germany have pursued very conservative policies towards the Third World, evident in their stances on South Africa and their efforts to tie aid to political requirements. Ireland is closest to the progressive policies exemplified by Denmark, Spain and the Netherlands. So although policy is now more heavily directed through the EC, that in itself entails an extensive world of political bargaining and negotiation.

However, Europeanisation of foreign policy does not seem to have improved one aspect of Irish policy implementation. Irish foreign policy tends to be highly reactive to events, a feature particularly noticeable with Third World affairs. To some extent this is inevitable. It is hard to be anything but reactive to events such as the assassination of Egyptian President Anwar Sadat in 1981 or the coup d'état in Haiti in 1992. However, it is possible to try to influence events in a more general fashion. For instance, the Indo-Pakistani wars of 1965 and 1971 and the Liberian civil war of 1991 were theoretically more amenable to prior influence. The Indo-Pakistani wars were the culmination of a long period of strained relations between the two countries, during which there was more scope to act in advance. The Liberian civil war was partly caused by the deteriorating economic and political situation in the country, which again might have been dealt with in advance.

What would be needed in order to exercise this more proactive role are contingency plans in order to be prepared to respond to events, and also a commitment to play an active part in promoting foreign policy initiatives. On both counts, Irish foreign policy is somewhat lacking, particularly in relation to the Third World. It concentrates more on monitoring political events rather than trying to pre-empt them. It could of course be argued that a small country like Ireland would only be laughed at should it try to intervene. That argument can be discounted by reference to two facts. First, Ireland was instrumental in initiating a number of proposals relating to disarmament in the UN, especially during the late 1950s and the 1960s, suggesting that small countries can take the lead on global foreign policy issues. Second, there is the greatly increased influence and muscle available to the country through the EC. However, Ireland has not yet made great use of Community membership to promote a more proactive or planned line.

This reflects two features of foreign policy implementation in Ireland. First, the small diplomatic network greatly hinders the development of a more proactive policy. The country does not have enough first-hand information available to support and strengthen initiatives. Nor does the Department of Foreign Affairs make full use of wider sources. The diplomatic information network has benefited considerably from information exchanges through EPC, but other potential sources of information tend to be ignored, especially Irish non-governmental actors in Third World countries. Second, Irish foreign policy is lacking in political direction. The political side of government is more concerned with Anglo-Irish affairs and the EC when it comes to foreign policy matters, and again it is the Third World that loses out. Without the political will to support them, it is very difficult for officials in the Department of Foreign Affairs to pursue a more proactive policy off their own bats.

This is again reflected in a further aspect of the implementation of Irish foreign policy. Although certain principles of foreign policy can be identified which are quite supportive of the Third World, it is quite difficult to translate these into concrete foreign policy actions. The principles that have emerged in the course of this book include commitment to decolonisation, to human rights, to peaceful resolution of conflicts and to a notion of international justice. It is harder to put flesh on these concepts. Beyond the more obvious actions such as votes in the UN General Assembly, there are few substantive elements that can be adduced. Perhaps the strongest action is in support of the notion of peaceful resolution of conflicts, through peacekeeping operations. But in other areas, there is a paucity of comparable examples. Rhetorical support for human rights or international justice has rarely been matched by action.

Again, this is largely a reflection of the lack of political will to adopt a more proactive role. However, it should be noted that political will is more forthcoming in other areas connected with the Third World. Political support for commercial and trading interests with the Third World is becoming increasingly evident. It seems to be the case that when material interests are involved, the political leadership takes notice and is prepared to provide material and moral support. However, when the country's moral interests are involved, the material support evaporates.

The evaluation process

The flaws identified above in formulation and implementation might be more generally evident and might be more readily countered if there was an effective evaluation mechanism available for the foreign policy process. However, the reasons for the absence of such a mechanism themselves reiterate some of the flaws. The rather inconsistent attention given to Third World affairs by the media and by public opinion sets a tone of disinterest. The absence of scrutiny through parliamentary committees is a more serious fault. Semi-state agencies have been discouraged from playing too active or too critical a role. Suggestions and critiques from NGOs and from other sources thus have no formal framework or setting where they can be aired. They can only be passed on to the Department of Foreign Affairs where their fate cannot be followed.

The limits on the public evaluation and assessment of Irish foreign policy are compounded by the situation pertaining in the European Community. The EC is widely recognised as suffering from what is termed a "democratic deficit", in other words an absence of accountability. This is exacerbated for Ireland by the weakness of the Oireachtas in dealing with Community issues. And the whole EPC procedure is particularly singled out as being a highly unaccountable and secretive process. At best, this means that the EC can frequently be used as an excuse for inaction or behaviour that has been criticised. At worst, foreign policy cooperation could become a cover for highly regressive policies. There is no reason to suggest that the latter is the case now or must inevitably come to pass – there are too many divisions within EPC to support that view. However, the supervision exercised in Ireland of the country's involvement in the Community and in EPC is far too lax. Ireland should not rely on the far stronger democratic supervision of other member states such as Denmark.

Evaluation needs to be made more open and more public at both domestic and EC levels. There is less point in establishing a foreign policy committee in the Oireachtas or giving semi-state agencies powers of assessment over foreign policy if similar mechanisms are not introduced with regard to the Community. Of course, there has always been a marked tendency towards secretiveness in diplomatic dealings in all countries. But public evaluation and scrutiny need not compromise the scope for diplomatic negotiation and compromise. Day-to-day diplomatic activities, the mechanics of policy implementation, can be kept secure. What is needed is a greater degree of accountability with regard to the overall political principles of foreign policy.

Conclusion

Irish foreign policy dealings with the Third World are now more extensive and important than ever before. The informal links which have come about through residual historical attachments, missionary and aid contacts and economic ties have inspired a growing range of more formal diplomatic ties. However, the Third World remains the poor relation among Ireland's overall foreign policy concerns. This is despite the best efforts of the main actor in the area, the Department of Foreign Affairs. Given the Department's size and resources and the political, economic and cultural environment it has to operate in within Ireland, it achieves a significant amount. Certain criticisms can be voiced with regard to the lack of openness of the foreign policy process, but these could be improved if a few institutional adjustments were made to allow more scope for general input and assessment of foreign policy.

What emerges most clearly from this book is the commitment that exists in Ireland to supporting the Third World, not just in a developmental sense but in a political sense as well. The acceptance of the need for progressive policies can be found in the Department of Foreign Affairs, among the political parties, in non-governmental agencies, in the media and in the public at large. The problem really lies in trying to ensure a consistent commitment to act upon these policies. Once again, this is reflective of the Third World's secondary status in the hierarchy of Irish foreign policy concerns. It is difficult to free resources to allow proactive and progressive activities to develop from the existing policies.

The major cause seems to come down to the lack of political will and commitment to pursue better relations with the Third World. It is difficult to establish with certainty why this should be the case. Partly it is due to the fact that foreign policy issues have never been significant in Irish elections, with the occasional exception relating to Northern Ireland. Irish political culture has meant that the electoral emphasis has always been on domestic economic and political concerns. This cultural dimension is equally evident in Ireland's dealings with the EC. The dominant concern of Irish Governments has been to secure economic benefits for the country rather than pursue wider political goals. This approach reflects Ireland's status as a small country, and in European terms, a relatively poor country – which should not be interpreted as saying politicians feel Ireland cannot afford to be supportive of the Third World, economically and politically. It is not a zero-sum game: Irish support for Third World development does not preclude the possibility of domestic economic development. Rather, the continuing cultural emphasis on Ireland's own development leaves fewer resources and time to pursue other concerns, such as relations with the Third World. Once again, it is worth noting the mismatch between the political support for policies which promise material advantages and those which promise moral advantage. However, the expansion of Irish contacts with the Third World should create an environment where the advantages of good relations are valued in their own right. Ireland's relations with Western Europe and the US might be rationalised in economic terms, but they are based upon a framework of cooperation and good relations that goes far beyond merely material motivations.

Ireland and the Third World are coming increasingly into contact with each other, and the country's one-time isolation and peripherality is increasingly irrelevant. However, although in practical terms the distance of Ireland from the Third World has been considerably diminished, the perceptual distance persists. If Irish people retain a perception of themselves as isolated and insular, then the Third World could remain the poor relation of Irish foreign policy. However, if they are prepared to see themselves not just as a part of a wider Europe, but of a wider world, as members of a global community, that can only reinforce the logic of foreign policy relations with the Third World and will inspire increasingly progressive relations also. To date, the relationship between Ireland and the Third World has been rather lop-sided. It is to be hoped that the relationship can develop to allow Ireland to learn from the many cultures and societies of the Third World.

Footnotes

1   Kirby 1992: 104-110.
2   Keatinge 1984a: 82.
3   Byrne 1974: 35-36.
4   ACDC 1991: 8.
5   *Sunday Tribune*, 17 May 1992.

6 *Ibid.*
7 *Dáil debates,* 5 December 1985, 362: 1385.
8 Matthews 1991: 200-201.
9 ACDC 1991: 63.
10 Keatinge 1984a: 112.
11 *The Irish Times,* 21 May 1992.
12. Questionnaires, 1991.

Appendix 1

The countries of the Third World

The phrase Third World is one which has clear political roots. It originally echoed the *tiers état* or third estate of the French system of government in the eighteenth century, when it referred to "the commons" in contrast to the clergy and the nobility. The *tiers monde* or Third World contrasts less developed countries with the first and second worlds of capitalist and communist industrialised states. The term was first used in France around 1950,[1] and quickly gained currency among certain countries as a means of distinguishing themselves from the two superpower blocs, and acquired a non-aligned connotation to some extent. However, the Third World has never been associated with non-alignment alone, and with the collapse of the Soviet bloc making a bipolar picture of world power even less tenable than before, clearly other interpretations of the term are more important.

Economically, the problems of poverty and underdevelopment do constitute an underlying theme across many Third World states, and this factor has been the most common means of identifying the Third World.[2] But economic indicators do not correspond in every case with the countries generally assumed to be in the Third World. The economic circumstances of Brazil are not those of Rwanda, and the GNP per capita of many Gulf states compares favourably with the developed western world, whatever about their nearer neighbours such as Afghanistan or Somalia. Similarly, although various social features such as low literacy levels, low life expectancies and high levels of disease appear common to most countries thought of as Third World, there are sufficient counter-examples to prevent social characteristics being made the basis for any hard-and-fast typology.

The interpretation which perhaps betrays the least number of counter-examples is drawn from history, and concentrates on the common experience and heritage of colonialism in Third World states. A few escaped direct take-over – for instance, Thailand, Ethiopia and Liberia – and there is also the slight problem posed by countries that were once colonies but are now firmly part of the developed world, such as Ireland, Norway and the United States. But this approach explains not only some of the reasons why the Third World came into existence, but also feeds back in to the economic and social features by helping to explain continuing circumstances. The colonial legacy includes persistent economic and social dependence and reliance which keeps Third World countries at a remove from the world's economic and political centres. As Clapham notes, "what distinguishes the third world is its peripherality".[3]

A final comment should be made concerning what actually qualifies for consideration as a country. The existence of some countries is in open dispute: Sahrawi, the former Spanish Sahara, is a case in point, where independence has not been secured from Morocco. Other areas are considered separately for some purposes, but again are not independent states: for example, Irish trade figures treat Hong Kong separately from the UK. Other areas in what is geographically the Third World are formally regarded as part of other countries: for instance, the French overseas departments such as Guadeloupe, Martinique and Guyane. Throughout this study, we have tried to restrict attention to fully independent, sovereign countries. However, we have made allowances for cases where source material has taken a different interpretation, such as with trade statistics which include Hong Kong and missionary data which include the French overseas departments. The list below is derived from the 1990 Annual Report of the Development Assistance Committee of the OECD.

Africa (53)

(a) LLDCs: Benin, Botswana, Burkina Faso, Burundi, Cape Verde, Central African Republic, Chad, Comoros, Djibouti, Equatorial Guinea, Ethiopia, Gambia, Guinea, Guinea-Bissau, Lesotho, Malawi, Mali, Mauretania, Mozambique, Niger, Rwanda, Sao Tome and Principe, Sierra Leone, Somalia, Sudan, Tanzania, Togo, Uganda

(b) other LICs: Egypt, Ghana, Kenya, Liberia, Madagascar, Morocco, Nigeria, Senegal, Swaziland, Zaire, Zambia, Zimbabwe

(c) LMICs: Angola, Cameroons, Congo, Côte d'Ivoire, Namibia, Tunisia

(d) UMICs: Algeria, Gabon, Libya, Mauritius, Reunion, Seychelles, South Africa

Asia (excluding Japan, 39)

(a) LLDCs: Bangladesh, Bhutan, Laos, Maldives, Myanmar (Burma), Nepal, Yemen

(b) other LICs: Cambodia, China, India, Indonesia, Pakistan, Philippines, Sri Lanka, Viet Nam

(c) LMICs: Mongolia, North Korea, Thailand, Turkey

(d) UMICs: Bahrain, Brunei, Iran, Iraq, Jordan, Lebanon, Macao, Malaysia, Oman, Qatar, South Korea, Syria, Taiwan

(e) HICs: Hong Kong, Israel, Kuwait, Saudi Arabia, Singapore, United Arab Emirates

Central and South America (46)

(a) LLDCs: Haiti

(b) other LICs: Bolivia, Guyana, Mayotte, St Helena

(c) LMICs: Anguilla, Belize, Colombia, Cuba, Dominican Republic, Ecuador, El Salvador, Guatemala, Honduras, Jamaica, Nicaragua, Paraguay, St Vincent and the Grenadines, Turks and Caicos Is., Wallis and Futuna

(d) UMICs: Antigua and Barbuda, Argentina, Aruba, Bahamas, Barbados, Bermuda, Brazil, Cayman Islands, Chile, Costa Rica, Dominica, Grenada, Guadeloupe, Guiana, Martinique, Netherlands Antilles, Panama, Peru, St Kitts-Nevis, St Lucia, St Pierre and Miquelon, Suriname, Trinidad and Tobago, Uruguay, Venezuela, Virgin Is.

Oceania (15)

(a) LLDCs: Kiribati, Tuvalu, Vanuatu, Western Samoa

(b) other LICs: Solomon Is.

(c) LMICs: Cook Is., Pacific Is. Trust Territories, Papua-New Guinea, Tokelau, Tonga

(d) UMICs: Fiji, Nauru, New Caledonia, Niue, French Polynesia

Footnotes

1 Wolf-Phillips 1987: 1311.
2 Grindle 1991: 15-17.
3 1985: 3.

Appendix 2

Ireland's diplomatic network

Country	Irish missions: status	Missions in Ireland: status
Algeria	Non-res.	Non-res.
Argentina	Embassy	Embassy
Australia	Embassy + HC	Embassy
Austria	Embassy	Embassy
Bahrain	Non-res.	Non-res.
Barbados	no links	Hon.Cons.
Belgium	Embassy + HC	Embassy + HC
Brazil	Non-res. + HC	Embassy
Brunei	Non-res.	Non-res.
Bulgaria	Non-res.	Non-res.
Canada	Embassy	Embassy
Chile	no links	Non-res.
China	Embassy	Embassy
Colombia	no links	Hon.Cons.
Cyprus	Non-res. + HC	Non-res. + HC
Czechoslovakia	Non-res.	Non-res.
Denmark	Embassy	Embassy + HC
Ecuador	Hon.Cons.	Hon.Cons.
Egypt	Embassy + HC	Embassy
El Salvador	Hon. Cons.	no links
Estonia	Non-res.	no links
Finland	Non-res. + HC	Embassy + HC
France	Embassy + HC	Embassy + HC
Germany	Embassy + HC	Embassy + HC
Ghana	Hon.Cons.	no links
Greece	Embassy	Embassy
Holy See	Embassy	Embassy
Hong Kong	Hon.Cons.	no links
Hungary	Non-res.	Embassy
Iceland	Non-res. + HC	Non-res. + HC
India	Embassy + HC	Embassy
Indonesia	Non-res. + HC	Non-res.
Iran	Embassy	Embassy
Iraq[a]	Embassy	Non-res.

(a) Mission temporarily suspended since 1991 Gulf War.

Country	Irish missions: status	Missions in Ireland: status
Israel	Non-res.	Non-res.
Italy	Embassy	Embassy + HC
Japan	Embassy	Embassy
Jordan	Non-res. + HC	Non-res.
Kenya	Hon. Cons.[b]	Non-res.
Kuwait	Non-res.	no links
Latvia	Non-res.	no links
Lebanon	Non-res. + HC	Non-res.
Lesotho	DCO	no links
Libya	Non-res.	no links
Lithuania	Non-res.	no links
Luxembourg	Embassy	Non-res. + HC
Malawi	Hon. Cons.	no links
Malaysia	Non-res. + HC	Non-res.
Malta	Non-res. + HC	Hon. Cons.
Mexico	Non-res. + HC	Embassy + HC
Monaco	Hon.Cons.	Hon.Cons.
Morocco	Non-res.	Non-res.
Netherlands	Embassy + HC	Embassy + HC
New Zealand	Non-res. + HC	Non-res. + HC
Nigeria	Embassy	Embassy
Norway	Non-res. + HC.	Embassy + HC
Oman	Non-res.	Non-res.
Pakistan	Non-res. + HC	Non-res. + HC
Panama	no links	Hon.Cons.
Peru	Hon.Cons.	no links
Philippines	Non-res. + HC	Non-res. + HC
Poland	Embassy	Embassy
Portugal	Embassy	Embassy
Qatar	Non-res.	Non-res.
Romania	Non-res.	no links
Russia[c]	Embassy	Embassy
Saudi Arabia	Embassy	Non-res.
Sierra Leone	Hon.Cons.	no links
Singapore	Non-res. + HC	Non-res.
South Africa	Hon.Cons.	no links
South Korea	Embassy	Embassy
Spain	Embassy + HC	Embassy + HC
Sudan	Non-res.[d]	Non-res.

(b) Full embassy between 1979 and 1987.
(c) Diplomatic recognition transferred from USSR.
(d) Development Cooperation Office between 1983 and 1987.

Country	Irish missions: status	Missions in Ireland: status
Syria	Non-res.	no links
Tanzania	Non-res. + DCO	Non-res.
Thailand	Non-res. + HC	Non-res. + HC
Tunisia	Non-res.	Non-res. + HC
Turkey	Non-res. + HC	Embassy
Uganda	Hon. Cons.	no links
UAE	Non-res.	no links
UK	Embassy	Embassy
USA	Embassy + HC	Embassy
Venezuela	Non-res.	Non-res.
Yugoslavia	Non-res.	Non-res.
Zambia	DCO	Non-res.
Zimbabwe	Non-res.	Non-res.

Irish missions to international organisations

Council of Europe	Non-res.
European Community	Perm. Rep.
OECD	Non-res.
United Nations	Perm. Rep. (New York and Geneva)
UNESCO	Non-res.

Abbreviations:

Non-res.:	Non-resident embassy
DCO:	Development Cooperation Office
Hon.Cons./HC:	Honorary Consulate
Perm. Rep.:	Permanent Representation

The Table above gives the extent of Ireland's formal diplomatic links with the rest of the world, both in terms of Ireland's embassies, consulates and other missions abroad and the missions of other countries in Ireland. The Table gives the level of diplomatic recognition involved, with the following hierarchy probably being most appropriate: embassies and permanent representations are the highest level, development cooperation offices next, then non-resident missions and finally honorary consulates. In many cases, however, an honorary consulate is maintained in conjunction with either a non-resident mission (as in Singapore) or a full embassy (for example, the consulate in Barcelona). Similarly, some foreign embassies maintain consulates outside Dublin. Ireland has general consulates, which are staffed by career diplomats rather than honorary appointees, in a number of cities in the USA. Ireland's non-resident missions are maintained from the following embassies: Argentina (Venezuela); Australia (Indonesia, New Zealand); Austria (Czechoslovakia, Hungary); China (Pakistan, Philippines); Denmark (Iceland, Norway); Egypt (Sudan, Tanzania); France (Morocco, OECD, UNESCO); Greece (Israel, Romania); India (Brunei, Malaysia, Singapore, Thailand); Iraq (Cyprus, Jordan, Lebanon); Italy (Libya, Malta, Turkey); Luxembourg (Council of Europe); Nigeria (Ghana, Zimbabwe); Poland (Latvia, Lithuania); Portugal (Brazil); Russia (Bulgaria); Saudi Arabia (Bahrain, Kuwait, Oman, Qatar, Syria, UAE); Spain (Algeria, Tunisia); Sweden (Estonia, Finland); Switzerland (Yugoslavia); USA (Mexico).

Source: Derived from IPA (1992)

Appendix 3

The ACP states

Africa:

Angola
Benin
Botswana
Burkina Faso
Burundi
Cameroon
Cape Verde
Central African
  Rep
Chad
Comoros
Congo
Côte d'Ivoire
Equatorial Guinea
Ethiopia
Gabon
Gambia
Ghana
Guinea
Guinea Bissau
Djibouti
Kenya
Lesotho
Liberia

Madagascar
Malawi
Mali
Mauritius
Mauretania
Mozambique
Namibia
Niger
Nigeria
Rwanda
Sao Tome &
  Principe
Senegal
Seychelles
Sierra Leone
Somalia
Sudan
Swaziland
Tanzania
Togo
Uganda
Zaire
Zambia
Zimbabwe

Caribbean:

Antigua &
  Barbuda
Bahamas
Barbados
Belize
Dominica
Dominican Rep.
Grenada
Guyana
Haiti
Jamaica
St Christopher
  & Nevis
St Vincent
St Lucia
Suriname
Trinidad &
  Tobago

Pacific:

Fiji
Kiribati
Papua New Guinea
Solomon Islands
Tonga
Tuvalu
Vanuatu
Western Samoa

Appendix 4

UN peacekeeping operations

Table 4.1: Contributing countries to UN peacekeeping operations, by number of missions supported, 1948-90[a]

17	Canada
13	Sweden
12	Finland
11	Denmark, **Ireland**, Norway
9	India, Italy
8	Australia, Austria
7	Ghana, Netherlands, New Zealand
6	Argentina, Brazil, Indonesia, Yugoslavia
5	Nepal, Nigeria, Peru, Poland
4	Belgium, Chile, Ecuador, Myanmar, Pakistan
3	Fiji, France, Iran, Malaysia, Senegal, Spain, Sri Lanka, United States
2	Bangladesh, China, Colombia, Congo, Czechoslovakia, Egypt, Ethiopia, Hungary, Kenya, Panama, Portugal, Soviet Union, Sudan, Switzerland, Thailand, Tunisia, United Kingdom, Uruguay, Venezuela, West Germany
1	Afghanistan, Algeria, Barbados, Costa Rica, East Germany, Greece, Guinea, Guyana, Jamaica, Japan, Jordan, Liberia, Mali, Mexico, Morocco, Philippines, Sierra Leone, Singapore, Togo, Trinidad and Tobago, Turkey, Zambia

Notes:
(a) This period covers 18 UN missions, with a total of 76 countries contributing personnel to those missions

Source: United Nations (1990: 419-449)

Table 4.2: Voluntary contributions to UN peacekeeping operations, by number of missions supported, 1948-90[a]

8	United States
6	Switzerland[b]
5	Japan[c]
4	Canada, Italy, West Germany
3	Australia, Soviet Union, United Kingdom
1	Greece, Kuwait, Morocco, Netherlands, New Zealand, Norway, Poland, South Korea, Sweden

Notes:

Apart from providing personnel, countries can also provide voluntary contributions. These usually take the form of transporting UN personnel of other countries to and from the zone of operations.

(a) This period covers 11 missions where voluntary contributions were required

(b) Switzerland has also undertaken to provide an emergency air ambulance service for all UN peacekeeping missions since 1988 (United Nations 1990: 420)

(c) All Japanese voluntary contributions have been purely financial

Source: United Nations (1990: 419-449)

Key [a]

UNTSO:	UN Truce Supervision Organization
UNMOGIP:	UN Military Observer Group in India and Pakistan
UNEF:	UN Emergency Force
UNOGIL:	UN Observer Group in Lebanon
ONUC:	UN Operation in the Congo
UNTEA:	UN Temporary Executive Authority
UNSF:	UN Security Force
UNYOM:	UN Yemen Observation Mission
UNFICYP:	UN peacekeeping Force in Cyprus
DOMREP:	Mission of the Representative of the Secretary-General in the Dominican Republic
UNIPOM:	UN India-Pakistan Observation Mission
UNDOF:	UN Disengagement Observer Force
UNIFIL:	UN Interim Force in Lebanon
UNGOMAP:	UN Good Offices Mission in Afghanistan and Pakistan.
UNIIMOG:	UN Iran-Iraq Military Observer Group
UNAVEM:	UN Angola Verification Mission
UNTAG:	UN Transition Assistance Group
ONUCA:	UN Observer Group in Central America
UNIKOM:	UN Iraq-Kuwait Observation Mission
ONUSAL:	UN Observer Mission in El Salvador
UNAMIC:	UN Advance Mission in Cambodia
MINURSO:	UN Mission for the Referendum in Western Sahara
UNTAC:	UN Transitional Authority in Cambodia
UNPROFOR:	UN Protection Force

(a) See page 150.

Bibliography

ACDC (1988) *The Development Cooperation policies of the European Community and the Contribution of Ireland to Those Policies*, Dublin, Advisory Council on Development Cooperation

— (1990) *Aid to Third World Countries: attitudes of a national sample of Irish people*, Dublin, Advisory Council on Development Cooperation

— (1991) *Ireland and the Third World: an overview of official development aid*, Dublin, Advisory Council on Development Cooperation

Barcroft, S. (1979) "Irish foreign policy at the League of Nations, 1929-1936" *Irish Studies in International Affairs* 1 (1): 19-29

Browne, V. (ed.), (1981) *The Magill Book of Irish Politics*, Dublin, Magill

Bulmer, S. and W. Wessels (1987) *The European Council: decision-making in European politics*, Basingstoke, Macmillan

Byrne, G. (1974) *Sources and Themes for Afro-Irish Studies*, Dublin, the author

Caherty, T. et. al. (eds.), (1992) *Is Ireland a Third World Country?*, Belfast, Beyond the Pale Publications

Chubb, B. (1982) *The Government and Politics of Ireland*, London and New York, Longman (2nd edition)

Clapham, C. (1985) *Third World Politics: an introduction*, London, Routledge

Commission of the European Communities (1990) *EEC Lomé IV 1990-2000*, Brussels, Commission of the European Communities (March)

Congood (1991) *75:25, Ireland in a Still Unequal World*, Dublin, Congood Development Education Commission

Connolly, J. (1992) *Riding the Tiger: Ireland, European security and defence, an examination of the issues in the light of Maastricht and beyond*, Dublin, Irish Commission for Justice and Peace

Coombes, D. (ed.), (1983) *Ireland and the European Community: ten years of membership*, Dublin, Gill and Macmillan

CTT (1986) *India – the market for telecommunications equipment*, Dublin, Coras Tráchtála

— (1990, 1991) *Annual Review and Outlook*, Dublin, Coras Tráchtála

Dinan, D. (1991) "European Political Cooperation" in: Hurwitz, L. and C. Lequesne (eds.), *The State of the European Community*, Boulder, Colorado, Lynne Rienner: 403-422

Dorr, N. (1986) "The Security Council of the United Nations" *Irish Studies in International Affairs*, 2 (2): 13-33

Edwards, G. and E. Regelsberger (eds.), (1990) *Europe's Global Links: the European Community and inter-regional cooperation*, London, Pinter

European People's Party, (1982) *European Digest 46*, Luxembourg, European People's Party

Fabian, L. (1971) *Soldiers Without Enemies*, Washington, DC, Brookings

Farrands, C. (1985) "Diamonds and impotence": the implementation of Giscard d'Estaing's African policies" in: Smith, S. and M. Clarke (eds.), *Foreign Policy Implementation*, London, George Allen and Unwin: 72-94

Farrell, B. (1983) *Seán Lemass*, Dublin, Gill and Macmillan

FitzGerald, G. (1985) "The Irish government and world development" in: Trócaire, *Ten years of action for justice for world development*, Dublin, Trócaire

— (1988) "Ireland's development policy: aid and trade" *Studies* 77 (307): 328-341

Fitzpatrick, J. (1985) "MFA IV – prospects for the textiles and clothing negotiations" *Trócaire Development Review*, 65-75

Fitzpatrick, J. and A. Storey (1988) "Economic benefits to Ireland of official development assistance" *Trócaire development review*, 51-68

Flaesch-Mougin, C. and J. Raux (1991) "From Lomé III to Lomé IV: EC-ACP Relations" in: Hurwitz, L. and C. Lequesne (eds.), *The State of the European Community*, Boulder, Colorado, Lynne Rienner: 343-358

Foot, R. (1979) "The European Community's voting behaviour at the United Nations General Assembly" *Journal of Common Market Studies 17*, 350-360

Ginsberg, R. (1989) *Foreign Policy Action of the European Community: the Politics of Scale*, Boulder, Colorado, Lynne Rienner

Gopal, S. (1975) *Jawaharlal Nehru: a biography Vol. 1 1889-1947*, London, Jonathan Cape

Grabendorff, W. (1990) "Relations with Central and South America: a question of over-reach", in: Edwards, G. and E. Regelsberger (eds.), *Europe's global links: the European Community and inter-regional cooperation*, London, Pinter: 84-96

Grindle, J. (1992) *Bread and Freedom: basic human needs and human rights*, Dublin, Trócaire/Gill and Macmillan

Harkness, D. (1970) *The Restless Dominion*, London, Macmillan

Heathcote, N. (1971) "Ireland and the United Nations operation in the Congo" *International Relations* 3 (11): 880-902

Heatley, R. (1979) *Poverty and Power: the case for a political approach to development and its implications for action in the West*, London, ZEDPRESS/RUA

Hederman, M. (1983) *The Road to Europe: Irish attitudes 1948-1961*, Dublin, Institute for Public Administration

Hennegan, M. (1989) Philippines: press release, Dublin, Philippines Consulate

Higgins, M. (1985) "Irish government: saint or sinner" in Trócaire: *Ten years of action for justice for world development*, Dublin, Trócaire

— (1988) "The case for an Oireachtas foreign policy committee", *Studies* 77 (305): 63-67

Higgins, R. (1980) *United Nations Peacekeeping 1946-1967: documents and commentary Vol. 3 Africa*, London, RIIA/Oxford University Press

Hill, C. (1983) *National foreign policies and European Political cooperation*, London, Allen and Unwin

Hobsbawn, E. J. (1978) *The Age of Revolution*, London, Abacus

Hogan, E. (1990) *The Irish Missionary Movement: a historical survey, 1830-1980*, Dublin, Gill and Macmillan

Holland, M. (1988) *The European Community and South Africa: European Political Cooperation under strain*, London, Pinter

Holmes, M., N. Rees and B. Whelan (1992) "Irish foreign policy and the Third World: voting in the UN General Assembly in the 1980s" *Trócaire Development Review*: 67-84

Horgan, J. (1987) "Africa and Ireland: aspects of a media agenda" *Trócaire Development Review*: 17-30

Horgan, J., M. Owens, and M. Sutton (1987) *Images of Africa: full-length Irish case study*, Dublin, Trócaire (unpublished)

Hurwitz, L. (1976) "The EEC and decolonization: the voting behaviour of the Nine in the UN General Assembly" *Political Studies* 24: 435-447

IPA (1991, 1992) *Administration Yearbook and Diary*, Dublin, Institute of Public Administration

Irish Commission for Justice and Peace (1980) *Ireland and the Third World – a Study of Government Aid*, Dublin, Irish Commission for Justice and Peace

Irish Congress of Trade Unions (n.d.) *Third World Development*, Dublin, ICTU

Irish Missionary Union (1976, 1982, 1990) *Survey of Personnel*, Dublin, IMU

Ireland (annual) *Trade statistics*, Dublin, Central Statistics Office

— (1979) A*nnouncement by the Minister for Foreign Affairs, Michael O'Kennedy, of the Government's 1979 Bilateral Aid Programme to Developing Countries* (15 March), Dublin, Government Information Services

— (1982-90) *Ireland's Official Development Assistance*, Dublin, Department of Foreign Affairs

— (1991) *State Directory*, Dublin, Stationery Office

Keatinge, P. (1970) "Ireland and the League of Nations" *Studies* 61 (234): 133-148

— (1973) *The Formulation of Irish Foreign Policy*, Dublin, Institute of Public Administration

— (1978) *A Place Among the Nations: issues of Irish foreign policy*, Dublin, Institute of Public Administration

— (1982) "An odd couple? Obstacles and opportunities in inter-state political cooperation between the Republic of Ireland and the United Kingdom" in: Rea, D. (ed.), *Political Cooperation in Divided Societies: a series of papers relevant to the conflict in Northern Ireland*, Dublin, Gill and Macmillan: 305-353

— (1983) "Ireland: neutrality inside European Political Cooperation", in: Hill, C. *National Foreign Policies and European Political Cooperation*, London, Allen and Unwin: 137-152

— (1984a) *A Singular Stance: Irish neutrality in the 1980s*, Dublin, Institute of Public Administration

— (1984b) "Ireland, Political Cooperation and the Middle East" in: Allen, D. and Pijpers, A. (eds.) *European Foreign-policy Making and the Arab-Israeli Conflict*, The Hague, Martinus Nijhoff: 18-30

— (ed.) (1991a) *Ireland and EC Membership Evaluated*, London, Pinter

— (ed.) (1991b) *Political Union*, Studies in European Union No. 1, Dublin, Institute of European Affairs

Keogh, D. (1989) *Ireland and Europe, 1919-1989*, Cork, Hibernian University Press

Kirby, P. (1992) *Ireland and Latin America: links and lessons*, Dublin, Gill and Macmillan/Trócaire

Laffan, B. (1988) *Ireland and South Africa: Irish government policy in the 1980s*, Dublin, Trócaire

Lindemann, B. (1976) "Europe and the Third World: the Nine at the United Nations" *World Today*, 32 (7): 260-269

— (1982) "European Political Cooperation at the UN: a challenge for the Nine" in: Allen, D., R. Rummel and W. Wessels (eds.), *European Political Cooperation*, London, Butterworth: 110-133

Lyons, F. S. (1974) *Ireland Since the Famine*, London, Collins/Fontana

MacKernan, P. (1984) "Ireland and European Political Cooperation" *Irish Studies in International Affairs*, 1 (4): 15-26

McDermott, A. (1988) *Egypt from Nasser to Mubarak: a flawed revolution*, London, Croom Helm

McSweeney, B. (1988) *Ireland and the Threat of Nuclear War: the question of Irish neutrality*, Dublin, Dominican Publications

Mahler, V. (1990) *Emerging North-South institutions? the case of the Lomé Convention*, Paper presented at the annual meeting of the American Political Science Association, San Francisco, 10 August – 2 September

Matthews, A. (1985) *The Common Agricultural Policy and the Less Developed Countries*, Dublin: Gill and Macmillan/Trócaire

— (1991) *EC Trade Policy and the Third World: an Irish perspective*, Dublin, Gill and Macmillan/Trócaire

Molle, W. (1990) *The Economics of European Integration: theory, practice, policy*, Aldershot, Dartmouth

Montecinos, V. (1991) *Latin America and the EC: closing gaps in cooperation*, conference paper, Biennial Conference of the European Community Studies Association, George Mason University, 22-24 May 1991

Nicoll, W. and T. Salmon (1990) *Understanding the European Communities*, London, Philip Allan

Nötzold, J. and K. von der Ropp, (1990) "Lomé IV: a chance for black Africa's return to the world economy?" *Aussenpolitik* 11: 181-192

O'Brien, C. C. (1962) *To Katanga and Back*, London, Hutchinson

— (1969) "Ireland in international affairs" in: Edwards, O. (ed.), *Conor Cruise O'Brien Introduces Ireland*, London, Andre Deutsch: 104-134

O'Brien, N. (1985) *Seeds of Injustice*, Dublin, O'Brien Press

— (1987) *Revolution from the Heart*, Dublin, Veritas Publications

OECD (1990) *Annual Report of the Development Assistance Committee*, Paris, OECD

O'Leary, M. (1985) "The presidency of the Council of Ministers of the European Communities: Ireland and its EC membership" in: O'Nuallain, C. (ed.), *The Presidency of the European Council of Ministers*, London, Croom Helm: 139-162

O'Neill, H. (1982) *Irish Aid: performance and policies*, Dublin, Centre for Economic Research, Policy Paper No. 3

— (1991) "Development policy" in: Keatinge, P. *Ireland and EC Membership Evaluated*, London, Pinter: 172-182

Oireachtas (1982) *Annual Report*, Dublin, Joint Oireachtas Committee on Cooperation with Developing Countries

— (1985) *Annual Report*, Dublin, Joint Oireachtas Committee on Cooperation with Developing Countries

Pijpers, A. (ed.), (1988) *European Political Cooperation in the 1980s: a common foreign policy for Western Europe*, London, Martinus Nijhoff

Potter, D. (1986) *India's Political Administrators, 1919-1983*, Oxford, Oxford University Press

Pryce, R. (1987) *The Dynamics of European Union*, London, Croom Helm

Quinn, R. (1980) *The Missionary Factor in Irish Aid*, Dublin, Dominican Publications

Radhakrishnan, S. (1965) *Speeches and Writings*, Delhi, Government of India

Riggs, R. E. and J. C. Plano (1988) *The United Nations: international organisation and world politics*, Chicago, The Dorsey Press

Rubin, S. (1966) *The Conscience of the Rich Nations: the Development Assistance Committee and the common aid effort*, New York, Council on Foreign Relations/Harper and Row

Rummell, R. (1988) "Speaking with one voice – and beyond" in: Pijpers, A. (ed.) *European Political Cooperation in the 1980s: a common foreign policy for Western Europe*, London, Martinus Nijhoff: 118-142

Salmon, T. (1990) *Unneutral Ireland: an ambivalent and unique security policy*, Oxford, Clarendon Press

Schmuck, O. (1990) "The Lomé Convention: a model for partnership" in: Edwards, G. and E. Regelsberger (eds.), *Europe's Global Links: the European Community and inter-regional cooperation*, London, Pinter: 45-56

Sharp, P. (1990) *Irish Foreign Policy and the European Community*, Aldershot, Dartmouth Publishing Co

Sifry, M. and C. Cerf (eds.), (1991) *The Gulf Reader: history, documentation, opinion*, New York, Times Books

Skogmo, B. (1989) *UNIFIL: international peacekeeping in Lebanon, 1978-1988*, Boulder, Colorado, Lynne Rienner

Sutton, M. (1985) "Comparative aid giving performance", *Trócaire Development Review* 36-43

— (1989) "The European Community and the Third World – Ireland's role" *Studies* 78 (311): 262-273

Thorp, W. (1985) "The DAC's expanding influence" in: Poats, R. et al. (eds), *Twenty-five Years of Development Cooperation: a review, 25th Annual Report of the Development Assistance Committee*, Paris, OECD, 45-49

Tomkys, R. (1987) "European Political Cooperation and the Middle East: a personal perspective" *International Affairs*, 63 (3): 425-437

Trócaire (1985) *Ten Years of Action for Justice for World Development*, Dublin, Trócaire

United Nations (1990) *The Blue Helmets: a review of United Nations peacekeeping*, New York, United Nations Publications (2nd Edition)

— (1992) *United Nations Peacekeeping Operations: information notes*, New York, United Nations Publications

UNICEF (1991) *UNICEF Annual Report*, New York, UNICEF

von Jagow, P. (1990) "European Political Cooperation: concerted diplomacy in an inter-regional context" in: Edwards, G. and E. Regelsberger (eds.), *Europe's Global Links: the European Community and inter-regional cooperation*, London, Pinter: 188-198

Wallace, W. (1975) *The Foreign Policy Process in Britain*, London, Royal Institute of International Affairs

— (1982) "National inputs into European Political Cooperation" in: Allen, D., R. Rummel and W. Wessels (eds), *European Political Cooperation*, London, Butterworths

Whelan, B. (1984) *Aspects of Irish Foreign Policy, 1945-51*, UCC, MA thesis (unpublished)

— (1985) *Anti-semitism in Ireland* (unpublished)

— (1992) "The Marshall Plan and Ireland" *Irish Economic and Social History* 19: 49-70

Willets, P. (1988) "The United Nations as a political system" in: Taylor, P. and A. Groom (eds.), *International institutions at work*, London, Pinter: 21-38

Wolf-Phillips, L. (1987) "Why 'Third World'?: origin, definition and usage" *Third World Quarterly* 9 (4): 1311-1327

Index

Trócaire World Topics

A new series on aspects of Third World affairs for the general reader – factual, accurate and up to date.

1. Bread and Freedom: Basic Human Needs and Human Rights

John Grindle

Basic needs – food, shelter, water, health, education, a living income and security – are the minimum human entitlement. Bread and Freedom outlines an approach to development which could provide these basic needs for all.

Political freedom and basic needs are inseparable. While great advances have been made in the Third World more progress is possible at little cost. All that is lacking is political will.

John Grindle has worked as an economic consultant in several developing countries and for the Irish Government.

"Some valuable ideas" *Sunday Tribune*

Trócaire and Gill and Macmillan, 1992,
£4.99, 0 7171 1967 X

2. Ireland and Latin America: Links and Lessons

Peadar Kirby

Our links with Latin America have always been strong through Irish missionaries, traders and soldiers. Part One of this book is a concise history of the region from pre-Columbus days to independence, military rule and democracy.

Part Two tells the story of leading Irish migrants to Latin America and Church and solidarity links. The author suggests Ireland and Latin America have much in common: both need to overcome a colonial legacy and find the right development model. Each can learn much from the other.

Peader Kirby, a journalist and author, has written widely on Third World development.

"a valuable insight... a fine read" *Sunday Tribune*
"a compact account" *Sunday Independent*
"fascinating and very readable" *Irish Catholic*

Trócaire and Gill and Macmillan, 1992,
£4.99, 0 7171 1969 6

Forthcoming

4. Third World Debt: Towards an Equitable Solution

Mary R. McCarthy and Thomas G. McCarthy

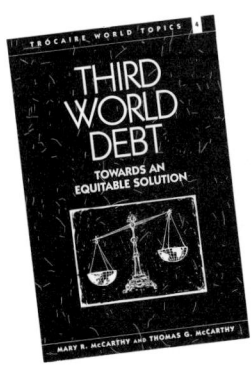

Third World debt payments cripple many developing countries. They reduce health and education spending, causing child poverty and malnutrition.

This book suggests the rich industrial countries are as responsible for the problem as debtor countries. The authors analyse responses to the crisis so far and propose a more attractive and equitable solution.

Mary McCarthy works with the EC in Brussels. Tom McCarthy lectures in Economics at St. Patricks College, Maynooth.

Trócaire and Gill and Macmillan, 1993,
£4.99, 0 7171 1968 8